LAND AND CLASS IN KENYA

During Kenya's transition to independence, a... changes took place in regard to land – that country's main econo... resource and most important political issue. These changes are described here and the evolution of agriculture analysed in a Marxist class framework. Leo shows how the settlers in the White Highlands helped create four classes – the landless, the peasants, the petit bourgeois, and eventually the haute bourgeois – and how each class participated in the move to independence and in its consequences. The Marxist notion of a succession of modes of production is, however, challenged by the facts in Kenya, for the peasant and capitalist modes are flourishing in tandem and are mutually reinforcing.

Professor Leo goes beyond the work of such analysts of Kenya as Colin Leys and Michael Cowan in developing and understanding the dynamics of African production and class relations. He concludes with an assessment of the likely effects of the agrarian and class systems on the country's chances of development or stagnation in the 1980s and of the policies that would help create the former.

All those interested in the history, political economy, and future development of Kenya, and indeed of other countries in the Third World, should learn much from this fresh, subtle, and informed study.

CHRISTOPHER LEO is an associate professor in the Department of Political Science at the University of Winnipeg.

THE POLITICAL ECONOMY OF WORLD POVERTY

a series edited by Albert Berry, Cranford Pratt, and Richard Sandbrook
at the University of Toronto

The books in this series aim at increasing our understanding of the
economic, political, social, and cultural processes and institutions that
promote or impede the development of the Third World and the
amelioration of its poverty.

CHRISTOPHER LEO

Land and Class in Kenya

UNIVERSITY OF TORONTO PRESS
Toronto Buffalo London

© University of Toronto Press 1984
Toronto Buffalo London
Printed in Canada

ISBN 0-8020-2532-3 (cloth)
       0-8020-6547-3 (paper)

Canadian Cataloguing in Publication Data

Leo, Christopher.
   Land and class in Kenya
   (The political economy of world poverty ; 3)
   Includes index.
   ISBN 0-8020-2532-3 (bound). – ISBN 0-8020-6547-3 (pbk.)
   1. Land tenure – Kenya – History. 2. Land use, Rural –
   Kenya – History. 3. Land reform – Kenya – History –
   20th century. 4. Social classes – Kenya – History.
   I. Title. II. Series.
   HD983.L46 1984   333.3′096762   C84-098464-2

For Deborah, Sarah, and Miriam, with love

Contents

viii Contents

Preface

This book began as a study of the politics behind the Million-Acre Settlement Scheme. It emerged, twelve years later, as an investigation of how class formation and the politics of land have influenced each other through Kenya's colonial and post-colonial history and how they continue to do so in the 1980s. The research began in April–June 1971 with a tour of the Million-Acre Scheme and a look at some large-scale co-operative farms. Starting at headquarters in Nairobi, the tour took me to Machakos, Nyeri, Nyahururu, Dundori, Nakuru, Sotik, Kisii, Kisumu, Kakamega, Bungoma, Kitale, Turbo, Eldoret, and points in between. It included visits to numerous settlement schemes and informal interviews with settlement administrators and technical people at various levels of the hierarchy, from agricultural assistant to area settlement controller and headquarters staff.

The next step was a series of intensive interviews with a 40 per cent random sample of the settlers in each of two units of the Million-Acre Scheme. The units were paired: geographically adjacent – located next to each other in Nyandarua District – but economically and socially very different from one another. One was Ol'Kalou West, a unit settled mainly by poor cultivators who had been landless before coming to settlement; the other was Passenga, whose settlers had had previous experience in farming or business and had come to settlement with a down payment of at least Shs 5000/- each. A total of 121 interviews – conducted from July to September 1971 and in February and March 1972 – inquired into the settlers' economic and family backgrounds, their places of origin, their experiences in relation to such historical events as the Emergency and land consolidation, and their attitudes on a variety of social and economic questions. With the exception of a few interviews in Swahili and English, most were conducted in Kikuyu with the help of interpreters.

The purpose of the interviews was twofold. They were designed 1) to elicit a certain amount of standardized, comparable data about the settlers' origins and their economic and social circumstances, and 2) to gain insights into the settlers' attitudes and values, their personal and political problems, and their perceptions of Kenya's recent history and of their own place in it. Accordingly, the interviews were structured as long conversations, provided the settlers were willing to take the time – and for the most part they were happy to do so. Typically, the interviews began with the interpreter posing the inquiries in the questionnaire in Kikuyu and translating the answers, which were written down verbatim. But if the settler initiated conversational gambits of his or her own, they were followed up. And I frequently posed supplementary questions, both as a means of stimulating the conversation and in order to check on accuracy and completeness of the questions and answers.

By this time, it began to be obvious that my study was raising as many questions as it was answering. For example, if it was true, as everyone seemed to agree, that settlement had been a concession to the problem of landlessness (cf. chapter 6 below), why had the formerly landless people I interviewed received such harsh treatment in the settlement process? How did it happen that some settlement schemes were supposedly populated entirely by former forest fighters, while elsewhere threre were pockets of former loyalists to the colonial regime? (Cf. chapters 6 and 7.) Why was Colin Leys' entirely plausible contention that there was little difference between high- and low-density settlement (chapter 1) so patently false on the ground? I launched a search for more information about the origins of settlement and the economic and political motivations behind it. The veritable library of published works about Kenya's colonial period proved a valuable source of enlightenment, as did documents from the Nairobi office of the World Bank, the Kenya National Archives, and the office of the Nyandarua district commissioner.

Over a ten-year period – mainly taken up with other professional commitments – the study yielded a PH D thesis, as well as two articles, one published in the *Journal of Modern African Studies* and another in the *Canadian Journal of African Studies*. The research concluded in February and March 1983 with another visit to Kenya, undertaken to update information that had grown venerable and to test some new hypotheses.

A stay in Nairobi was followed by another tour, including return visits to Nyahururu, Ol'Kalou, Nakuru, Eldoret, and Kitale, as well as fresh looks at the Ol'Kalou Salient, at the Wanjohi area, and at a number of settlement schemes along the coast, in the Kilifi–Malindi area.

Despite the fact that I accumulated a mountain of paper, my most valuable source was not documentary, but situational. It was my love for Kenya, and my two-and-a-half-year residence there – in Nairobi, in Sabugo, a remote part of Nyandarua District, and in Nyahururu – that yielded the most useful knowledge. Regular perusal of the English and Swahili media as well as numerous conversations along the road and in houses, fields, pubs, and offices helped to shape the conceptions of Kenya's political economy presented in these pages.

I had a great deal of help. Cran Pratt, Jonathan Barker, Richard Stren, Colin Leys, and Jonathan Kariara all offered valuable critiques of earlier drafts. Steven Langdon's encouragement and advice helped pave the way for a final draft, which, in turn, occupied a great deal of Richard Sandbrook's time. He is that rare editor whose toughness in pointing out a manuscript's weaknesses is fully matched by his perceptiveness in identifying and developing its strengths. Lydia Burton's thoughtful and thoroughly professional copy editing further strengthened the manuscript, while Betty Harder and Virginia Hart did a superb job of typing. Needless to say, any weaknesses that remain are my responsibility.

The research done in the early 1970s was made possible by generous financial assistance and moral support from the Canada Council and the University of Toronto's International Studies Program, and that in 1983 by a grant from the Social Sciences and Humanities Research Council of Canada. The University of Winnipeg gave me time off from other duties and offered supplementary financial assistance. This book has been published with the help of a grant from the Social Science Federation of Canada, using funds provided by the Social Sciences and Humanities Research Council of Canada, and a grant from the Publications Fund of University of Toronto Press.

Numerous officials of the Kenya government assisted me, both in clearing administrative obstacles to my research and in explaining various aspects of Kenya's agrarian system to me. I am indebted to Mwaniki Wangai and Stephen Ngotho, who put in many hours of hard work acting as interpreters for the field survey, and to the residents of the Ol'Kalou West and Passenga settlement schemes, who invited me into their homes and shared their thoughts with me. I am particularly grateful to Danson W. Ngotho and his wonderful family, whose courtesy and frequent, warm hospitality touched my heart in the early 1970s and whose friendship remained undimmed by a decade's absence.

Christopher Leo
Winnipeg

LAND AND CLASS IN KENYA

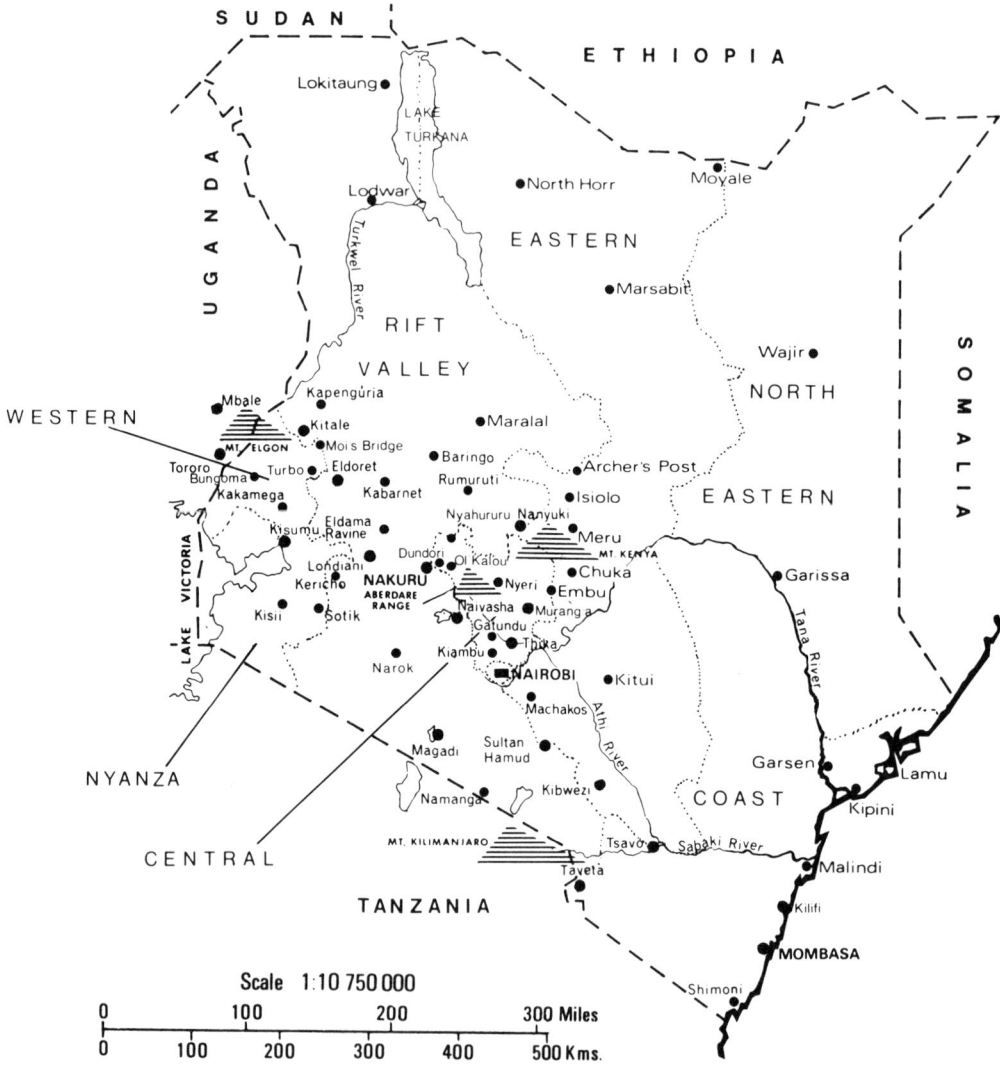

Figure 1 Kenya: cities, towns, and provincial boundaries (adapted from
Kenyatta by Jeremy Murray Brown [New York: Dutton 1973])

1

Introduction

Anyone – African, European, or Asian – who last lived in Kenya's high-lands in the early 1950s, would, upon returning in the 1970s, not only have failed to recognize many familiar places, but also have been quite at a loss about how to behave. In less than twenty years, this fertile agri-cultural region underwent a complete transformation in its politics, economy, society, and even to some extent its geography. This transfor-mation was at the heart of the changes that Kenya itself underwent during those same years, the years of its transition from colonial status to independence. In those few years, forces that had been building for half a century were released in a great social upheaval which, in turn, set the stage for the decades to come.

In the 1950s, colonial Kenya's European community, although it com-prised less than one per cent of that country's total population, was so important politically that Kenya was referred to, quite accurately, as White Man's Country.[1] The Europeans enjoyed status, stability, and in-fluence. Kenya had not only been a base of operations for the usual cast of colonial characters – the government administrators, missionaries, and representatives of metropolitan commercial interests – but had, in addition, become the permanent home of a prosperous European settler community. As owners of farms and ranches, the settlers had a signifi-cant personal stake in Kenya. Moreover, many of them were people of independent means, well connected abroad. Kenya's White Highlands were an influential factor in the economics and politics, not only of Nairobi, but also of London.

The White Highlands – as the European or scheduled areas of Kenya continued to be called until 1960 – took in some three million hectares of land, which was divided into 3 600 farms and ranches, most ranging in size from 400 to upwards of 12 000 hectares.[2] The European area was an almost solid block of land, constituting about one-fifth of Kenya's highlands. Railway lines, connecting all major centres in the scheduled areas with the Kenya coast, carried the agricultural produce of the Europeans to local and world markets. Substantial commercial areas and plush residential districts in the small towns dotting the White Highlands attested to their prosperity. For the owners of the farms and ranches surrounding these towns, life was rough without being hard: murram roads, rocky or muddy depending on the season, led to exclusive clubs – for Europeans only – and to stone mansions where bevies of house and garden servants and plenty of cheap African labour for the fields contributed to the peculiar bucolic opulence of European life in Kenya. Many of the Europeans worked hard and lived plainly, but in the 1950s they did not suffer the hardships we usually associate with a frontier existence. It was an appealing and well-established life.

In its 'upper class' ambience and its influence abroad, European Kenya was unlike the other major centre of permanent British settlement in that part of Africa, Southern Rhodesia (later to be renamed Rhodesia and then Zimbabwe). White Kenyans disdainfully referred to Rhodesia as 'the sergeant's mess,' conveying their perception that it did not provide the suitable environment for officers and gentlemen that Kenya did. From the viewpoint of Africans, however, Kenya was not at all unlike Rhodesia, or, for that matter, unlike South Africa. In Kenya, as in those other white-ruled areas, Africans were subjected to rigid social and geographical segregation and their rights were strictly circumscribed by the privileges of Europeans.

Upon arriving in Kenya, Europeans had taken their pick of the fertile, well-watered highlands, as well as some drier land for ranching. In order to ensure freedom to develop the land they had chosen, the Europeans confined the Africans to 'native reserves' – as they came to be called – each one consisting of a block of land reserved for an African ethnic group. Thus, there was a Kikuyu reserve, a Luo reserve, a Kamba reserve, and so forth. Within the reserves, most people lived a peasant life, meaning that they engaged in small-scale agriculture and animal husbandry, relying heavily on family labour and rudimentary technology, producing partly for their own subsistence and partly for the market.

Life in the reserves was strictly controlled. Colonially appointed chiefs and headmen ruled with a firm hand, ensuring not only the maintenance of law and order but also the collection of the heavy taxes levied by the colonial authorities and the maintenance of numerous restrictions on commerce and agriculture. In addition, they recruited labour – for, to Europeans, the reserves were first and foremost a reserve of labour – often by pressure and sometimes by out-and-out force. Restrictions on agriculture included not only a ban on the growing of a variety of cash crops, but also numerous measures designed to promote 'correct' agricultural practices – the 'proper' spacing and arrangement of crops, contour ploughing, terracing, etc. – measures that were sometimes ill calculated and therefore failed to achieve the desired result.

The restrictions in the reserves motivated some Africans to leave and seek work on European farms or in the towns – even without being pressured to do so. However, although some of the work-seekers found a measure of relief from the watchful eye of the headman, they did so at the cost of exchanging the indirect encounter with colonialism – mediated by local administrators – for a direct confrontation with a racist system of rule. On the roads and in the towns, they were in constant danger of being stopped by police, ever on guard for violations of the numerous restrictions on travel, residence, and commerce. On the European estates they had to learn to tip their hats to white people and behave in a manner befitting their station. Often they found the educational opportunities for their children even more limited in European areas than in the reserves. Worst of all, many who migrated for work lost their rights to land at home. Without land or education and without regular employment, they had good reason to fear a bleak future for themselves and their children.

The Mau Mau war, which broke out in 1952, signalled the beginning of the end for that system, and Kenya's achievement of independence on 12 December 1963 sealed its fate. By then, the White Highlands had been opened to Africans, a substantial proportion of them being subdivided for smallholder occupation. Much of the panoply of colonial restrictions on commerce and agriculture had been abandoned and African entrepreneurs seized economic opportunities by the fistful. The school system mushroomed and colonial symbols of segregation and obeisance – the separate washrooms and tipping of hats – gradually disappeared. Indeed, it became the turn of the Europeans and Asians to learn a few things about *African* ideas of *heshima* – respect. For the first time in Kenya's history, it began to be important to an immigrant's or expatriate's success to understand, for example, that, to Africans, the term 'old man' is a respectful designation, not a disdainful one; and that losing one's temper is a very serious gaffe, not a mark of virility. In the past, Europeans and Asians had been able to dismiss such information (if they knew about it at all) as quaint curiosities. Now they had to pay attention. In twenty short years, for expatriates as well as Europeans, life in Kenya had changed drastically.

At the same time, much about Kenya – including much that is fundamental – remained unchanged. After the dust of independence had settled, Kenya was still primarily an agricultural country – indeed still mainly a peasant society. The White Highlands were no longer European power-centres, either economically or politically, and growing numbers of the farms were being hived off into smallholder agriculture. But large estates remained an important factor in agriculture and politics. And Kenya still lacked a substantial industrial base, wages were still low, extreme poverty and great wealth still existed side by side.

This book deals with the changes that took place during Kenya's transition to independence and beyond, and assesses their significance for Kenya today. It does not, however, try to cut a wide swath through all the changes that occurred. Such an undertaking would be unlikely to produce anything more than a recitation of the obvious. My focus, rather is on the two interrelated topics of *land* and *class*. The significance of *land* is that it constitutes the single most important political issue in Kenya. That statement is one of those rare ones that can be made without any qualification. It was true when Kenya became a colony dominated by European settlers. It remained true through the Mau Mau war and the transition to independence, both of which revolved around competing demands for land. And it remains true in the 1980s, in a country in which rich and poor alike consider land the single most important form of personal wealth and are deeply concerned with its distribution and use. A study of land, therefore, involves looking at much that is basic to Kenya's political economy.

The other focus, on *class*, involves a study of the evolution of Kenya's society in relation to the land issue. In using the term 'class,' I am adopting the Marxian criterion of relationship to the means of production. A study of land and class, therefore, looks at how changes in agricultural production, and in the way people are employed (or unemployed) in agriculture, have brought about changes in the stratification of Kenya's society. Thus, we will look at how the establishment of European large-scale agriculture contributed to the formation of a class of landless people, a peasantry, a petty bourgeoisie, and eventually a high bourgeoisie, or upper bourgeoisie, as I will call it. We will then look at how each of these classes became involved in the struggle against European rule and what happened to them after the colonial regime came to an end.

This book draws heavily upon Marxist thought. At the same time, I am critical of some of the less well-considered Marxian notions. A basic problem of Marx's – and one that becomes particularly obvious upon close study of an African society and polity – is that he believed he could understand the problems of what we now call the third world without necessarily knowing a great deal about actual third-world countries. Marx's followers also are inclined to make sweeping assertions about imperialism, about the expansion of the forces of production and development of the relations of production, sometimes in countries they barely know and often in countries they do not understand in any depth. The assumption, apparently, is that if we have a sufficient grasp of the economic laws governing society, we need not trouble ourselves with the tedious details of actual human endeavour and intercourse. In this, Marxists sometimes bear a striking resemblance to the colonialists of the capitalist world.

One of the most basic Marxist notions is that of a historical succession of modes of production, with each mode spawning a particular constellation of classes that must change fundamentally to make way for a succeeding mode of production. For example, peasant society, based upon smallholder agriculture, hand implements, and petty trade, may be succeeded by a capitalist society dominated by a bourgeoisie and based upon industrial technology. That picture did not jibe with what I observed in an intensive study of Kenya. One of the most obvious facts about Kenya society, and one that becomes the more firmly rooted the more one pursues the matter, is that the peasant and capitalist modes of production are not succeeding phases, one retreating while the other advances. Rather, they are flourishing in tandem and mutually reinforcing. In the long run, to be sure, the development of Kenya's society may well run the course mapped out for it in the Marxist scenario. In the short run, however, Kenya is gripped by a paradox: Capitalism is being built, not upon the rubble of a disintegrating peasant society, but upon the firm and well-established foundation of a peasant mode of production that is still developing and expanding. In referring to this state of affairs as paradoxical, I am stating my belief that it does not pose a fundamental challenge to Marxian thought. But it certainly does challenge some of the more conventional interpretations of Marx. And it is so central to the development of Kenya's economy that it needs to be examined with care.

In this study, I pursue my concept of Kenya's agrarian class system, building it piece by piece out of a careful analysis of Kenya's society and politics. The primary purpose of the study, however, is not to reconstruct Marxist theory. Although my observations lead me to rethink a number of cherished Marxian conceptions, my main concern is to develop a clearer understanding of Kenya's political problems and the options available for addressing them. My theory serves concrete rather than abstract ends. We already have more Marxist theory about the third world than anyone has time to read. What we are short of is concrete understanding of the problems of third-world countries. Marxian theory can be a great help in seeking such an understanding, but the tools of production should not be allowed to crowd out the product. Let us begin this study by placing it in relation to the relevant literature.

THE AGRARIAN SYSTEM AND ECONOMIC DEVELOPMENT

The question with which this book is ultimately concerned is one that preoccupies many writers, while constituting an important undercurrent in Kenya's politics and a major consideration in policy-making: What are Kenya's chances for agricultural development? To put it more precisely: Is Kenya's agrarian system and its constellation of classes evolving in such a way as to build a viable basis for future prosperity? Or is the productive potential in agriculture being dissipated so as to contribute to that familiar third-world spectacle of economic stagnation and continuing or even worsening poverty for the majority of people? The question is obviously difficult and intricately ramified. Before we can even approach it directly, we have to dispose of a number of preliminary questions:

1 What kind of development are we assuming?
2 How does agriculture contribute to development?
3 What kind of agrarian system leads to development and what kind brings about stagnation?
4 What constellation of classes is desirable?

The answers to the first two questions are the common property of Marxists and non-Marxists, while for the last two I will rely primarily upon Marxists for guidance.

Common property. In the context of Kenya, the answer to the first question is easy: 'development,' in practice, means 'capitalist development.' Capitalism in Kenya is anchored in a prosperous and powerful bourgeoisie. Moreover, it enjoys substantial popular support. To be sure, a coup was attempted in 1982 in which the participants were said to be shouting Marxist slogans, but no one has seriously suggested that the attempt, had it been successful, would have resulted in the abolition of capitalism. A more likely alternative would have been another capitalist regime reflecting a new alliance of interests and perhaps trying to project a different image.

Indeed, Marxists writing about Kenyan politics – as opposed to more ethereal literary and philosophical Marxists – do not take a non-capitalist development route seriously as an alternative for Kenya. In fact, if we ignore terminology and mode of analysis to focus on policy alternatives, we find that the alternatives being considered by Marxists are essentially identical to those being debated within Kenya's Ministry of Economic Planning and Development. As we will see, one Marxist faction favours policies that encourage large-scale agriculture and technologically sophisticated industry and accepts the growth of sharp income differentials, while another advocates serious limitations on multinational enterprise in order to foster the development of decentralized, smaller-scale industry and agriculture and the widest possible distribution of income. The former is identified in Marxist terms as favouring the upper bourgeoisie and the latter as being oriented toward the petty bourgeoisie and the peasantry. Non-Marxists, who are well familiar with the same sets of alternatives, identify them as, respectively, an orthodox capitalist development strategy and a social democratic approach. Both lines of policy posit a substantially private enterprise economy working in tandem with a strong interventionist state. The approach actually being pursued in Kenya lies somewhere between these extremes, leaning somewhat toward the former. In short, Marxists and non-Marxists are as one in their acceptance of a capitalist development path for Kenya.

Given that reality, it is difficult to see why many Marxists continue to strike the esoteric poses of a revolutionary underground, to represent themselves as belonging to a select group of seekers of truth and justice. In these pages, although I draw freely upon the considerable sophistication of Marxist thought in this attempt to understand problems of land and class, I eschew revolutionary poses which, in any event, are spurious in Kenya's context. In particular, in considering possible solutions to problems, I emphasize those that are likely to be of assistance to Kenyans over those that might be imaginable in a different set of circumstances. Anyone with a conscience and with a knowledge of the extremes of oppression to which many human beings are subjected will have to admit that there is a time and a place for revolution, but few would seriously argue that Kenya in the early 1980s is the time or the place.

Given, then, that Kenya's most likely development is a capitalist one, the next question is: How does agriculture contribute to capitalist development? Here too, as was noted, there is substantial agreement between Marxist and bourgeois commentators: Agricultural development is an essential of economic development, especially in a country like Kenya, which is capable of a lavish abundance and a wide variety of agricultural production, both for home consumption and for export, and at the same time lacks any other major natural resources. T.J. Byres, in a typical formulation drawing on Marxist thought, argues that in order to contribute to capitalist development, 'agriculture must perform two crucial functions. On the one hand, it must generate and release in sufficient quantity and on reasonable terms the surplus that is necessary if growth is to take place outside of agriculture; on the other, it must contribute to the creation of the home market.'[3] Non-Marxists might prefer 'profit available for reinvestment' to 'surplus,' but otherwise there is little here to argue about.

Marxian property. As we turn to questions three and four, however, we find ourselves moving onto Marxist territory because the questions assume a close connection among levels of technology (or modes of production), forms of social organization, and development paths. It is both the genius and the Achilles heel of Marxist thought that it paints on a broad canvas, seeking to show how apparently disparate phenomena are related to each other and how they work together to produce development or stagnation, revolution or stability. It is genius in that it can produce valuable insights, and Achilles heel in that it can become suffocatingly convoluted – a hazard I will seek to avoid. In any event, Marxist thought is particularly well suited to addressing the questions of what kinds of agrarian systems and what constellations of classes are needed to bring about economic development.

The short answer is that there is no one correct answer. Development can be produced by many different systems and many different class configurations. Byres offers a formulation that ably sums up a great deal of other literature. In the past, he argues, the development of agriculture, and the class formation that accompanies it, has taken place in 'complex and varied' ways,

... growing out of simple commodity production, here via the landlord class and there via a peasantry which gradually became differentiated (so providing, at the extremes, a stratum of rich peasants who ultimately became capitalist farmers and a stratum of poor peasants who were transformed into agricultural labourers or who joined the urban proletariat); slowly penetrating the countryside; developing the forces of production in manifold ways and raising agriculture's productiveness ...[4]

The development of agriculture, therefore, has always involved class formation and differentiation, but the particular class configurations whereby this took place have varied. Nor is it only technologies and class configurations in the process of development that can vary. As Arghiri Emmanuel argues, the role and importance of agriculture within a developed capitalist system can vary from country to country. Conventionally, one tends to equate development with industrialization. Emmanuel points out, however, that there is a difference between mechanization and industrialization. A capitalist country may be fully developed (he cites Australia, New Zealand, and Denmark as examples), while continuing to rely on highly mechanized agriculture as an economic mainstay. To be sure, a country will not reach such a stage without also developing a significant industrial sector. The point, however, is that the development of agriculture may be an important final goal, and not just a transitional stage.[5] In other words, although we know that the development of agriculture under capitalism involves class formation, there is no rule to tell us either which classes are the appropriate vehicles of development or even how great a role agriculture must play. The answers are not written on the universe; we will have to seek them for ourselves, through an analysis of the concrete situation in Kenya.

Having answered our preliminary questions, we are now free to turn to the question that is our ultimate concern: Is Kenya's agrarian system evolving toward prosperity or stagnation? The remainder of this chapter is concerned with what others have written on the subject. First I review some important discussions of Kenya's overall development and then turn to writings that provide some background to an understanding of the agrarian system.

DYNAMICS OF DEVELOPMENT IN KENYA

Throughout the 1960s, the preponderance of literature on third-world politics was sympathetic to the regimes in those countries, many of which had but recently won their independence from colonial rule. Writers chose such themes as 'mass mobilization,' 'national integration,' 'political development,' and 'rural development' to express their concern for the maintenance of stability and the growth of prosperity. Societies were seen, ideally at least, as unified wholes, and any rents in the social fabric tended to be treated as undesirable manifestations.

In the late 1960s, a reaction appeared to this line of inquiry in the form of a Marxist literature that criticized bourgeois regimes and capitalist economic development on behalf, especially, of the third-world's poor.[6] This literature, adopting the rubric of 'dependency,' suggested that capitalists' use of the term 'development' to describe their policies was bogus, because it was capitalist development in some areas of the world, and some parts of society, that was the prime cause of underdevelopment in others. The causes of poverty in the third world were to be sought, on the one hand, in the international political and economic system, which systematically plundered its poor, and on the other, in local class systems, in which a few prospered at the expense of the majority, while the national economy stagnated. Third-world countries were not being 'developed,' they were being 'underdeveloped.' And they were not unified wholes; they were divided into classes, with the bourgeoisie enriching itself through links with foreign economic interests, while much of the rest of the population languished in poverty.

In Kenya, the most prominent of the Marxian commentators was Colin Leys. In an argument built on the premises outlined above, Leys contended that Kenya's agrarian system was serving the interests both of foreign capital and of a Kenyan 'auxiliary bourgeoisie.'[7] While foreign investors were earning high returns in manufacturing, tourism, and estate agriculture, Leys argued, large-scale mixed farming, which would probably not have been viable in an unrestricted market, was being subsidized to appease the Kenyan bourgeoisie and British investors, both of whom had interests in that sector. Meanwhile, among smallholders, freehold landownership was replacing older systems of land tenure: 'property relations were brought into line with the dominant productive relations so as to ensure that peasant production would be adapted to and would supplement capitalist production, not challenge it.'[8]

Just how the maintenance of pre-colonial systems of land tenure in smallholder areas would have challenged the capitalist system – or, for that matter, how either domestic or foreign bourgeoisies were benefiting from failure to develop agriculture as fully as possible – was not clear from Leys' argument. It was not on these points, however, that he was challenged. Reaction, rather, focused on the question – particularly associated with Nicola Swainson's work[9] – of whether Leys was right in his assertion that Kenya's bourgeoisie was 'auxiliary' and was leading the way to chronic dependency and stagnation. Leys himself had some second thoughts about his interpretation and, in 1977, reversed his earlier position by declaring 'that "underdevelopment" and "dependency" is no longer servicable and must now be transcended.'[10] The thrust of his argument was that the underdevelopment/dependency theory he had earlier advocated had since proved unenlightening and problematic, that it had failed to have a 'practical impact in favour of the popular forces in the struggles in third world countries,' and that in fact it had shown 'a marked tendency ... to be co-opted by developmentalists allied to international capital.'[11] In a subsequent article, he argued that the primary causes of poverty in the third world lay, not in the exploitation of poor countries by the world capitalist system, but in the failure of productive investment within the poor countries themselves. 'What produces *under*development is not the "transfer of surplus" appropriated by metropolitan capital from the periphery of the metropole, significant though this may be. Rather, such a transfer should be seen as an *effect* of structures at the periphery which militate against the productive investment of the surplus at the periphery.'[12]

What is needed, Leys argued, is the development of a local bourgeoisie that is capable of investing on a sufficient scale to build an industrial base. He made it explicit that he was favouring large-scale enterprise over development based on less technologically sophisticated businesses and small farms when he said of the indigenous bourgeoisie: 'If it is "progressive," it is progressive in relation to the petty-bourgeoisie, which seeks to defend, in general, relations of production – especially small-holding and petty trade – in which the exploitation of the workers does not expand the forces of production (however much that defence is couched in the rhetoric of populism and petty-bourgeois socialism).'[13]

Leys' advocacy of a conventional capitalist route to Kenya's development was not greeted with universal applause. Indeed, it ignited a spirited and sometimes labyrinthine debate[14] that has unearthed a wealth of information about Kenya's bourgeoisie and about the activities of multinational corporation in Kenya, but has predictably failed to produce a definitive reading on whether Kenya is on the road to development or stagnation. Rafael Kaplinski and Steven Langdon, prominent opponents of Leys' position, have argued that multinational enterprise is not helping to develop Kenya's economy and that the local bourgeoisie are too closely tied to multinational interests to be capable of building Kenya's prosperity. Langdon, in a forcefully argued and carefully documented indictment of the effects of multinational corporations on Kenya's economic development, devoted some attention as well to the policy implications of the Kaplinsky-Langdon position. He argues that the government should limit the role of multinational corporations as part of a strategy to encourage smaller-scale, local enterprises and to redistribute incomes and assets. Some multinational corporate subsidiaries, which are engaging in essential production, might be taken over by the state or by co-operatives. Some might be allowed to produce for export only and others – which are making particularly important contributions through technological innovation – might be allowed to continue their activities unhampered. All of this, he says, could only occur if there was a 'fundamental transformation of power and orientation in Kenya's political economy.'[15]

Langdon does not address the question of what kind of transformation would be needed to bring about the policies he advocates. And that is the problem with the discussion to this point: we lack a clear picture of the class dynamics of either development path. The regime favoured by Leys and Swainson would be based on the power of a national bourgeoisie and the Langdon-Kaplinsky alternative would obviously have to be built largely on a petty bourgeois and peasant base. But that does not take us very far, because none of these classes are undifferentiated. Which fraction of the bourgeoisie can be relied upon to pursue an independent development path? Indeed, what fractions are there? Is there a landed bourgeoisie and an industrial one, or are they mixed up together, or differentiated in some other way? What kind of an alliance is possible between peasants and the petty bourgeoisie? Which elements would be left out of such an alliance, and how strong would they be? No one knows the answers to these questions in their entirety, but writings focusing on Kenya's agrarian system have made some important headway in addressing them.

KENYA'S AGRARIAN SYSTEM

'Peasantization.' An early contribution to the study of Kenya's agrarian class system came from Colin Leys, who wrote an article entitled 'Politics in Kenya: The Development of Peasant Society,' a draft of which was being passed around by his colleagues as early as 1969.[16] Although the

article has been subjected to a great deal of criticism, it stands up surprisingly well to a rereading in the 1980s. Directing himself at Marxist commentators who were looking for signs of a transition to capitalism – the formation of a bourgeoisie and a proletariat – Leys imaginatively assembled evidence from a variety of sources to document his contention that the most striking feature in the development of Kenya's forces of production is not proletarianization, but 'peasantization.' He argued that small-scale agriculture based on family labour, far from being displaced by other forces of production, was expanding its scope and displacing large-scale agriculture.

This trend was more than obvious in Kenya's settlement program, which the present volume describes in some detail and which, in 1969, was devoted to the purchase of European estates, their subdivision, and their resale to African smallholders. Leys also pointed out, however, that many European estates that had supposedly been conveyed intact into African hands had in fact been bought by partnerships and co-operatives and then subdivided into smallholdings by informal arrangements – another example of the expansion of the peasant mode of production. A perspicacious observation in the late 1960s, this has since become a central fact of rural life in Kenya.

How could the peasant mode of production be displacing capitalism, turning European history on its head? Leys' argument hinged on the existence of a frontier (in the American sense of space for expansion) consisting of European estates not yet Africanized, as well as unoccupied and underutilized land. A substantial majority of Kenyans, Leys argued in effect, either want to own land, or indeed need it to survive. As long as this is the case, and as long as there is a land frontier, the course of least resistance for farmers wishing to expand is to move onto the frontier rather than to displace their neighbours. And the multiplicity of demands for land make it likely that the frontier – where it consists of large tracts of land – will be subdivided into smallholdings rather than being turned into large farms. The net result is the multiplication of smallholdings, rather than their consolidation into larger farms.

Leys' argument did not suggest that this was a permanent reversal of the usual historical sequence, nor that other classes, besides the peasantry, were in retreat – except, of course, for the European bourgeoisie. There continued to be a substantial number of large farmers. Furthermore, many people were becoming owners of more than one smallholding, thereby building their economic base by leapfrogging rather than expansion. And, as Leys acknowledged, there was a fringe, albeit a small one, of urban proletarians who had no rural base. All of that, however, did not prevent the multiplication of smallholdings, which, as Leys saw it, would be likely to continue as long as there was a land frontier. The impression of an expanding peasant mode of production was strengthened by the fact that even the urban petty and upper bourgeoisies were engaging in 'peasantization' as they supplemented their incomes or provided some additional security for themselves through the ownership of smallholdings.

To anyone who knows rural Kenya in the 1980s, this is a remarkably clear-sighted view of the society that was emerging through the 1960s and 1970s. The article is not without faults. At one point, for example, Leys refers to lack of room for expansion in Central Province and Embu and Meru districts,[17] forgetting apparently that the people living in those areas have found plenty of room to expand beyond them. He mistakenly minimizes the distinction between high- and low-density settlement,[18] a point dealt with in chapters 5, 6, and 7 of this study. And the social services that he credits former European settlers with supplying for their workers[19] are ones that the former workers consulted in the present study (see chapter 7) would only have known about had they read Leys' article. But these are quibbles.

The article's most important shortcoming is that it conveys no real sense of the social and political dynamics of the society it describes. It draws a picture of a society developing gradually, perhaps, but essentially static for the long-term future. Class alliances and class struggles, and the process of differentiation among classes and class fractions, which one would expect to find in any society, including peasant society, are not in evidence. An attempt to supply this missing element is found in the work of Michael Cowen, an ascerbic and respected *éminence grise* of the Kenya Marxist community, whose wellnigh unreadable prose fails to conceal a shrewd and penetrating intellect. Cowen offers two propositions that are important for our purposes.

Middle peasants and the bourgeoisie. The first is an elaboration of the 'peasantization' thesis. Directing himself, as Leys did, at commentators looking for signs that Kenyan peasants were becoming proletarianized, Cowen asserts that Kenya's middle peasants – far from being squeezed and oppressed by capital – were being assisted by foreign investment to achieve a stable and economically viable existence as a group. Cowen defines middle peasants as small-scale farmers who rely almost exclusively on household labour. They do not hire labour from other producer households or from the ranks of the unemployed, nor do they 'in the main ... supply local agricultural labour to larger holdings.'[20] Their economic base is the production of such commodities as tea and coffee that has been established with the help of international aid agencies and has been made possible by investments of multinational firms and the state in processing facilities. Furthermore, the presence of international capital has, within this group, helped to promote a tendency toward equalization of incomes.

This analysis, based on careful empirical work, goes beyond Leys' assertion that peasant society can survive in an economy dominated by international capital to specify one of the class alliances which makes that survival possible. At the same time – in response to some of the more simplistic versions of underdevelopment and dependency theory – it points out that an analysis that makes international capital the all-purpose villain responsible for poverty in the third world does not stand up to examination. In Cowen's work, all the fondest dreams of a Unilever public relations agent – economic growth fostered by multinational firms and accompanied by equalization of incomes – are confirmed by a Marxist analysis, at least as far as the middle peasants covered by his studies are concerned.

Cowen's second proposition is that the existence of a strong middle peasantry acts as a deterrent to the growth of an indigenous bourgeoisie, and thus to the establishment of a domestic industrial base. There are various reasons for this. For one thing, the stabilization of middle peasants allows them to remain independent producers instead of (in the classic scenario of capitalist development) being forced off the land to become labourers. Thus the would-be indigenous capitalist class is denied both a source of labour and a source of land that might otherwise serve as a base for the accumulation of capital. For another, the controls on marketing and on quantities of production that accompany multinational investment in processing facilities reduce the opportunities for local traders to make profits in commodity trading – another potential source of capital accumulation. At the same time, the local would-be bourgeoisie miss out on the possibility of investing in their own processing facilities.[21]

The suggestion, therefore, is that there is an objective antagonism between the peasantry and international capital on the one hand, and the urban bourgeoisie, perhaps allied with the rural bourgeoisie, on the other. To be sure, Cowen does not picture this as an unchangeable feature of Kenyan society. On the contrary, he explicitly allows for the possibility of a shift in class alliances, with the indigenous bourgeoisie and the peasants taking sides against international capital.[22] This, presumably, is his elliptical way of telling his readers that nothing is cast in bronze – that if even the remote possibility of a bourgeois/peasant alliance exists, then surely other, more readily conceivable outcomes are possible. Nor should one conclude that a durable alliance between the peasantry and international capital would spell chronic dependency and stagnation for Kenya. That conclusion would be valid only (remembering the passage from Emmanuel cited in an earlier section of this chapter) if we assume the British or German, rather than the Danish or Australian, route to development. The expropriation of peasants by a rural bourgeoisie that then generates a surplus for industrial development is not the only possible route to prosperity. It is equally conceivable that small-scale farmers producing commodities for an international market might create a significant amount of prosperity directly and generate a surplus for industrialization on a less massive scale than that of Britain or Germany.

In any case, Cowen has got us beyond broad generalizations about 'dependency,' 'embourgeoisment,' and 'peasantization' to the point where we can consider in more concrete terms the class antagonisms and alliances that are the raw materials of the development process – or the lapse into stagnation, as the case may be. His discussion of peasants, however, has been restricted to only one segment of peasant society: middle peasants who are tied to international capital. A wider-ranging look at peasant society will be helpful in filling out the background to the present study.

Capturing the peasant. We have noted that peasant cultivators rely heavily on family labour for the pursuit of their enterprises, but that is not the distinguishing feature of peasant society. Traditional cultivators rely on family labour too, as do many capitalist farmers in Europe and North America. What sets peasants apart from others is that they live simultaneously within two economies – a subsistence economy in which they produce for their own consumption and a cash economy in which they work for wages, sell commodities, or engage in small-scale business enterprise. By straddling[23] two economies, they gain a measure of security and a measure of freedom from the market as well as from the government – both of which are capable of being particularly harsh in their dealings with the poor.[24] If, for example, there is a crop failure, they can go to work for wages. If wages are low or commodity traders are squeezing them hard, their gardens protect them from starvation.

Because they occupy a position of ambivalence toward the market, peasants cannot be counted upon to obey its laws. Chayanov cites some interesting examples: a reluctance to use economically viable labour-saving devices because there was no economic benefit in allowing family labour to stand idle; the use of an economic advantage, say an improved market, not to increase profit, but to gain leisure.[25] The peasants' position also gives them opportunities to evade the dictates of government. A retreat into subsistence agriculture may serve as a way of avoiding taxes or a resort to wage labour may provide an escape from onerous regulations upon agriculture.

Their ability to defy both laws and categories has made peasants the despair of intellectuals and policy-makers of all stripes. To Marxists, the peasants' resistance to capitalism means they are blocking the course of social evolution that will lead through capitalism to socialism. Marx himself had already lost patience with the French peasantry by 1850. Discouraged at their lack of revolutionary *esprit*, he could not resist salting his analysis of their situation with such angry descriptive words and phrases as 'stupidity,' 'prejudice,' 'superstition,' 'fanatical defence of their imaginary property,' and 'incapable of asserting their class interest.'[26] Nor did it take socialist policy-makers long to despair of the peasant. The modern history of conflict between agricultural officials and small-scale producers began in the Soviet Union, where repeated attempts to bring about an agrarian revolution failed, with the result that the government carried out a brutal, forced collectivization of agriculture, which, to this day, has not been turned into a success. Bourgeois commentators and officials have also found that peasants defy their dictates and overturn their analyses and have responded by calling them rigid, tradition-bound, and irrational. Much of this invective stems from a failure to appreciate the differences between the lives of intellectuals and policy-makers on the one hand, and that of peasants on the other.

Goran Hyden, in a recent book,[27] has broken new ground in the attempt to apply these insights to an examination of policy. Focusing on Tanzania, he argues that peasants will not make a contribution to national economic development as long as they retain their independence. Since Tanzania is a peasant society, it follows that peasants must be 'captured' – their exit options blocked – if poverty is to be overcome. In this context, Hyden offers some qualified support to the Tanzanian government's attempts (which include coercion) to increase the productivity of small-scale agriculture. He argues, by implication at least, that it is better that the peasantry be captured by a social democratic regime – which has not lost its social conscience – than that the job be left to either robber barons or Stalinists.

Hyden's conclusions about Tanzania are peripheral to this study, but his approach has applications to Kenya. As we will see, much of that nation's peasantry has already been captured, but some of it has not. Hyden's analysis helps us to understand regional inequalities in Kenya and it is potentially useful in deciding what kinds of development and welfare resources are best allocated to different parts of the country and different segments of society. We return to this subject in chapter 8.

EVALUATION

The studies we have been looking at differ from each other in important ways, but they also have a number of features in common. In the first place. all of them involve class analyses in which class is conceived of as a relationship to the means of production. This form of analysis is tailor-made to the study of economic development, or stagnation. Economic development, after all, takes place when a society is organized to permit successful exploitation of a productive apparatus. The peasantry, the petty bourgeoisie, and the upper bourgeoisie are all defined according to their relationships with the means of production and it is through those relationships – and the organization of production that they constitute – that development will either succeed or fail.

Second, the studies deal, not only with the question of whether development is taking place, but also with the quality of development. The language used is not always well calculated to make that point clear, but it is implicit. The term 'underdevelopment,' as it was used by dependency theorists, is an ill-wrought coinage. For one thing, the intention of the term is to indicate a trend, a direction of change, while the word 'under' refers to a particular place, not movement in a direction. The term does not say what it means, therefore, and grates on the fastidious ear. More important, the meaning itself is ill conceived. A country suffering from 'underdevelopment' may not in fact be failing to develop or moving backwards. On the contrary, there may be a great deal of development, with multinationals investing, buildings going up, people being employed, goods being produced, and services purveyed. The problem, rather, is that the development is not, in the long run, benefiting the majority of citizens; indeed, it may be impoverishing them. It is not underdevelopment, but *perverse* development. Perverse development is in fact what Langdon and Kaplinsky maintain – and Leys denies – is happening in Kenya. Cowen seems to be hinting that the middle-peasant/international-capital alliance could lead to perverse development, by blocking industrialization.

A third feature of the studies reviewed is that they offer a set of guidelines – loose, but a useful starting point for further analysis – about the ways in which economic development can take place. First of all, we established that capitalist agriculture will be an important feature in Kenya's development. Then Byres, making generalizations about the third world, observed that capitalist development in agriculture can take place through a variety of class configurations, involving landlords and/or peasants at one stage of development and varying alliances among peasants, petty-bourgeois elements, and capital at another stage. Emmanuel, also speaking of the world in general, pointed out that the role of agriculture can vary from country to country, serving as little more than a stepping stone to industrialization at one extreme and, at the other, constituting a major element in the development process and occupying a prominent place in the economy once development has taken place.

Moving beyond the generalizations of Byres and Emmanuel to a more specific appreciation of Kenya's circumstances, we know from Leys' 'peasantization' thesis that peasants occupy a prominent role in Kenya's political economy and that they are not about to be displaced by other classes. From Cowen's example of the middle-peasant/international-capital alliance, we can gather that the position of peasants is sustained by an alliance or series of alliances with other classes. If those alliances promote the mutual interests of peasants and the petty bourgeoisie – or, for that matter, some of the less moneyed sections of the upper bourgeoisie – we can expect that Kenya's development path such as it is, will follow loosely the lines laid out by Langdon and Kaplinsky, involving smaller-scale industry and agriculture and a relatively wide distribution of income and assets.

How alarming or comforting we find that prospect depends on our estimate of the likely role, respectively, of industry and mechanized agriculture in Kenya's future. If we believe that it will be possible for Kenya to become prosperous in an economy in which small-scale, mechanized agriculture plays a prominent role, we will likely welcome the Kaplinsky-Langdon scenario. If, however, we agree with Leys (not the young Leys of 'peasantization' fame, but the more mature one who advocates conventional capitalist development) that the industrialization essential to Kenya's future prosperity would be blocked by a dominant petty-bourgeois/peasant alliance, we will hope that the bourgeoisie manage to forge an alliance unfavourable to the continued advance of 'peasantization' and the growing prosperity of the petty bourgeoisie.

We have learned one other thing about the process of economic development. In looking at the works of Chayanov and Hyden we discovered that not all peasants are capable of making contributions to modern economic development, capitalist or otherwise. It is only a captured peasantry – one pressured or otherwise motivated into a firm commitment to market agriculture – that is prepared to abandon its traditional independence and to contribute to the generation of surplus for investment in productive assets. Until that point is reached, smallholder agriculture cannot contribute to economic development.

APPLICATION

That, in brief, is what can be learned about land and class in Kenya by consulting other writers. It is a tribute to the quality of the literature that it yields so much knowledge. The remainder of this book tries to build on that base. It also modifies it in important ways. Part I traces the formation of agrarian classes during the colonial era, showing how the arrival of a European settler community gradually transformed local societies consisting of cultivators, herdsmen, and petty traders into a landless class, a peasantry, and a petty bourgeoisie. At the same time, it emphasizes the differences between Africa and the West, focusing on the significance of land in African society and its importance in the minds of Africans. In the process, there emerges an explanation of how Marxists have misunderstood land and class in Kenya and how the colonial regime, on the basis of similar misunderstandings, miscalculated its policies.

Part II deals with the education of the colonial authorities and Kenya's transition to independence. It traces the process whereby the authorities came to a more realistic understanding of the dynamics of the society they had been trying to govern for three-quarters of a century, and how they used their new-found knowledge to lay the basis for the survival of an agrarian bourgeoisie in the face of an expanded peasant sector. It outlines the roles played by various classes and class fractions; and it details how each one fared as a system that had been dominated by an expatriate agrarian bourgeoisie became adjusted to the demands of African majority rule. In the process, it corrects a number of misunder-

standings in the literature about the character of the transition to independence.

Part III looks at Kenya in the 1970s and 1980s, describing how the
peasantry and the capitalist classes flourish and expand side by side and
showing how they reinforce each other even as they engage in the conflicts of getting and spending, being exploited and striking back. Here,
too, the analysis refutes some of the Marxian conventional wisdom. This
book ends with a discussion of how the evolution of Kenya's agrarian
system and class system in the 1980s affects that nation's prospects for
development or stagnation in the future, and with analyses of the policies that are being followed – or might be followed – in pursuit of prosperity.

Part I

Historical background: class formation and land in the colonial era

The Mau Mau took to the forests in the 1950s in a bloody, seemingly hopeless battle with handmade weapons against the might of the colonial regime. In the kind of contradiction that never seems to deter purveyors of media myths, much of the Western press portrayed them as blood-thirsty savages on the one hand and crafty agents of communism on the other. To Africans in Kenya, they have come to be known as the Land Freedom Army, and in retrospect it is clear that their apparently suicidal assault on the colonial regime was in fact a turning point on the road to Kenya's independence.

Land Freedom Army: The linkage of 'land' and 'freedom' expresses the ideas for which forest fighters gave their lives. An understanding of that linkage is fundamental to an understanding of land and class in Kenya, even today. For those Africans who suffered most at the hands of the colonialists, it was loss of land and land rights that were at the heart of their suffering. The colonial system dealt a double blow to Africans who were relatively poor to begin with or who were less able than others to adapt to the changes brought about by British rule. First it led to the loss of land rights they had enjoyed in pre-colonial society and then it spurred the development of an economy within which landless Africans were the most helpless and exploited group. A knowledge of this course of events helps to explain the extraordinary importance of Kenya's land, both as a political symbol and as a material resource well worth fighting for.

Part of this story has already been told well enough for our purposes and part of it has not. Thus we proceed selectively, looking at pre-colonial society, drawing on secondary materials, and correcting some mis-conceptions those materials have not redressed. What we need to know about the history of colonial land alienation can be read out of two accounts, Sorrenson's *Origins of European Settlement in Kenya* and the Kenya Land Commission *Report*. The relevant parts of the two accounts are summarized here. The history of class formation in colonial society has been touched upon in various accounts without receiving the systematic treatment supplied here, again in summary form. On the other hand, we skim very lightly over the Mau Mau war – a story that is at the heart of the history of land and class in Kenya, but which has been told and retold elsewhere, almost as much as it deserves to be, and better than our sources allow.

2

European encroachment: the roots of class conflict

When the first Europeans arrived in the Kenya highlands, they found a society largely untouched by capitalism. Social organization was focused on the extended family and people earned their livelihoods by agriculture, cattle-keeping, handicrafts, and barter. The colonial era brought both the benefits and the disruptions of capitalism to Kenya. Europeans introduced modern agriculture, commerce, and industry. In the process, new wealth was created side by side with new poverty, and each was contingent upon the other. Much of the wealth was based upon the exploitation of agricultural land, while a good bit of the poverty stemmed from loss of land and from exploitation of labour upon the land.

The settlement of Kenya's land question at independence was a direct outcome of these changes. It was an arena for the resolution – for good or ill – of the class conflicts surrounding land that were a legacy of the colonial era. In order to understand the relationship between land and class at independence, therefore, it is necessary to have some idea of how the classes originated and how each was shaped by the economic and political forces of colonialism. First, let us begin by looking at some relevant aspects of pre-colonial African society, and then let us look at how colonialism encroached upon that society and laid the basis for the establishment of a new social and economic order in Kenya.

PRE-COLONIAL SOCIETY: COMMUNAL OR INDIVIDUAL?

The question of how best to describe pre-colonial social organization has become so suffused with polemics that it is difficult to look at it in a detached way. The polemics have focused on a dispute over whether

African society was 'communal' or 'individualistic.' The opening salvo in this war of words was fired by colonialists who early on concluded that African society was communal in nature. In order to understand the significance of this description, it has to be viewed in the context of the all but universal assumption among Kenya Europeans that individualism and capitalism represented the 'highest' stage of human development. 'Communal,' therefore, was a shorthand for 'primitive' or 'inferior.'

Because they really did believe in the inferiority of Africans, the Europeans reckoned without the sophistication of their opponents. Jomo Kenyatta, who spent a generation (much of it in exile and detention) as the premier Kikuyu politician before becoming independent Kenya's first president, was quick to grasp the significance of individualism as a political symbol in colonial Kenya. Concerned to bolster Kikuyu land claims in particular and political claims generally, he wrote a political book disguised as an anthropology book, designed at least in part to rehabilitate what would nowadays be called his people's image, and to stamp them with the individualist imprimatur that was a sine qua non of political respectability in colonial Kenya.

Facing Mount Kenya is deservedly a literary classic, for it is extremely well written. Indeed, even as an anthropology book it is an indispensable source, certainly for the non-specialist. But it is best understood if the reader bears its political purpose in mind. On the question of land ownership, Kenyatta replied to European arguments as follows:

The sense of private property vested in the family was ... highly developed among the Gikuyu, but the form of private ownership in the Gikuyu community did not necessarily mean the exclusive use of the land by the owner, or the extorting of rents from those who wanted to have cultivation or building rights. In other words, it was a man's pride to own a property and his enjoyment to allow collective use of such property. This sense of hospitality which facilitated the communal use of almost everything, has been mistaken by the Europeans who misinterpreted it by saying that the land was under the communal or tribal ownership, and as such the land must be *mali ya serikali*, which means government property. Having coined this new terminology of land tenure, the British Government began to drive away the original owners of land.[1]

In other words, the sharing of land and other property, which was an obvious feature of Kikuyu society, should not be interpreted as in any sense qualifying Kikuyu commitment to individualism and private property. Clearly, this argument is better politics than anthropology. Certainly it served Kenyatta's political purposes admirably and gained wide acceptance. In the 1960s, however, as Kenya gained its independence, and the respectability of colonialism waned, it became acceptable, even among opponents of colonialism, to emphasize the 'communal' aspects of traditional society. Leading the way this time was Julius Nyerere, president of neighbouring Tanzania, who made political virtues out of 'traditional' values under the rubric of *ujamaa* (familyhood).

In the 1970s, the pendulum took another swing, propelled this time by the Marxists' delight in finding conflict and disharmony every-where – except of course in that society which has not yet been created. Writers like Michael Cowen and Apollo L. Njonjo once again empha-sized, as Kenyatta had, the individualist aspects of pre-colonial society. By 1981, Cowen apparently felt that his 'revisionist' conventional wis-dom had been enshrined to the point where he could dismiss opposing arguments without bothering to examine them. In the *Review of African Political Economy*, he congratulated Njonjo, in one sentence, for 'debunk-ing' the idea that 'pre-colonial landed ownership was essentially commu-nal rather than private' and then moved on to matters he regarded as more important.[2]

This seemingly endless debate has been as wearisome and repetitive as it has been unenlightening, because it has been conducted in the wrong terms. Both the concept of 'individualism' and that of 'communal society' are Western. The former has a long history of associations with the mainstream of the Greek-Judaeo-Christian tradition and more recently represents an idealized model of capitalist society. The latter is asso-ciated with countless communities and ideologies that have reacted against individualism and capitalism. African traditions are different and they are not readily understood as long as they are being used as a political football on an alien playing-field. They deserve to be examined and understood on their own terms. Such an examination suggests, as we will see, that pre-colonial society was neither individualist nor com-munal in the Western sense of those terms. In our discussion we focus on that aspect of African society most relevant to our concern: land tenure.

LAND TENURE

African land tenure was a kaleidoscope of regulations that varied according to ethnic group,[3] to the type of land in question, and to the status of each individual. One common feature of African tenure, how-ever, was its tendency to permit very widespread – perhaps universal –

access to land. In the case of nomadic pastoral groups, this was axio-matic, because typically they ranged freely over large areas and an individual did not require long-term rights to a particular piece of land.[4] Members of agricultural groups, on the other hand, did acquire rights to a particular plot, but these rights did not as a rule have the effect of barring any members from access to land.[5] Certainly this was true in the case of the Kikuyus, who are especially important for our purposes because it was Kikuyu grievances over land that eventually became Kenya's most controversial political issue. It is especially worth our while, therefore, to understand some of the customs that consti-tuted traditional tenure among the Kikuyus.[6]

Regular inheritance. A basic unit of Kikuyu society was the *mbari*, or lineage, which consisted of the descendants of a single man. The mem-bers of a *mbari*, who usually numbered in the hundreds, were the joint owners of a piece of land, called their *githaka*. The original acquisition of a *githaka* took place when a man undertook the first clearing of virgin land or when he purchased land. Thereafter, his descendants would inherit pieces of that land for their own use. After the death of the founder of a *mbari*, the lineage would select a *muramati*, 'a leader of the *mbari* in matters of land. His chief duty was to control the allocation and use of the land ... The *muramati*, as far as can be ascertained, had no more cultivation or building rights than his brothers. He had the power to adjust the allotment of holdings with the *mbari* and to admit or refuse tenants.'[7] Land was distributed to members of each successive genera-tion according to their need for it. When a *githaka* became overcrowded, more land might be acquired, or part of the *mbari* might split off and move to unclaimed land elsewhere, thereby founding, if they wished, a new *mbari*. As one generation followed another, therefore, the Kikuyu people were steadily expanding the boundaries of their territory. And, in the normal course of events, each person was able to claim a piece of land for his or her own use as the need for it arose.

Tenancies. In addition to the regular process of land inheritance through the *mbari*, there were also ways in which a man could obtain the use of land from a *mbari* other than his own. In order to acquire such tenancy rights, he had to establish one of several possible types of rela-tionships with someone who would be in a position to offer him the use of land. These relationships might involve either a simple contractual arrangement focused specifically on land use or a more far-reaching status-tie in which the tenancy was only one part of the total relationship.

There were three types of contractual tenants. One was a *muhoi*, a person who acquires cultivation rights on the basis of friendship, offering no payment in return other than an annual tribute of beer and the first fruits of the harvest. Another was a *muguri*, someone who is given the use of land in return for a loan of livestock. A third type of contractual relationship involved a *muthami*, a person who acquires the right to build his home on the *githaka* of a *mbari* other than his own. A *muthami* and *muhoi* or *muguri* might be one and the same person, having acquired cultivation rights and building rights as well within the strange *githaka*.

The literature available for the present study lists four kinds of more substantive status-ties that conferred land-use rights. One was the *muthoni* tie, usually involving a son-in-law and his father-in-law. The latter could not refuse to give land rights to the former, provided he needed them. (This was not the regular inheritance procedure, as a man would normally inherit from his father rather than his father-in-law.) Another person whose status included land rights was the *mwendia ruhiu*, a man who lived with, but was not married to, a widow. A third status-tie involved a landless stranger who gained full rights in a *mbari*. He is a *muciarua*, 'a man (often a foreigner) who has no rights in any *githaka* and is "adopted" by a wealthy man, given a wife and land; his children belong to the adopted *mbari* and inherit from it.'[8] Finally there is the *ndungata* – possibly another name for *muciarua* – who gets a wife and land from a rich man.

Discussion. These arrangements, clearly, are neither individualist nor communal. The land is not held in common, but demarcated by boundaries. Individuals hold land and exercise authority over it as a personal privilege and responsibility. There are wealthy people and poor people and, by implication, there is also exploitation. The head of a household, whether a *muramati* or another male *mbari* member, can acquire wives, children, and tenants and, therefore, increase his power and access to material resources by deploying the labour of others. On the other hand, property owners do not have licence to do whatever they please with their property. They have obligations, in the first instance to family, but also to friends in need. The terms 'individualist' and 'communal' are at best over-simplifications and at worst entirely misleading.

It is important for us to move beyond the over-simplifications because, in order to understand problems of land and class in the colonial era, we must know how things changed for Africans when Europeans arrived and how they reacted to those changes. Three observations are important in that context. The first is that the Kikuyu system of tenancy required the existence of an open frontier, so that when a *githaka* became overcrowded, some members of the *mbari* could move out to new land. When Europeans arrived, they claimed unrestricted rights to seize unoccupied land. Such seizures robbed the Kikuyu land tenure system of its dynamic element and very quickly brought about distortions, not only in land tenure, but also in the social system as a whole. From the Kikuyu perspective, therefore, the mere presence of Europeans on the fringes of their territory – even without all the more blatant aspects of colonialism – meant the end of a way of life.

Second, it is worth underlining the fact that pre-colonial land rights among the Kikuyus were, for all practical purposes, universal. Not only did *mbari* members gain rights to the land they needed as part of the regular process of inheritance; in addition, there was a variety of means whereby people – even those who had no rights in any *githaka* – could become tenants. Thus when the colonial system began to spawn landlessness, it was inflicting, from the African point of view, an unheard-of deprivation and committing an unspeakable outrage. That is one reason why the land issue never lost its impact. Europeans wondered why Africans kept harping on the same old land grievances decade after decade, even after the colonial system had brought new economic opportunities in commerce, industry, and the public service. But Africans – especially those who became landless while being denied access to the new opportunities – could not so easily forget that the liquidation of traditional land usages had cut the heart out of their way of life.

Finally, it is important to note that pre-colonial land use involved a mutually reinforcing mixture of the personal and familial with the economic. This is in sharp contrast to Western society, where we try very earnestly (though not always successfully) to separate these two aspects of our lives. In pre-colonial society, land was distributed on the basis of family ties or friendship and in exchange for livestock, labour, or commodities. In later chapters, we will see that the use of land as a means of simultaneously building one's personal relationships and one's economic fortunes has been adapted to the post-colonial economy and society and has become a central feature of the development of peasant society.

TRADITIONAL ENTREPRENEURSHIP

Agriculture and animal husbandry were the main sources of subsistence in pre-colonial society, but they were not the only economic activities. A very important activity, and one which proved particularly adaptable to the colonial economy, was trade. Although much less has been written about the history of traditional entrepreneurship than one would like to know, there is material available that gives a vivid, if fragmentary, picture of its character. Peter Marris and Anthony Somerset, using the data from a series of interviews with old men in the Mahiga Location of Nyeri District, give an account of how Kikuyu traders exploited the commercial opportunities offered by pre-colonial society.[9] Their halcyon days were those of the Masai trade, when Kikuyu entrepreneurs were among the wealthiest and most respected people in their communities. The Mahiga traders led caravans numbering from 30 to 200 over Nyandarua – called the Aberdares Mountains by Europeans – to trade the various products of Kikuyuland for the livestock of the pastoral Masai. A leader of a caravan had to be fluent in the Masai language and he needed to maintain contacts among the Masai that would protect him and his caravan from attack. In organizing a trading expedition, the caravan leader first had to make arrangements with his Masai contacts, setting a time and place for his caravan's safe conduct. Next he would set about assembling the goods that he would sell on the expedition.

Millet flour would come from his own farm, and honey from his hives, but for other goods he might have to travel widely over Kikuyuland. Ochre, for instance, was cheaper in Chinga, ten miles to the south; the best gourds grew in Murang'a, twenty miles south; tobacco and snuff were available locally, but the Masai valued higher the tobacco from Ndia and Embu, thirty or forty miles to the east; a Mahiga blacksmith would forge spearheads and knives, but the ingots had to be obtained from Murang'a, where iron ore was mined and smelted. To acquire all these goods, the trader had to drive livestock for exchange. He travelled with porters, but unless he had an experienced assistant, he supervised his own purchasing, since quality was important. Gourds, for instance, had to be of the right shape and colour: young Masai women much preferred the straight, unblemished gourds and curved or blotched gourds would only sell to older women at a discount.[10]

When the entrepreneur had assembled his goods, he would set off with his caravan on the hazardous journey over the mountains to keep his appointment with his Masai contacts. He would trade his goods for livestock, which, in Kikuyu society, was the basic component of a wealthy man's fortune.[11] The Kikuyu entrepreneur, although he was a formidable businessman, was closely tied to the land. Most of his products – as well as the animals that represented his profits – were agricultural goods. The coming of European settlement, as we will see, put an end to the Masai trade, but entrepreneurship remained an important feature of African society throughout the colonial era. And although the cash nexus replaced that of livestock, the reciprocal relationship between trade and agriculture remained strong, not only for the remainder of the colonial period, but after independence as well.

EUROPEAN SETTLEMENT

When European settlers first came to the region that was to be called Kenya, they had very little knowledge of African society. But that did not prevent them from developing strong opinions. From the outset, Africans were assumed to be inferior to Europeans, not only in the sense of having a more rudimentary technology, but in some kind of vaguely conceived absolute sense, which was thought to have both intellectual and moral dimensions. Those assumptions led, not surprisingly, to the conclusion that European rights should prevail over those of Africans. Espeth Huxley, one of the most articulate defenders of settlers' rights and prerogatives, explained that colonialization was founded, among other things, on

an inherent conviction that civilization in itself was good. In [the early days of settlement], when abstract morality had a concrete meaning, when there was a Right and a Wrong, people did not doubt that it was better to be civilized than savage. Civilization was good, savagery was bad. The logical corollary of this belief was that anyone who spread civilization was doing right, was conferring a benefit on the people he helped to civilize ... There could be no question therefore, but that the white man was paramount, and must remain so until the native became – if he ever did – the intellectual equal of the European.[12]

As European settlement spread through Kenya's highlands[13] early in this century, considerable amounts of African land were included in what became known as the White Highlands. In later years, defenders of European settlement found a variety of justifications for these aliena-tions of land. Some land, it was said, was unoccupied or was so sparsely settled as to be virtually unoccupied; some was taken by right of con-quest; some areas, it was maintained, were buffer zones between hostile 'tribes' and European settlement was merely a means of bringing peace to the land; and in other cases, mistakes were allegedly made and later on some minimal compensation was offered.

For the most part, such justifications were for public consumption, to satisfy the Colonial Office in London and the British public. Among themselves, Kenya's European settlers did not seriously question their right to alienate any African land that seemed to them to be underutilized. (The fact that they themselves were occupying far greater acreages than they would be able to utilize in the foreseeable future did not figure in their reasoning.) Their belief in the superiority of European civilization and the European economy served to justify, to themselves at least, the primacy of their rights over those of Africans. Elspeth Huxley summarized the position crisply: 'The idea that the interests of ... untutored tribesmen ... should be exalted over those of the educated European would have seemed ... fantastic.'[14] The settlers not only took their primacy for granted, but also seemed to lack any great concern for minimizing the harmful effects of European settlement upon Africans. On the contrary, it was the effect of the *African* presence upon *Europeans* that was viewed with alarm. Many settlers feared that what one referred to as 'the foolish negrophilist sentimentality'[15] of British authorities would lead to undue restrictions on European expansion. Sir Charles Eliot, commissioner of the East Africa Protectorate until 1904, was an early and vigorous advocate of European settlement. In response to complaints that Europeans were moving into 'thickly cultivated' African areas, he warned a subordinate 'to be careful not to deprive intending [European] settlers of any right or privilege to which they may be entitled under the existing regulations.'[16] On another occasion, a Kenya official declared testily: '... if the Highlands are to remain a White man's country a very firm stand must be taken against allowing *any* of the existing [African] Reserves to be extended.'[17] The spirit of European expansion in Kenya was a self-confident belief in a personal and cultural superiority that could justify almost anything. In order to get a sense of the realities that shaped African attitudes toward the land issue, it is useful to take a look at how the landholdings and land reserves of some of Kenya's major ethnic groups were affected by that expansion.

Kikuyus. The land transactions that turned out to have the greatest long-term impact upon Kenya's politics were those involving Kikuyu country, located on the eastern side of the Aberdares Mountains between Nairobi and Mt Kenya. European settlement in this area took place under the influence of the policy that Eliot referred to as 'interpenetration,' whereby European holdings were allowed to be interspersed among existing African areas instead of being restricted, as they later were, to blocks of land reserved entirely for themselves. Eliot, who saw European settlement as a civilizing mission to the indigenous popu-

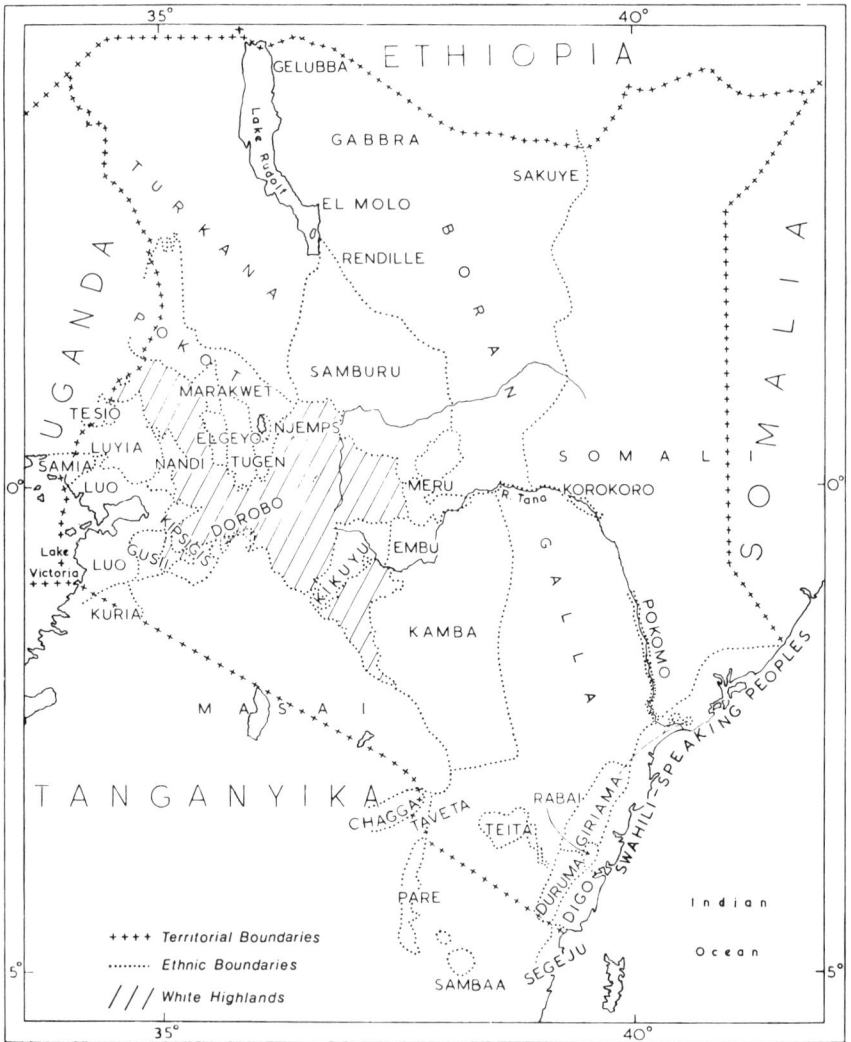

Figure 2 Ethnic groups, colonial Kenya (drawn by J.K. Mbazira, Makerere Institute of Social Research; used by permission)

lation, felt that interpenetration, by bringing Europeans and Africans close together, would hasten the process of civilization.

Interpenetration had another consequence, which was perhaps not entirely unanticipated. It put Europeans in close proximity to some of the finest farmland in Kenya, making it readily available for take-overs. A rash of land seizures followed. To be sure, there is a possibility that some of these alienations were the product of mutual misunderstandings. Europeans were not familiar with African land tenure systems and there was a tendency to assume that *githaka* rights were nothing more than temporary rights of usufruct rather than the permanent rights that they in fact were. That assumption made it easy for Europeans to claim any piece of *githaka* land that was temporarily not being used. Africans, for their part, may not have understood in the early days that when Europeans offered money for land they were after permanent and inalienable rights. In some instances, they may have believed they were granting the kinds of tenancy rights described earlier in this chapter and which, in Kikuyu custom, were normally revocable.[18]

As Africans and Europeans got to know each other better, however, the likelihood of such misunderstandings grew less. There developed a regular procedure, administered by the colonial authorities, for the alienation of Kikuyu land. Settlers were required to pay the previous occupants two rupees per acre for cultivated land in the presence of a local official. M.P.K. Sorrenson describes how Kikuyu rightholders thus became squatters on what had been their own land.

Once Kikuyu had been paid compensation for their occupiers' rights, they lost all claim to the land and could be moved at the will of the settler concerned. The settler could then obtain a title to the portions of the land formerly occupied by Kikuyu, according to the Crown Lands Ordinance. In fact, many of the Kikuyu who received compensation for land were encouraged to stay to provide labour. In this case the government drew up labour contracts which allowed the employees to cultivate up to one acre per [person]. Through the compensation and labour agreements the Kikuyu thus became, in terms of law, mere squatters.[19]

Between 1903 and 1906, according to Sorrenson, some 25 000 hectares of Kikuyu territory were alienated in the Kiambu-Limuru area in the vicinity of Nairobi. Years later, the Kenya Land Commission worked out the following totals for Kiambu District. Something less than 4000 rupees had been paid to some 8000 Kikuyus at the rate of two rupees per acre (five per hectare) to compensate them for their rights of occupation. Another 3000 Kikuyus, the commission acknowledged, had received no compensation for the rights they had lost.[20]

The shift from a policy of interpenetration to the creation of 'tribal' reserves made African land less readily accessible to individual Europeans, but it failed to provide absolute protection. Establishment of reserve boundaries remained a colonial responsibility and colonial authorities often proved highly susceptible to settler pressure. Even after they had been established, boundaries were not necessarily sacrosanct, as Sorrenson points out. The boundaries of the Kikuyu reserve were published in 1912, he notes, but 'In January 1913 a block of land between the Amboni and Chania rivers, near Nyeri [in norther Kikuyuland], was cut out of the reserve and surveyed for settlement. The land was said to be almost entirely unoccupied. The government wanted Europeans to occupy it to prevent Kikuyu from doing so.'[21]

Masai. Like the Kikuyus, the Masai suffered what were probably their most significant losses during the period of interpenetration. Among the early settlers, those who were interested in farming headed first for the green highlands of central Kenya; those who wanted to go into ranching were most attracted to the Rift Valley, 'not merely because the railway passed through the valley [but] also because the best of the Rift Valley pastures were already inhabited by the Masai, a sign that the land and climatic conditions were suitable for ranching.'[22] Europeans should be permitted to settle in the Rift, it was decided. In support of that decision, Sir Charles Eliot argued: '... as a matter of principle, I cannot admit that wandering tribes have a right to keep other and superior races out of large tracts merely because they have acquired the habit of straggling over far more land than they can utilize.'[23]

When the policy of reserves began to take precedence over that of interpenetration, European primacy in the Rift Valley became a *fait accompli*. Among the disunited Masai, colonial authorities were able to find leaders who were prepared to give their official assent to the *fait* in return for the promise of secure boundaries in the future. The Agreement of 1904 was an arrangement for the Masai to move 'away from the railway line and away from any land that may be thrown open to European settlement' and to occupy two reserves: one to the south and another in Laikipia to the north. The agreement, which specified that the Masai had decided of their 'own free will ... that it is for our best interest to move our own people, flocks and herds into definite reservations ...' was to be 'enduring as long as the Masai as a race shall exist.'[24]

In 1911, the Masai were still very much in existence, but the Agreement of 1904 was abrogated in favour of a new arrangement in which they vacated Laikipia in return for an extension of the southern reserve. The Agreement of 1911, like the earlier one, involved an elaborate display of the Masai's alleged voluntary acquiescence. But other reasons for the land exchange were not far to seek. 'A full and complete statement of the objects and reasons of the [agreement],' the Kenya Land Commission acknowledged, rather sheepishly, 'would require mention of the fact that the Northern Reserve was to be vacated partly for European settlement ...' The commission was at pains to emphasize, however, 'that the paramount chief of the tribe and the representative chief and elders of the Northern Masai agreed to the move for the reason set out in the preamble of the Agreement, namely that they were "satisfied that it is in the best interests of their tribe that the Masai should inhabit one area."'[25] Henceforth, the Masai reserve was restricted to an area south of the railway. The question of how satisfactory, or unsatisfactory, this exchange of land was from the Masai point of view is a controversial one that cannot be settled within the scope of the present study. But it is not open to dispute that the earlier loss of the fine grazing land in the Rift Valley was a Masai sacrifice to the advance of European settlement.

Ukambani. The home of the Kamba people, located to the east of Kikuyuland, was the scene of two incidents of land alienation worthy of mention. One of them occurred in Kikumbuliu, which was set aside in 1906 as a closed district, reserved for African use. The area was sparsely populated and the railway ran through it. In the period that followed, land along the railway was taken up by Europeans. In 1909, new boundaries were established, 'which amounted to a reduction of the Kikumbuliu reserve by three-fifths.'[26] Those Africans who were resident on the European estates established along the railway, it was noted, would be able to stay on as labourers. It was another case of Africans being reduced to the status of labourers on what had been their own land.

Another district set aside for Kamba use in 1906 was the Ulu reserve, which took in the Mua Hills, a well-watered area suitable for cultivation. Only a small part of the hills had been occupied by the Kamba before 1895.[27] Beginning in 1906, European settlers had taken up ranching on the Athi plains outside the reserve and in 1908 they applied for small tracts of land in the hills to supplement their drier land. The request was granted and in the following year further inroads were made on the reserve. By 1909, the hills were being taken from the Kamba altogether.

According to Sorrenson, a colonial official reported that other land 'had been found further north and was to be given to the Kamba in exchange for the Mua hills.' Sorrenson adds: 'He neglected to say that the land, the Matungulu hills, was already occupied by other Kamba. The Colonial Office accepted the "exchange" without further enquiry.'[28]

Nandi. The stiffest resistance to European encroachment came from the Nandi on the Mau plateau west of the Rift Valley, who, in the 1890s and the first part of the present century, harassed European caravans and railway workers and forced some early settlers to retreat. The defeat of the Nandi, therefore, was regarded as a prerequisite for European settlement in the western highlands. In 1905 the defeat was accomplished, and the peace settlement of that year provided for the removal of part of the Nandi people from areas adjacent to the railway. After their removal, some 3200 square kilometres of 'evacuated Nandi country' was made available for European settlement.[29] The Nandi were left with a reserve of about 1800 square kilometres. Despite the fact that the reserve boundaries had been defined, they were changed in the next few years. The Kenya Land Commission claimed that the changes were made 'after the agreement of ... Nandi chiefs had been obtained' and that they resulted in a net gain of some 180 square kilometres to the Nandi. Sorrenson found evidence to show that there was strong dissatisfaction among the Nandi over the changes.[30]

But there was more to come. In 1912, the colonial authorities began to alienate land within the Nandi reserve for European settlers. 'For some reason which is not fully explained,' the Kenya Land Commission noted, the colonial authorities 'overlooked' the fact that the land was in the Nandi reserve and alienated some 155 square kilometres in the Kaimosi and Kipkarren areas, leasing the land to European settlers. In the Kipkarren area, compensation at the rate of 50 rupees per hut was paid to all Africans who were 'disturbed.' After the alienations were already under way, according to the commission's account, the colonial authorities belatedly 'realized' that their actions were out of line with government commitments to the Nandi people. In recognition of Nandi rights, the colonial authorities then began to pay to the Nandi Local Native Council the proceeds from the leases in the Kaimosi and Kipkarren area. The Kenya Land Commission placed its stamp of approval on this arrangement, maintaining that it was in the best interests of all concerned.[31]

Sotik area. In 1905, the year the colonial authorities were at war with the Nandi, another successful campaign was being waged directly to the south against a people who today are called the Kipsigis.[32] During the next few years, some 520 square kilometres of Kipsigis grazing land in the Sotik area were alienated to Europeans.[33] In 1933, the Kenya Land Commission approved the alienations, but expressed sympathy for the Kipsigis, who, it was noted, 'have an excellent war record and merit generous treatment.'[34] In compensation for the Kipsigis claim to Sotik, the commission recommended that the colonial authorities refrain from alienating Chepalungu, a nearby area encompassing roughly 390 square kilometres that local Europeans had wanted as an addition to the White Highlands.[35]

The idea of refraining from one alienation in order to compensate for another was perhaps the most novel concept the commission invented in its feeble defence of African land rights, but it stands as a succinct characterization of the climate of thought prevailing at the time. The historical and legal claims of Africans to their land meant little in the face of European economic and military power. The commission had been given the task, among other things, of considering 'the needs of the native population'[36] and a reading of the report leaves the impression that the commissioners were making some effort to resist settler pressures. But those efforts did not have much effect. Africans were in a subject position and they were left no choice but to accept what was offered and relinquish what was taken. They did not forget their grievances, however, and eventually their lost land became a central preoccupation of Kenya politics, contributing first to the Mau Mau rebellion and then to the nationalist ascendance that led to Kenya's independence. In the end, it took the land settlement at independence to satisfy the land claims that the Kenya Land Commission's recommendations had supposedly settled three decades earlier. But by then, the colonial system had given rise to a host of new grievances.

THE COLONIAL SYSTEM

It had been the task of the Kenya Land Commission to help legitimize the racial and tribal boundaries formed as a result of European expansion into Kenya's highlands. In order to be viable, the colonial system of landownership had to be sustained by laws that rigidly separated Europeans, Asians, and Africans into strata of differential status, rights, and privileges. The division of land was the keystone of the system.

The White Highlands. An area of land totalling some three million hectares was reserved for European agriculture and Africans were barred from owning land within it. Roughly half of the European area was arable land and the other half consisted of land suitable mainly for grazing. The pastoral half was occupied by very large ranches, including a dozen units of 20 000 hectares or more. The land was relatively arid and unsuitable for more intensive use.

The other half of the European area consisted of land with higher potential – having more rainfall and yielding a wide variety of crops and high-quality grasses. At the end of the colonial era, the majority of the farms in this agricultural zone ranged in size from 400 to 800 hectares. A small, but very valuable, part was devoted to coffee, tea, and sugar plantations. The largest proportion of the arable part of the White Highlands was mixed farmland, supporting a variety of crops, notably cereals and vegetables, and dairy cattle as well.[37]

The reserves. According to a colonial estimate,[38] the White Highlands constituted 21 000 of Kenya's 356 000 square-kilometre area. If the European share seems small, it must be borne in mind that some two-thirds of the country (243 000 square kilometres) is a remote area, very thinly populated by nomadic peoples. Most of Kenya's six million Africans lived within an 84 000 square-kilometre area reserved for them and referred to popularly as 'the reserves.'[39] The quality of the agricultural land in the reserves was described in a World Bank report as 'variable, but [including] large areas with a high production potential.'[40]

The reserves, as we have seen, were not a single area but a collection of land units, each one reserved for the use of a particular ethnic group. We have noted that the Kenya Land Commission's acknowledgment of African historical land claims was feeble at best. The commissioners, however, were instructed, not only to look into historical rights, but also to consider the present and likely future land needs of each ethnic group, and in this regard the inadequacies of their report became especially obvious in later years. The East African Royal Commission concluded twenty years later that 'the estimation of future need [was not] made on any uniform of even rational basis, and the consequent rough and ready assessment of this is perhaps the least satisfactory part of the report.'[41] The result (discussed in chapter 3) was ever-growing population pressure in the reserves as the available agricultural land became more and more inadequate to the task of supporting an expanding population.

The squatter system, which was part of the legal framework supporting large-scale agriculture in Kenya, assured European farmers of a supply of cheap African labour, while at the same time maintaining the exclusiveness of their rights of landownership and permanent residency in the highlands. In the early days of European settlement, the system consisted of a patchwork of varying labour and land-use arrangements between European settlers and African squatters or labourers. In 1918, the basis for a uniform squatter system was laid in the Resident Native (Squatters') Ordinance,[42] which provided for a government-supervised labour contract. Under the contract, the squatter agreed to work a specified number of days per year and in return the settler allowed him and his family to live on the farm and cultivate a plot of their own. Africans were forbidden to reside in the White Highlands in any status other than that of squatter and were liable to eviction at the expiration of their respective labour contracts. As Ghai and McAuslan observe, one of the objects of the Resident Native Ordinance 'was to destroy the relationship of landlord and tenant between the European farmer and the African, and so destroy any rights the African might have in the land by reason of the tenancy. A relationship of employer and employee involving elements of involuntary servitude was substituted, and one of the prime objects of later legislation in this field was to maintain that relationship and to prevent the development of a system of tenancy.'[43]

From the beginning, the establishment of a settler community had meant that Africans had to yield to the demands of Europeans. Now a system of law and administration had been erected to legitimize and protect the European position. Chapter 3 looks at how the economic changes that took place within that system helped to bring about the formation of classes within African society.

3

Class formation and the growth of landlessness

We have seen how the colonial regime undermined traditional land tenure and imposed a racialist system of administration. Like a boulder crashing into a pond, these actions made waves which, during the colonial era, rippled through African society, changing it forever. Most Africans were forced to abandon traditional modes of production and become peasants, producing partly for their own subsistence and partly for the market. But, as noted in chapter 1, the margins of peasant independence in Kenya, especially in those areas most affected by the colonial presence, were not wide. Chapter 2 showed in more detail why and how these margins became narrowed: the mere European presence on land adjacent to African areas undermined the traditional system of land distribution and land grabs further limited African access to land. In addition, the colonial administration imposed taxes and numerous restrictions on African agriculture and commerce. The result was that many Africans never enjoyed even the limited freedoms of a peasant's existence. They were rudely snatched from the life of a traditional cultivator and thrust into the pressure cooker of cash agriculture, where they were forced either to become successful market producers or to live by selling their labour.

All of that involved changes in relations to the means of production and in class consciousness. And it was not just a peasantry and a landless class that was being created. A petty bourgeoisie was becoming established as some people parlayed surpluses generated in agriculture or other savings into business ventures while others acquired an education and found their way into administrative positions. At one end of the social spectrum, therefore, people were forced off the land and, gradually, into destitution. At the other end, some were able to prosper within the colonial system. Many of them were undoubtedly spurred on by the narrow margins of peasant existence, which forced them to look for alternatives. In short, colonialism produced class formation within African society. In this chapter, we look at that process and examine its consequences.[1]

THE SQUATTERS: IMPOVERISHMENT

For many Africans, their first contact with the modern economy was the experience of working as a labourer on a large-scale farm. In the early days of settlement, such employment was not necessarily perceived by Africans as an unattractive proposition. On the contrary, for many people it represented (or seemed to represent) a real economic opportunity, especially in the areas where European settlement had closed the frontier for expansion to new land. Rebmann M. Wambaa, a perceptive observer of African social and political life in the large-scale farming areas, describes the situation as follows:

At the time that several families from ... Dagoretti [in the Nairobi area] were going up to the Rift Valley in the late 1910s and early 1920s, there were several influences at work which attracted them to go to the large white farms. The principal force was the popular rumour that you could become rich in a day, since your sheep and goats could multiply, and you got to cultivate as much land as you wanted. Indeed, there was a tale that went around to illustrate this. A man called Nguwa Waikama had gone to the Rift to clear a garden. The very first day he came across a lot of sheep whose Somali owners had been killed by lions. So he suddenly became wealthy.

These rumours were spreading fast, particularly among those who found that their old life in the reserves was not nearly so free nowadays. Naturally those *ahoi*[2] who had no land of their own were attracted by this talk of getting as much land as you cared for; but so also were the rich men who simply wanted to gain extra space for their many goats and sheep. They had been used to shifting on [to new land] in earlier days, and suddenly it had become difficult as the reserve boundaries got closed to expansion ... They knew they would have to do some work for the *mzungu*[3] up on the farms, but Kikuyus were not afraid of that ... They did not mind some wage labour provided they could continue their old social life and get space for their stock and for cultivation.[4]

During the early period of settlement, there was a degree of coincidence between the interests of settlers and those of their labourers. As long as there was plenty of space and freedom on European farms, life on a *githaka* in the reserves did not necessarily offer any great advantages over a squatter's existence. In some ways, in fact, life on large-scale farms was preferable. It included cash wages while offering relief from land shortages, taxation, and the administrative restrictions that were becoming an increasingly distasteful feature of life in the reserves as the colonial administration became stronger.

The coincidence between settlers' interests and those of squatters, however, was not a permanent feature of their relationship. It was a temporary consequence of the particular position in which Europeans found themselves in the first decades of settlement. In 1920, there were only 1122 farms and ranches in the highlands, less than one-third of the 1960 total.[5] Agriculture was relatively undeveloped, indeed was still to a large degree experimental. During this period, as the East African Royal Commission points out,

settlers required labour and they frequently held areas of uncleared land which could be prepared for farming operations by allowing African families to practise their shifting methods of cultivation. The absence of many European farmers during the First World War, the early years of uncertainty regarding methods of farming, and doubts as to profitability, accentuated the need for labour which was cheap in cash outlay and, since there was little prospect that farms would be brought immediately into full production, the uncontrolled use of part of the farmer's land was held out as an inducement to the African to offer his services.[6]

At this point, therefore, the abundance of land available in the areas expropriated by Europeans was ameliorating the effect of land losses upon African society. But large-scale agriculture was developing. The 1920s were a period of rapid expansion in some of Kenya's most important crops. The acreage of coffee, which was concentrated in the plantations of the Nairobi area, tripled during that decade. In some of the more remote districts, maize and wheat expanded at yet faster rates. To be sure, European husbandry remained rather unsophisticated by modern standards. 'Most farmers were content to grow only one or two crops and took little interest in livestock farming, except in areas where pastoralism was being practised. As a result of this the [1920s have] been referred to as the "period of monoculture." This ... was regarded as unsatisfactory in a country considered to be very suitable for mixed farming, especially in the arable districts.'[7]

But as agriculture continued to develop the economic advantages of the squatter system gradually diminished. When settlers cleared new land it became unavailable for the cultivation and cattle-keeping of labourers. There were other problems as well. The Africans' 'zebu' cattle, although resistant to disease themselves, posed the hazard of disease to the more productive grade cattle that were in many cases preferred by Europeans. And settlers who were developing their land maintained that the Africans' practice of traditional methods of cultivation on their allotted plots brought with it the danger of soil deterioration.

The effects of these changes were not uniform, because European farms were developing at different rates. Farmers who had the capital for development tended to favour the removal of squatters, while relatively poorer farmers continued to find that the squatter system worked to their economic advantage. Nevertheless, as early as 1933, the development of European agriculture had reached a point where the future of squatters was beclouded. In that year, the Kenya Land Commission commented:

It is scarcely to be supposed that the European area will always afford accommodation for all the squatters and their natural increase or for their stock. While nobody can foretell how many extra labourers expansion of agricultural industry may be able to employ, there is at least an indication that the numbers have for several years been in excess of requirements, and there has been a set of the tide back towards the reserves. This tendency, although it may be only a temporary phenomenon due to the current depression, has caused a justifiable apprehension, and it is possible that it may become a problem of the first magnitude how and where accommodation is to be found for squatters who are surplus to the requirements of the European Highlands.[8]

As it turned out, the phenomenon was not temporary and the apprehension proved amply justified. Squatters became less and less welcome on European farms, while the problems of finding alternative accommodation for them mounted steadily. In 1937, the Resident Natives Ordinance, described in chapter 2, was repealed

and replaced by a version giving greater powers of control over labourers and their cattle. The employer-occupier might fix the number of cattle the resident labourer could keep and it thereupon became unlawful for him to keep more. A magistrate was empowered to order the removal of labourers from undeveloped farms. District Councils, which were purely European in composition, were empowered to limit the number of labourers which could be employed on a farm, limit or prohibit their keeping stock, and fix the number of days in a year labourers were required to work for their employers.[9]

In so far as such legislation implied removal of squatters from the White Highlands and their return to the reserves, it was more readily written than put into practice, because their land rights at home were no longer assured. As early as 1932, according to M.P.K. Sorrenson, some Kikuyu squatters were already losing their land rights in the reserves.[10] The British government declined to allow the legislation to go into effect until land could be made available for the resettlement of squatters who would be evicted. In the end, however, the British authorities yielded; although land for settlement did not become available until 1942, the ordinance was brought into effect in 1940.[11]

In the years that followed, the authority granted under the ordinance was used to impose limits on squatters' stock and on the size of their cultivation plots, to increase their work loads, and even to get rid of some of them.[12] To squatters, the enforcement of these regulations meant that they were gradually being reduced from a quasi-peasant status to that of landless labourers, living under conditions of steadily mounting impoverishment. Cash wages had always been low and, as we have seen, it was the cultivation rights and the opportunity to keep substantial numbers of livestock that had provided much of the incentive to move to the highlands. In practice, squatters had derived a substantial part of their subsistence from cultivation and livestock. The limitations meant progressive reductions in their real income, even in the face of increases in the pittances that passed for their wages.[13]

There was another aspect of the squatters' situation which, in future, would place obstacles in the way of their recovery of peasant status. Many – and probably most – of them spent their working hours doing simple, routine tasks from which they could learn nothing about modern agriculture and animal husbandry or the marketing of produce. While many of their relatives in the reserves were, as we will see, gradually being introduced to modern agriculture on their own small-scale farms, squatters were dividing their time between mind-stopping manual labour and whatever subsistence agriculture they were permitted to do on their own plots. As a rule, they were not given responsibility and remained mere cogs in a machinery the working of which they had no opportunity to learn. As one of them himself recalled years later, even the squatters who milked the cows did not know where the milk went.[14]

Not all Africans fared as badly under colonialism as did the squatters. For some people, the colonial economy brought opportunities – a chance of a missionary education, a relatively well-salaried job, or a profitable enterprise. In responding to such opportunities, they acquired the skills and accumulated the capital necessary for participation in the fast-growing modern sector of Kenya's economy. In the process, the kaleidoscope of classes and class fractions characteristic of a nascent capitalist economy took shape: a peasantry, the most prosperous part of which soon began to build an agricultural base for capital accumulation; a petty bourgeoisie, including traders, merchants, and a salariat; and wage workers, many of whom – by virtue of part-time pursuit of petty trade and/or continued attachment to land – were more akin to an embryonic petty bourgeoisie, or a peasantry, than a proletariat. These classes were amorphous, because people moved freely back and forth between them and because the peasant practice of straddling two or more occupations (noted in chapter 1) carried over into the rest of society. But they were developing rapidly, and the process of their formation set the stage for the swift and brutal changes that were to take place in the latter part of the colonial era.

Trade. The traditional pattern of African commerce changed drastically as a result of the coming of Europeans, but it proved adaptable to the new conditions, despite the favoured position enjoyed by immigrant races during the colonial era. The Masai trade described in chapter 2 was wiped out by the Agreement of 1904, whereby, as we saw, Masai vacated the area across the Aberdares Mountains from Kikuyu country and moved north to Laikipia. For a time, Kikuyu caravans travelled to Laikipia but that trade too was ended when the Agreement of 1911 restricted the Masai to the remote district south of the railway. In time, Kikuyu traders among the Masai found that the advantages of the traditional caravan trade were evaporating and began to set up stationary trading depots, which gradually developed into retail stores. By the 1920s, at least 18 Kikuyu businesses in Narok District had become shops, open the year around and employing assistants.[15]

Throughout the 1920s and 1930s, travelling traders continued to find opportunities that were not yet pre-empted by retail stores. One trading partnership bought sheep and goats from the Tugen in the Lake Baringo area and sold them to Kikuyu squatters in the Rift Valley.[16] The European settlers themselves offered a good market for itinerant traders during this period. Food was bought from African farmers, brought by donkey into the European areas, and sold there. 'So long as prices were lower than a settler would pay to the Asian shops in Nyeri – and he sometimes telephoned to check – the market was assured. But by 1940, Asian traders had begun visiting [African areas] themselves with lorries to buy maize, and Kikuyus left the business for other more promising opportunities.'[17]

The European presence provided the opportunity for another type of mobile trade that was more viable in the modern economy. It involved buying surplus produce from squatters and transporting it to markets in the cities and towns.[18] Even earlier than the 1930s, Africans other than the shopkeepers in Masailand were finding their way into more modern types of trade. Partnerships raised the Shs 12000/- to 15000/- needed to buy a water mill for grinding flour. The viability of water mills was undermined by the introduction, some time later, of mechanical grinders. After that, Asians moved into the mill business and Africans were forced out. But there remained numerous other outlets for African entrepreneurial talent, despite the restrictions of the colonial system and the immigrant races' monopolization of sources of supply for many goods. In the African areas of cities and towns, there were opportunities to open hotels, butcher shops, teashops, and *maduka* (provision stores). In town markets, Africans traded in farm produce. Some were able to get into transport and others produced charcoal or supplied firewood.[19] Unfortunately, there has been little systematic study of African enterprise during this era, even though it was plainly important and widespread. In a 1957 sessional paper outlining its development program, the colonial regime unintentionally acknowledged both the importance of African business and its own ignorance concerning it. The paper noted that about 25000 non-Africans in Kenya were employers or self-employed. 'For the African community,' it added vaguely, 'the total is probably several hundred thousand.'[20]

Many of the details of African involvement in enterprise during the closing years of the colonial era, therefore, remain unrecorded. It is clear, however, that changing relations to the means of production and changing class consciousness were contributing to the class formation that was becoming an increasingly obvious feature of African society.

Education. Since entrepreneurship had been part of pre-colonial society, access to it was relatively unrestricted. In the early days, as we saw, African traders were able for some time to follow trading patterns that varied little from the traditional ones. It was not long, however, before it became obvious to African observers of the European scene that the colonial economy offered far better opportunities, but that these were closed to people without a European-style education. Already in the early years of this century, Africans who had had some mission education were able to use it as an entrée, not only to new opportunities for trade, but also to lower-level white-collar jobs, which were far better paid than the more readily available manual positions.[21]

The impetus to European education came, not only from personal ambition, but also from the collective needs of African communities. African leaders saw that

... knowledge of the European's way of life and his language, gained at schools, made the 'educated' person a possible intermediary between the local community and the officials, whose authority as the final court of appeal in legal matters was rapidly being established. Some individuals saw opportunities for personal gain in this, but by far the most significant happening was the recognition by increasing numbers of elders and adults in the African communities that once their interests could no longer be effectively protected by hostility and rejection, a knowledge of how to use the white man's legal system was essential. White settlement and the sudden alienation of land in areas like South Kiambu gave tremendous impetus to this attitude, particularly amongst the Kikuyu.[22]

Missionaries who came to Kenya had established schools, usually at their central stations, as part of their program for attracting converts. Once Africans saw the value of the education, however, the demand for schooling outran both the available facilities and the capacity of the missions to augment them. It soon became common practice for local communities to make land available, to erect the buildings, and, in time, to offer significant financial support.[23]

As time went on, a growing number of African communities, dissatisfied with the educational opportunities offered by the government and the missions, launched their own schools. The independent school movement began in western Kenya, where John Owalo founded the Nomiya Luo Mission which, from 1910 onward, established primary schools in the Nyanza District. In Kikuyu country, independent schools began in the 1920s and developed very rapidly in the 1930s. In 1939, one of the earliest Kikuyu independent schools was converted to an institution of higher education, the Kenya African Teachers' College at Githunguri.[24] By that time, the colonial government had given its somewhat grudging recognition to the importance of the work being done by independent schools. Education Department figures for 1938 show that more than 1800 elementary schools were offering two to six years of education. Of these, only 37 were directly financed by the government and 367 were mission schools receiving government grants, leaving almost 1400 to provide education without government aid.[25]

Virtually all of the independent schools were primary schools. Secondary education in Kenya for Africans did not begin until 1926 and for a long time thereafter it remained the province of a handful of schools. The founding of the Protestant Alliance High School, which opened in 1926, was followed in 1927 by that of a Catholic secondary school at Kabaa, later to move to Mangu. In the late 1930s, secondary education was instituted at Maseno and then at Yala.[26]

It was not until the post-war era that the 'parsimonious, short-sighted and gradualist'[27] colonial approach to African education began to yield to more enlightened policies. In 1950, there were five government secondary schools for Africans in Kenya and the government was aiding six other schools. In 1960, thirty-three African secondary schools were receiving government funds and by 1963 that figure had reached eighty-two,[28] still woefully inadequate to the needs of a population of more than eight million Africans, but certainly a marked improvement.[29] In 1962, 918 boys and 154 girls passed their Cambridge (Secondary) School Certificate examinations.[30]

Another route to jobs within the modern sector of the economy was technical education and training for skilled trades. Already in the pre-World War II period, some government departments had opened training programs to Africans. Among these were the Post Office Training Centre, the Police Depot, and the Medical Training Centre. The materials available for this study do not offer detailed descriptions of the nature of such programs, but it is clear that they were not enabling significant numbers of Africans to rise above subordinate positions in their respective departments. Training for trades throughout the colonial era suffered from misdirection. Large numbers of carpenters and masons were trained for jobs that often did not exist, while other potentially more viable training programs were neglected.[31]

The most fervently sought-after opportunity of all was university education and it was the hardest one to come by. No degree courses were available in East Africa until Makerere College in Uganda began to offer them in 1949. Until then, getting a university education meant going abroad. Peter Mbiyu Koinange, who was the first Kenya African to go abroad for a full university education, returned in 1938 with an MA in Education from Columbia University.[32] Through World War II and in the immediate post-war period, opportunities for Africans to attend university were very scarce. As late as 1949, only fourteen Africans held bursaries or scholarships. It was left to African politicians to undertake the first really serious and large-scale program of support for Africans seeking university degrees. In the late 1950s, Tom Mboya participated in the formation of the African-American Students Foundation, which raised money to pay students' fares to the United States and Canada, thus setting in motion the famous 'Mboya airlift.' In 1956, Kenya had only sixty students in the United States, but by January 1963 more than 1100 were studying in North America.[33] By that time, significant numbers of Kenyan students were taking university courses in various European countries, both East and West.[34]

The available statistics do not give a detailed account of the cumulative effect of the colonial education system upon Kenya's African population, but the general trends outlined above are sufficient for our purposes. What is clear is that by the eve of Kenya's independence, a significant number of Africans had acquired enough education to affect their potential or actual class position in Kenya's society. For people with good secondary or university educations, the position was clear-cut. Their education qualified them – or soon would – for well-salaried jobs, good business opportunities, and perhaps top leadership positions in politics or the civil service. People with only primary schooling and/or technical training were less fortunate, but were far from unfortunate. As long as their education was sufficient to qualify them for jobs or individual enterprise within the modern sector of the economy, the possibilities for their economic advancement were numerous, especially in the post-independence wave of Africanization. Anyone with a modicum of education had a clear chance to achieve petty-bourgeois status, and at least some opportunity to become a member of the bourgeoisie proper.

Agriculture. One might have expected that enterprising African agriculturalists would have jumped at the opportunity to supply the domestic and foreign markets created by colonialism and the influx of European settlers. However, it was not until the 1940s that Africans began to turn their main occupation into an important asset in the modern economy. Why so long? One reason, undoubtedly, was that prospective cash farmers found their ambitions blocked by the obligations they had incurred under pre-colonial land law. Some Marxists have been reluctant to accept the suggestion that traditional usages could have retarded the spread of capitalism. This reluctance is based on the broad assertion that pre-colonial society was accumulative/individualist rather than communal and must therefore have been receptive to capitalism. In chapter 2, I have shown why this line of argument flows from an inadequate appreciation of traditional usages. It is particularly important, in this study, to insist on that point because if we assume that African land usages have always been fundamentally capitalist, it is impossible to understand the outrage that later erupted over the issue of landlessness. That outrage, in turn, is an important determinant of late colonial and post-colonial history.[35]

In any event, Africans interested in cash farming did in time begin to free themselves of traditional obligations, but, as they did so, they played a role in the creation of landlessness, a phenomenon which, as we saw in chapter 2, was new to Kenyan society. We have seen that traditional land tenure among agriculturalists was based upon the principle of universal (or at least very widespread) access to land. The viability of that system rested upon the existence of an open frontier, which guaranteed that succeeding generations would have new land to move to as the population increased. European settlement and the subsequent establishment of 'native' reserves involved the fixing of the boundaries, hence the elimination of the frontier. For some ethnic groups, this development had no immediate significance, because their traditional lands were sufficiently underpopulated to allow for a considerable amount of future expansion. Others, who had lost a lot of land to the Europeans or who were close to the point of full utilization of their existing lands, found themselves restricted to land that soon became insufficient for their needs.[36]

The loss of the frontier did not result in the immediate abolition of the principle of universal access to land. Young men continued to inherit land from their fathers in the old way, while tenants continued to exercise the various land rights that existed outside the regular process of inheritance. With growing populations trying to accommodate themselves on static acreages, there was nothing to do but to try to make more intensive use of existing lands. The first resort was to reduce the periods during which land lay fallow in order to restore its fertility. Inevitably, that meant loss of fertility and lower yields. Soon a point was reached at which fallow periods could be reduced no further. The only remaining alternative, then, was to subdivide existing fields, fragmenting them into ever smaller plots. As the East African Royal Commission observed: 'With increasing population, higher, not lower, yields are needed, yet there is no hope of producing a greater surplus per acre because of the

fragmentation and subdivision of "shambas"[37] into tiny, scattered holdings with different crops and fallows mixed up together.'[38]

Traditional land claims were still valid – in fact they were enforceable
in the local-level courts or native tribunals – but under the circumstances
they were obviously being granted more grudgingly and were leading to
growing amounts of litigation.[39] Plainly the situation was not one that
offered encouragement to farmers who might wish to adopt modern
farming methods. Declining fertility of land was steadily restricting the
scope for the production of surpluses, while growing density of population, occupying disorganized and fragmented plots, made the expansion
of acreages for cash cropping ever more difficult.[40] People who continued to exercise various sorts of traditional rights on other peoples'
land found their position more and more precarious, especially if, as in
the case of the *ahoi*, it was based simply on friendship. 'Their precarious
position encourages them to "mine" the land and inflates the growing
sense of insecurity.'[41] All this no doubt contributed to the comparative
tardiness of African farmers' entry into the modern economy.

In time, however, some individuals did begin to acquire larger acreages, a process that, in the more crowded areas, necessarily involved the
displacement of others from the land, the gradual breakdown of pre-
colonial land usages, and the appearance of embryonic social classes. In
Kiambu District, the outright sale of land – as opposed to the traditional
practice of redeemable land transactions – had been going on since the
late 1920s or early 1930s. There, too, traditional land ties were less
binding than in other parts of Kikuyuland, and by the 1940s a significant
number of better-off people had taken advantage of the opportunity to
expand their acreages. Among them were chiefs, elders of native tribunals, and some of the early beneficiaries of European-style education. In
1941, the Kiambu district commissioner reported that such sales during
the previous ten or fifteen years had amounted to 'hundreds, possibly
even thousands of acres ...'[42] Other Kikuyu districts were following suit,
and during the 1940s, administrative officials repeatedly took note of
the steady growth of a privileged landowning class in Kikuyu country.
By 1944 the first fruits of class formation at the top of the social ladder
were becoming noticeable at the bottom. In that year, the Kiambu District Annual Report referred to a 'large landless class growing up in this
district ...'[43] The traditions that had always provided for widespread
access to land were beginning to break down under the pressures of land
shortage and the lure of agricultural markets.

It was in the 1940s, too, that the colonial authorities began seriously to encourage the expansion of African cash cropping. Before then, they had shown little enthusiasm. Kikuyu farmers were actually prohibited from growing coffee because it was assumed that they would allow their coffee plants to contact diseases that might spread to European plantations.[44] Potentially progressive African farmers were also hampered by the lack of credit available to them. But the experience of World War II brought the beginnings of a new official attitude toward African farmers. 'The war acted as the great catalyst of change. It forced the administration to see the reserves as essential productive units and adopt laws and policies accordingly ...'[45] In 1947, the African Land Utilization and Settlement Board (ALUS) was established and was given the task of helping to bring about land improvement in African areas. In the 1950s, ALUS, now renamed ALDEV (African Land Development Board), began to administer a scheme making credit available on the personal security of the borrower. At the same time, financial incentives were introduced. Farmers who met specified development standards were awarded tax rebates.

These early provisions for African agriculture were paternalistic and often coercive. Improvement of African agricultural land, for example, could be secured through land preservation orders that were made by administrative officers and might be carried out by the use of forced labour. The credit made available through ALDEV was primarily short term. As late as 1955, the East African Royal Commission recommended continued restriction of long-term credit on the grounds that 'the whole conception of long-term borrowing presupposes a maturity of mind, which, as yet, is only in evidence among a small number of East African cultivators.'[46]

Nevertheless, the colonial authorities were supporting the improvement of African agriculture.[47] And gradually they also began to allow Africans to participate in the administration of the programs. Beginning in 1955, new marketing boards were established to regulate the cultivation, storage, processing, and movement of a wide range of African farm produce. Some of the members of the boards were chosen from nominees of the producers. It was 'the first occasion that legislation provided for direct participation by African producers in a system of control of African producers.'[48] The boards were intended to stimulate production increases. As an example of their success, Ghai and McAuslan cite the earliest of them to be established, the Nyanza Province Marketing Board, which, in its third year, had a gross turnover of more than

£2 000 000. In its first four years, it marketed an annual average of 600 000 bags of maize.[49]

Unlike maize and other crops, coffee was under the jurisdiction of the Coffee Marketing Board, which handled both European and African produce. In the mid-1950s, Africans began to be co-opted to the board and in 1960, new legislation provided for 'full African representation at delegate conferences and on the [board].'[50] The legislation applied identical cultivation controls to all planters, regardless of race. In that year, the number of African coffee planters rose to more than 100 000.

Perhaps the best-known reform of the 1950s was the program of land consolidation and registration,[51] which was designed to abolish traditional tenure and replace it with individual ownership of land. We have already seen how the elimination of the Kikuyu frontier had distorted the traditional system of land tenure, resulting in fragmentation of holdings, loss of fertility, and declining yields. The solution the government chose frankly favoured better-off farmers, on the assumption that their successes at cash cropping would result in increased yields and would generate employment opportunities for others who were left landless. The program called for each existing plot to be measured; for all the fragments held by an individual to be consolidated into a single holding; and for that holding then to be registered in the individual's name as personal property no longer subject to the obligations of traditional tenure. Such far-reaching and thorough-going changes were bound to be met with resistance. But the declaration of an Emergency in 1952 gave the government extraordinary powers, which it was able to use to force the program through. Land consolidation and registration was being put into effect in the Kikuyu districts in the 1950s and was credited with having contributed to the expansion of cash-crop production there.[52]

By 1959, total revenue from cash sales by African farmers had reached £9 million. It was not a high figure measured against European large-farm production, which amounted to £34 million,[53] but it represented a 40 per cent increase in two years. The dizzying rise of peasant agricultural production was the final stage in the colonial era of the class formation spawned by the colonial system. Small farmers joined merchants and educated people in the scramble for wealth as a social system encompassing peasants and capitalist classes began to take shape.

Land and freedom. But while some Africans were beginning to prosper, Kenya's landless people were experiencing a different fate. The development of agriculture, both in the White Highlands and in the reserves, was working to the detriment of Kikuyus who had little or no land of their own. In the White Highlands, squatters, whose place in the modern economy was becoming increasingly insecure, were suffering a steady decline in their standard of living. In the reserves, economic development, class formation, and overpopulation were undermining the African tradition of ready access to land and causing the growth of a landless class. Throughout the 1930s and 1940s, the majority of squatters resident outside of the reserves were Kikuyus and their numbers were growing. A 1945 labour census showed about 100 000 Kikuyu resident labourers on European farms and some 20 000 more employed by government departments, most of them by the Department of Forestry.[54] Large numbers of other Kikuyus besides squatters were resident outside of the Kikuyu reserve as well, living in towns or in other 'tribal' reserves. In 1948, Kikuyus living outside the reserve numbered more than 290 000 or almost thirty per cent of their people.[55]

As the economic pressures to which squatters were being subjected intensified, they became more discontented and their discontent escalated by stages into open revolt. In 1946 and 1947, there were demonstrations. In 1948, the name Mau Mau, soon to be a grim byword of Kenya politics, received its first official mention when a Nakuru district administrator reported the existence of a 'politico-religious sect' called the 'Maumau association' and 'emanating from the Kikuyu reserve,' with branches in Naivasha and Ol'Kalou. In the next two years, Mau Mau steadily gained support among resident labourers.[56]

The phenomenon of 'Mau Mau' and the events of the Emergency occupy a literature in themselves[57] and need not be reviewed here at length. The so-called Mau Mau referred to themselves as the Land Freedom Army. Their organization was loosely knit and it lacked a well-articulated program, but its name summed up the most pressing concern: opposition to colonial rule and bitterness over the landlessness that was becoming the fate of growing numbers of Africans. They organized themselves and sought popular support by means of oathing ceremonies. The oaths contained appeals to Kikuyu traditions and exhortations to unity, discipline, and self-sacrifice in the name of national liberation.[58]

On 20 October 1952, Kenya's governor, Sir Evelyn Baring, declared a state of emergency in response to a series of events – including the assassination of a Kikuyu senior chief – which colonial authorities interpreted as a threat to law and order. There followed a trial, ending in the imprisonment of Jomo Kenyatta and a group of nationalist leaders. The fol-

lowing March there was a successful raid by dissident Africans on a
weapons cache at the Naivasha Police Station, while at Lari another
group massacred a loyalist chief, his family, and other residents, leaving
ninety-seven people dead. The anti-government forces found refuge in
the forests of the Aberdares Mountains and Mt Kenya.

Among the first steps the government took in trying to put an end to
the dissidence was one which was to have tragic consequences for many
landless people. Noting that the Land Freedom Army consisted mainly
of Kikuyus, who – together with the neighbouring and related Embu
and Meru peoples – numbered about thirty per cent of the African
population,[59] the government decided to isolate them from other Africans in order to keep the dissidence from spreading. Accordingly, large
numbers of Kikuyus resident outside the reserve – including squatters
and other landless people – were 'repatriated,' i.e. sent back to the reserves. Once there, they were forbidden to leave without a pass. In 1953,
regulations were proclaimed authorizing the repatriation of Kikuyus, as
well as Embus and Merus.[60]

The eviction of squatters from the European areas got under way in
that year, with the result that

in the early months of the Emergency the Kikuyu reserves, already bursting at
their seams, had to receive a further influx of refugees, some of whom were
second and third generation inhabitants of the Rift Valley.[61] Indeed, some families had had only a tenuous contact with the reserves for thirty or forty years.

So they came, by the tens of thousands, on foot, by bus, by truck, and by train,
many leaving behind all they had – goats, maize, beds, and houses – to be sold by
the Government, who would forward the proceeds to their 'district of origin.'
They arrived with their pots and pans, the clothes they stood up in, and small
packs of the beans or maize they had salvaged. Some of the children got lost on
the way. Many of the young men walked straight from the point of arrival to the
sanctuary of the forest. Those who remained in the reserves found, after the
warmth of the initial greetings from long-forgotten relatives, that the burden of
existence grew rapidly beyond all human strength. By the end of 1953, the
Government estimated their numbers at 100 000, of whom perhaps a third required Governmental aid for subsistence.[62]

The wave of evictions spread to Nairobi in 1954. In 'Operation Anvil,'
25 000 troops and police surrounded the city and systematically searched
it. All Kikuyus, Merus, and Embus were held. Twenty-seven thousand

were detained and another twenty thousand were expelled from the city. Kikuyus resident in other reserves and in Tanganyika and Uganda were repatriated as well.[63]

With the Kikuyu reserve sealed off from the rest of the Kenya population, the next step in the government's strategy was to isolate the rebels from their fellow Kikuyus. This the government did with what have since become familiar tactics of anti-guerrilla warfare. Inhabitants of the Kikuyu districts were forced to build villages for themselves that were fortified against the dissidents. Where the inhabitants did not co-operate readily with the government, their village was placed under a 23-hour curfew and they were allowed out only one hour each day, under armed guard, to get food. A deep ditch was dug for more than 100 miles along the forest perimeter to keep the rebels away from the rest of the population. Cut off from their sources of supply, they could then be hunted down more readily in the forest.

Captured rebels, and anyone else suspected of Mau Mau activities, were sent to detention camps, where they were pressured to give up their ideas of dissidence. By the end of 1954, 77 000 people, most of them Kikuyus, were in detention,[64] some of them in punishment camps in remote areas like Hola on the Tana River and Manyani in an arid district to the southeast. Any land belonging to rebels was ordered confiscated.

The government was determined, not only to eradicate Mau Mau, but to build a new Kikuyu society, bringing the majority who were passive supporters of the Land Freedom Army firmly under the influence of the minority who remained fiercely loyal to the colonial regime. These opponents of the rebels came to be collectively referred to as 'loyalists.' Included in their ranks were the Kikuyu Home Guard, which was organized for military resistance to the Land Freedom Army, as well as the Tribal Police, some government servants, and mission adherents. They were not only a distinct minority, but also a relatively prosperous one. One colonial official estimated that they constituted about ten per cent of the population and there is a variety of evidence to indicate that they were, for the most part, relatively well-off landowners. The government intended that in the future the loyalists would be 'the hard core of the new society, of the "reconstruction of the Kikuyu people." They would be the new elite cadre round which the district officers could shape the future of the tribe. Their advice would decide whether a man should be detained and when he should be allowed to return from detention.'[65] While landless people from the Rift Valley were being evicted to the reserves or sent into detention, therefore, landed loyalists were being given new power and greater prestige. What had begun as a revolt against colonial rule and European occupation of African land was taking on the aspect of a Kikuyu civil war, a class conflict pitting Kikuyus with land against the swelling ranks of the landless.

The conflict inflicted heavy punishment upon the poor. It helped to swell the numbers of landless people and sometimes to enrich others at their expense. Confiscated rebel land disappeared in the land consolidation and registration process, to the advantage of all who were not stigmatized as rebels. The government also tried, in the early days of land consolidation, to give loyalists control over the adjudication of land claims, a power offering wide scope for abuse.[66] But more important, the Emergency inflicted a heavy toll of personal suffering, especially upon those who had been repatriated from their place of residence outside the reserve. At a time when large numbers of people fretted over the insecurity of their land claim in the face of consolidation, the return of long-lost clansmen was bound to escalate the already chaotic conflict. Murders over land were a common occurrence, as were all sorts of physical deprivation and abuse. At the same time, government prosecution of the war led to ever more Draconian measures. Capital punishment was introduced for a wide variety of offences and by the end of 1954 the rate of hangings had reached fifty per month. People who were detained faced beatings, short rations, and hard labour.[67]

The Emergency was a brutal and bloody conflict, a rebellion turned civil war, which, by the end of 1956, had claimed almost 13 500 African lives – compared with 95 European and 29 Asian lives.[68] In retrospect, it seems reasonable to wonder how many lives could have been saved had the colonial government instituted a program of settlement for landless people instead of herding large numbers of them into an already overcrowded reserve under conditions that were positively bursting with potential for mutual antagonism, exploitation, and the settling of old scores. Development of such a program, however, would have implied a reversal of the basic assumptions of half a century of colonial land policy, which, from the outset, had accepted, even welcomed, the idea that large numbers of peasants would be forced to become labourers. The colonial establishment, surveying history with that serene detachment that comes with financial security, had viewed the impoverishment of squatters as an inevitable part of the development of capitalism. In making these assumptions, however, they reckoned without the African attitude toward landlessness. Mau Mau might have been a warning to them that they were on the wrong track, but they were not ready to listen. Mau Mau, after all, was a proxy war, in which Africans were the main sufferers. It was only later, when European livelihoods were at stake, that the colonial authorities finally faced the fact that the politics of Kenya demanded a direct attack on the problem of landlessness.

By 1957, administrators were ready to start sending Kikuyu repatriates back into the European areas. In that year, 18 000 people were moved out of Kiambu District to Nairobi, the Rift Valley, and the Kericho tea estates. Thousands of others were moved out of Nyeri District and as emergency restrictions were gradually relaxed, more left the reserve.[69] In 1960, the Emergency was lifted and free travel in and out of the reserve became possible. In November of that year, the minister for agriculture acknowledged that there were 130 000 landless families in Kenya. Most of them, he said, had plots to cultivate, but they were 'very small acreages of land, in other words, well below the subsistence level.'[70] The colonial authorities, by allowing the squatters to return to the White Highlands, were expressing their confidence that the squatter problem could still be contained within the framework of the colonial land system. But the system was about to be abolished and the big question for the future was what kind of expression the squatters' accumulated grievances would find when the edifice of the White Highlands crumbled.

TOWARD LAND TRANSFER

The Mau Mau war was the climax of a long series of events. Many years before the Emergency, as we have seen, an expanding population of poor people were gradually being reduced from the relatively independent position of squatters with substantial cultivation rights to that of impoverished agricultural workers who truly had nothing to sell but their labour. At the same time, the members of another segment of society were taking advantage of the land they owned and/or the skills they commanded to improve their economic position.

It was during the years of the Emergency that these changes were consolidated. The evictions from the scheduled areas proved to any squatters who might still be living the dream of freedom and wealth in the Rift Valley that they were totally subject to forces beyond their control. At the same time, land consolidation and registration resulted in the consolidation, not only of land, but also of the positions of landed people.

In 1959, even before the Emergency was lifted, the colonial government declared its new policy of removing racial considerations from the regulations governing ownership and management of agricultural land.[71] In addition, the authorities resolved to undertake land transfer schemes designed to promote the purchase of land by Africans. To Africans in all walks of life as well as to Europeans, these developments signalled the imminence of a period of very rapid change, of once-in-a-lifetime opportunities as well as great risks. In order to understand the events of the next few years, it is necessary to consider the position of Kenya's major economic groups – and, for the moment, especially those of better-off Africans and European settlers – vis-à-vis the land-transfer schemes that were soon to begin.

Prosperous Africans. We have already seen that Africans who were moving rapidly into modern agriculture and education in the post-war era were swelling the numbers of people who would be able to participate profitably in the cash economy. But Africans were moving into the capitalist economy with more than just credentials. Many of them had accumulated capital as well.

Not a great deal is known of the details of capital accumulation among Africans in colonial times, but it is clear that a good deal of saving was going on, sometimes in surprising places. The point is amusingly illustrated by Waruhiu Itote, who returned from wartime service overseas with a rather patronizing attitude toward the rustic environment of his father's home, as he himself admits. 'With my 1000 shillings Army gratuity burning holes in my pocket,' he related, 'I was ... somewhat too big for my boots.'

Perhaps this was why my father, Itote, one evening called me, my mother, Wamuyu, and my wife Leah into his hut and said that I must now be a very rich man as I had stayed in the Army so long. He suggested that we put our total wealth down and count it, and that whoever had the most should take the other's money as well. Brash and big-headed and with that fabulous sum tucked inside my army greatcoat pocket, I readily agreed. How on earth could the old man have saved up that amount from his herd of scrawny old goats? ...

I gaily slapped my one thousand shillings down on the table. This was going to be easy money. Itote was looking steadily at me, not speaking. He took [his] damp-smelling bundles of notes and handed them to me. Quietly he suggested I should start by counting them. When I had reached 3000 shillings there was still much more to come. I did not know where to look ... I went outside and walked, or rather ran, the five miles to Karatina where I took a train to Nanyuki. The thousand shillings were left with my father, and I have never mentioned the episode to him again from that day to this.[72]

By the late 1950s, opportunities to earn money – as labourers, small entrepreneurs, clerks, teachers, and farmers – had been available to Africans for a long time. Even if they had not, on the whole, been very lucrative, they had offered the possibility to some of saving money and even of investing and reinvesting it in growing enterprises. Some African enterprises had reached a respectable size long before the 1960s. Rosberg and Nottingham cite the example of the Kiambu Chicken and Egg Dealers who in 1945 'could afford to buy property in the Nairobi Bazaar for £8,000.'[73] Thanks to the rapid growth of cash crop production in the 1950s, African agriculture, too, was becoming a source of new savings and an investment outlet for accumulated capital.

Now that the colour bar was being lowered, African capital was free to move into the highlands. In short order, the first Africans would begin to buy large-scale farms from Europeans. Others would buy smaller subdivisions of formerly large-scale operations, but many of them would hope to be able to expand their acreages in time. In the process, some Africans would begin to identify their interests with those of large-scale agriculture. The opening of the highlands to Africans, therefore, had fundamental implications for the future of Kenya's politics. It blurred the racial lines that before had been so clearly drawn, while emphasizing the class differences within African society that were just developing.

European settlers. The changes in African politics resulting from the opening of the highlands ultimately worked to the advantage of European settlers, strengthening their bargaining power in the negotiations that set the terms of land transfer and of independence itself. But many settlers failed to recognize their good fortune or to enjoy it. A way of life was about to end forever and many Europeans could see no future for themselves in Kenya.

Their idea of the new life ahead was conditioned by their notions about Africans. Even in the late 1950s, many settlers continued to think of Africans, patronizingly or with hostility, as 'primitive' and not very able. The position of superiority that Europeans still enjoyed in their day-to-day dealings with Africans no doubt helped them to maintain that belief. When the Mau Mau war got under way, many Europeans saw in those bitter hostilities a confirmation of their view that the alleged savagery of traditional life had not been overcome. In that era especially, it was not uncommon to hear views that today sound like unvarnished bigotry expressed openly and without hesitation, revealing attitudes that might otherwise have remained hidden. At the now notorious trial of Jomo Kenyatta, for example, the magistrate, a former Kenyan Supreme

Court justice, seemed to see nothing wrong with commenting on a witness's testimony with a brusque 'I cannot follow the African mind.'[74] In delivering his judgment at the close of the trial, the magistrate told Kenyatta, rather melodramatically: '... you have taken the fullest advantage of the power and influence which you have over your people and also of the primitive instincts which you know lie deep down in their characters.'[75]

Fred Majdalany, in an account of the Mau Mau struggle that fairly trumpets its sympathy with the settler viewpoint, makes some equally improbable observations. For example, he refers to Waruhiu Itote, who later became assistant director of Kenya's National Youth Service, as a 'mentally backward tribesman' whose 'intelligence quotient was by western standards that of a child of perhaps eleven ...'[76] Such statements are obviously overwrought reactions to difficult times and would not bear repetition here except for the fact that they capture something of the spirit of those times. They offer a point of reference from which we can well imagine the reactions of many settlers to the revelation that the White Highlands of Delamere and Grogan were about to be opened to African ownership and that ordinary Africans would soon be electing Kenya's political representatives.

What did such reactions mean in concrete terms? An extreme view was that Africans were not (or not yet) capable of governing a modern nation and that chaos would be the inevitable result of *uhuru*. A less apocalyptic view focused on the possible economic consequences of political uncertainty. The approach of independence meant that there would be a political struggle and no one could be sure what kind of government would emerge, what its agricultural policy would be, and what would happen to land prices. In the meantime, if large numbers of farmers cut back their production, or even abandoned their farms, those who remained might find their position seriously jeopardized. This point can be, and has been, exaggerated. There was no reality in the spectre of economic 'collapse' or the suggestion of imminent popular upheaval that is sometimes associated with the politics of the early 1960s (see chapter 5). But uncertainty there was. For a large-scale landowner, it was a time of crucial decisions: whether to sell out and leave Kenya or to stay; whether to invest or liquidate investments. And in the circumstances, these decisions would involve a larger-than-usual element of risk.

But it is important to point out also that for anyone who was willing to gamble on political stability, there was a real incentive to stay on and to invest. Large-scale agriculture in Kenya was not only very profitable by the late 1950s, but it held out considerable promise for the future. It had come a long way since the 1920s when a relatively low-yield, single-crop type of agriculture was the dominant farming pattern in the arable districts. The more sophisticated and capital-intensive mixed farming – in which a farm is devoted partly to livestock and party to crops to achieve a high level of productivity per acre – was being developed in the 1930s, but it did not really take hold in the highlands until after World War II. When it did take hold, it expanded very rapidly. For example, grass leys, which were a key to mixed farming, took up about 12 000 acres in 1946. By 1960 that figure had grown to almost 220 000,[77] indicating that the profit potential of mixed farming was beginning to be realized in earnest.

But even in 1960, the trend toward continuing development of agriculture did not show any indication of having spent itself. On the contrary, a 1961 assessment of highlands agriculture noted that 'Only a portion of the land of high productive potential has yet been developed for intensive use and there is considerable scope for further intensification. On much of this land the development period has been short, not all settlers have a farming background and many prefer livestock as their principal enterprise, even on land which is well adapted to the production of cash crops that yield higher returns.'[78] It seems plain, therefore, that there remained plenty of room in the 1960s for further development of the agriculture of the highlands, hence real possibilities for future investment. Neither African majority rule nor African ownership of land in the highlands, in themselves, posed any threat to these possibilities. For Europeans, then, the alternative of staying on after independence was a live one, provided large-scale agriculture did not lose its political support.

However, it was important from their point of view that they use the political influence they had left in the final years of colonialism to secure their economic interests. Their aims varied. For those who were willing to stay on in Kenya, the important thing was that the system of large-scale agriculture be maintained and the economic prerequisites for its functioning – the markets in land, labour, supplies, and produce – remain undisturbed. For those who wanted to leave, the hope was that there could be full compensation for the property they were leaving behind. These were the objectives for which Kenyan Europeans pressed at the bargaining tables of the 1960s, and the settlement program that emerged from the bargaining was designed to help meet them.

Landless people. Considering the events of the Emergency and the role of landlessness in that conflict, one might have thought that the colonial authorities' program of inter-racial land transfer would be devoted, in the first instance, to settling people who had no land and no saleable skills. That was not their idea, however. They hoped, rather, to preserve the fundamentals of colonial agrarian policy, and to settle the land question through an arrangement with more prosperous Africans, without becoming involved in the class struggle that had been simmering for so long beneath the surface of colonial politics.

Part II

The transition to independence

In 1959, the colonial authorities resolved to eliminate racism from their agrarian policy and in 1963 Kenya became an independent nation under African majority rule. In the four intervening years, the class struggle described in part I was relocated from the fields, forests, and towns to the bargaining table, as political representatives wrangled and manoeuvred over the rights and prerogatives of the European agrarian bourgeoisie, a nascent African bourgeoisie and petty bourgeoisie, a peasantry, and a landless class. In four short years, tensions that had been building up for more than half a century were forced to a resolution. In the process, the colonial patterns were broken, and Kenya was cast into a new mould, one which would remain very much the same for a long time to come. An examination of the events of those four years, therefore, sums up a great deal of Kenya's past and offers important insights into its present and future.

The colonial government's 1959 decision was followed in 1960 by Britain's concession in principle of Kenya's independence. In short order, the authorities set out to develop a government-assisted program for the transfer of land from European to African hands. The program evolved, in stages, into a number of schemes aimed at different groups and designed to meet different needs. The most important and best known of these was the massive Million-Acre Settlement Scheme, the name of which has become synonymous with land transfer in Kenya's transition to independence, and which – although it was developed in the twilight of the colonial era – subsequently became a corner-stone of post-colonial land policy. As a result, it has become thoroughly identified with the government of independent Kenya. In the eyes of friends of the Million-Acre Scheme, that identification legitimizes it, proving that it is genuinely responsive to the needs of African people. The evidence in chapters 4 to 7 clearly refutes that interpretation. In the eyes of its critics, the scheme's identification with an independent government marks the program as a product of neo-colonialism, an example of how international political and economic forces can capture the leadership of an African country and bend the latter to their will.[1] That characterization has a very real element of truth, but it over-simplifies somewhat.

The more complicated truth is that the Million-Acre Scheme was a product of two phases of development, the first colonial and the second neo-colonial. In the first phase, the colonial authorities tried to implement a settlement program aimed at a very limited number of relatively prosperous Africans – designed, in fact, to favour, not just any prosperous Africans, but those who had been loyal to the colonial regime. In this phase, official thinking was guided by an unsophisticated view of both Kenya's society and its political dynamics. In the second phase, the authorities greatly expanded the scheme to offer benefits to Africans of all classes and political tendencies, but – by skilfully dangling carrots and wielding sticks – managed to avoid conceding anything fundamental. Needless to say, the neo-colonial phase was marked by a more sophisticated understanding of Kenya's society and politics.

Part II traces Kenya's agrarian class struggle through these two phases and into the era of independence, outlining the roles of the various groups participating in the struggle and noting how each of them fared. This builds on the class analysis presented in chapter 1 and on the historical material covered in chapters 2 and 3.

4

Yeomen and peasants:
the colonial phase of settlement

One of the most subtle and fascinating Marxist concepts is that of forces of production, which are made up of particular means of production and the labour power used to exploit them. The notion underlying the concept is that human minds and human hands, working in tandem, constitute a kind of energy resource, a raw power capable of transforming the earth. The same power also transforms society, often in bloody and brutal ways. When new means of production become available, people grasp the opportunities they represent, and new forms of social organization – the factory system, the plantation system, slavery, and so forth – are forged to exploit them. In the process, relations of production are transformed: the class system changes and people's social, economic, legal, and even personal relations change accordingly – all in response to the organizational requirements of the changed mode of production.

The concept is not a narrowly mechanistic one. The reader should not conclude that society is regimented by technology. Rather, Marxists see a dialectical relationship between modes of production and forms of human interaction – one in which influence is exerted in both directions, although it is the mode of production that is ultimately the dominant force. Thus, a newly available mode of production may, initially at least, have different impacts on different societies, depending on the pre-existing differences in those societies. Industrial technology, for example, is one thing to a peasant society and quite another to a society dominated by traders and administrators. Within a society, too, a new mode of production may unleash a struggle over how society will be reorganized to take advantage of it.

This is the kind of transformation that was under way within African society in Kenya in the early 1960s as colonial restrictions were relaxed to make mechanized agriculture, motorized trade, and modern industry fully available to Africans for the first time. And it was clear from the start that the transformation of agriculture would, in fact, occasion a struggle over the future organization of Kenya's agrarian system, pitting the peasantry and the landless class against the bourgeoisie. Peasants, who together with the landless would-be peasantry were harbouring a pent-up demand for more land to support and employ expanding families, would be clamouring for the breakup of large estates into small-holdings where they could engage in subsistence agriculture and small-scale commodity production. The bourgeoisie, needless to say, would be fighting for the survival of large-scale agriculture. The colonial authorities, well aware of the pitfalls ahead, set out on a search for a settlement of the land question that would avoid them. In the first year and a half of their search, their strategy was to look for allies within the African population, while holding the majority of the population and their political leaders at arm's length.

The bulk of the African leadership was to be found in the Kenya African National Union (KANU), which in the 1961 elections had polled 67.4 per cent of the vote.[1] However, KANU initially demanded that independence be granted quickly and its leaders wanted to wait until after independence for a final settlement of the land question. The colonial authorities were having none of that, and they had an alternative. The Kenya African Democratic Union (KADU) was the second-strongest African party, having, however, polled only 16.4 per cent of the popular vote. It represented members of minority ethnic groups who feared that KANU rule would lead to political dominance by Kenya's two largest groups, the Kikuyu and the Luo. Taking advantage of these ethnic tensions, the authorities engineered the formation of a government without KANU, consisting of KADU members, liberal Europeans, Asian and African splinter groups, and nominated members. It was this still very much colonial regime that presided over the first phase of the search for a resolution of the land question.

Colonial dominance in that search was reflected in the membership of the Land Development and Settlement Board (LDSB), which the government had appointed at the beginning of 1961 to administer a settlement scheme for almost 8000 families.[2] The LDSB was mainly representative of the colonial regime and the settler community. Of seventeen members, four were appointments of the minister of agriculture;

seven were members of the Board of Agriculture (Scheduled Areas), which represented the settlers; and three were top colonial civil servants. Only three were Africans, and these were nominees of the Board of Agriculture (Non-scheduled Areas), an organization with an African majority that continued, however, to be under strong influence from the colonial administration.[3] In short, African representation on the LDSB was token. Europeans were giving themselves a free hand in developing a program of land transfer and, beyond that, the settler community was being given a strong voice in its planning and implementation.

THE IDEA OF SETTLEMENT

The problem of land, as it was articulated by the colonial authorities, was twofold. On the one hand, there was a need for a significant transfer of formerly European land into the hands of Africans as a demonstration that the lowering of racial barriers to landownership would not remain, in the words of Col. B.R. McKenzie, minister of agriculture, 'a pious expression of intention only ...'[4] On the other hand, there were the fears of European settlers, many of whom felt betrayed by what they saw as their abandonment by the British government. To reassure them, it was necessary to demonstrate that independence would not result in their losing the assets they had built up over the years, either by confiscation or by a drop in the prices for land under conditions in which they would feel forced to sell.

The proposed solution came in the form of a development project, an international aid program with funds from the World Bank and the Colonial Development Corporation (CDC) designed to effect a measure of inter-racial land transfer and to reassure Europeans of the continuation of a market in land. The idea was to make land transfer an economic proposition by combining it with a program for the intensification of agriculture in selected parts of the highlands. Africans would be lent money to enable them to buy European land. With the help of the intensification program, they would then be able to farm the land profitably. On paper, it looked like a good idea.

Land purchase and subdivision. The LDSB would purchase from Europeans parcels of high-potential, underdeveloped land capable of being converted to the production of tea, pyrethrum, or coffee. A significant amount of land in the highlands was regarded as underdeveloped and suitable for the introduction of higher-yield crops (see chapter 3). A World Bank report on the plans for the project noted that 'many [European settlers] prefer livestock as the principal enterprise even on land which is well adapted to the production of cash crops that yield higher returns.'[5] The potential gains from a conversion to cash crops were substantial. An acre of grassland supporting sheep was capable of producing an annual gross cash return of less than £5, the report pointed out. If it were suitable for coffee, that same acre might gross £130. Comparable figures for pyrethrum and tea ranged from £60 to £90, although, the report added, 'labour and other costs incurred in cash crop production reduce net returns considerably.'[6] Nevertheless, the potential gains from the conversion were substantial.

Land selected for purchase would be valued according to the prices prevailing in 1959, 'as that year was the most recent in which a reasonable volume of transactions occurred.'[7] Purchase would be on the basis of 'willing buyer–willing seller' negotiations between the LDSB and the prospective seller, with the board empowered to vary the appraiser's figure by 25 per cent either upward or downward. After take-over by the board, the land was to be subdivided into two types of holdings: a 'yeoman' or 'assisted-owner' farm of about twenty hectares, which would yield a net annual income of Shs 5000/- in addition to loan repayments and the personal living costs of the plot-holder and his family; and a 'peasant' holding of approximately 6 hectares with a target income of Shs 2000/- per year. The LDSB was instructed to settle 1800 yeomen and 6000 peasants on 73 000 hectares of land by September 1963.[8]

Expected benefits. This scheme, it was hoped, would placate Africans by providing for genuine and conspicuous inter-racial land transfer, while at the same time restoring European confidence by supporting the land market. The most conspicuous racial integration would take place through the yeoman (or assisted-owner) program. As the World Bank report noted, 'land for assisted owners would be bought in the interior of the Scheduled Areas [i.e. White Highlands] in neighbouring but non-contiguous parcels totaling about [2000 hectares] per unit. Solid African "islands" are to be avoided for social reasons ...'[9] The 'yeomen' would begin as smaller farmers than their European neighbours. But by being integrated into the highlands and scattered through various parts of them, they should be able to become, both economically and to some extent socially, a part of the highlands. The scattered pattern of settlement would have practical advantages as well. Since Africans would be unable, within the financial limitations of the scheme, to afford the grandiose residences that were a part of the settler scene, they might be able to buy an undeveloped portion of an existing farm, not including the residence, thereby concentrating their investment on productive resources. In addition, the scattered pattern of settlement would enable the new settlers to take advantage of 'the informal technical guidance' that their European neighbours could offer them.

Participants in the peasant program, on the other hand, were not to be integrated into the large-scale farming areas. 'Smallholder settlements,' the World Bank report noted, '... generally would be made on the periphery of existing African reserves in solid blocks of about [2000 hectares]; in this way ... whole units could be absorbed for local government purposes into the jurisdiction of adjacent African District Councils.'[10] Although they were not actually being integrated into the highlands, the clients of the peasant program would be given an opportunity to buy excellent smallholdings in areas that had previously been barred to Africans. They, too, would serve as a demonstration that colonialism was coming to an end.

But the main thrust of the program was directed at the security of large-scale agriculture and it was clear that the LDSB's best efforts were being directed at satisfying their settler constituency. The first sentence of the board's *Review of Activities* reflects the board's priorities in regard to land transfer. 'Any appraisal of the activities of the Land Development and Settlement Board,' the *Review* notes, 'must take into account the acute fears of the European landowner about the sanctity of his land title ...'[11] Many settlers were deeply demoralized by the approach of independence and the land transfer program was intended to demonstrate to them that the bottom was not about to drop out of the land market, that their investment was secure, and that, despite independence, they would still be able to liquidate it, if they chose, and realize their capital.

The settlers were not easily placated. Their fears, the board reported, 'were reflected in the immense suspicion with which they greeted the introduction of the settlement scheme.' When the settlement program was first announced, the terms of purchase offered to prospective settlers by the British government were one-third in cash and the balance in promissory notes bearing 5 per cent interest and payable in equal instalments over seven years. The landowners objected to 'such a protracted method of payment.' They also expressed fear that exchange controls might be introduced to prevent them from transferring their money out of the country. In negotiations with Kenya's minister of agriculture, the British government was persuaded to make a new offer: one-half in cash, the other half payable in three equal, annual instalments. If he wished, the vendor might take payment in sterling currency in London. 'This final offer of the British Government,' the LDSB reported, 'was reluctantly and with suspicion accepted by the landowners ...'[12] Purchases on that basis began in November 1961.

These provisions were intended to help compensate Europeans who wanted to leave the country. But the program was also designed to encourage Europeans who were prepared to stay on. The offer to buy significant acreages at 1959 prices was concrete evidence that the government intended to help sustain land prices through the transition to independence and thereby to provide an underpinning for the continued security of large-scale agriculture.

Another source of reassurance to Europeans who wanted to stay would be the fact that, while the program provided for integration of 'yeomen' or assisted owners into the highlands, it refrained from integrating 'peasants.' Although some Europeans were changing their attitudes about peasant agriculture, many remained convinced that the proximity of African smallholders was detrimental to good agriculture and, perhaps more to the point, to the maintenance of the social milieu to which the settlers had grown accustomed. The program assisted the integration of upwardly mobile Africans into the highlands, but it also provided a bulwark against what many Europeans would have perceived as frighteningly rapid social change.

It is important to note that the people for whom the yeoman and peasant schemes were designed were all either members of the petty bourgeoisie or better-off peasants. This was true even of prospective participants in the peasant scheme, who in order to be eligible for settlement had to produce at least Shs 1000/- working capital and satisfy the district agricultural officer that they had sufficient farming experience to 'farm a low density plot whose development costs are to be met from loan funds provided by the I.B.R.D. or C.D.C.'[13] It was all the more true of 'yeomen,' whose capital requirement was Shs 10000/- and who likewise had to offer proof of their ability as farmers.

In order to get an idea of the social chasm separating successful applicants for these settlement schemes from landless people, it is instructive to think of down payments of Shs 1000/- and 10000/- in the context of squatters' wages. A 1946 study calculated the average squatter family's real income – including the value of cultivation and cattle-keeping – at about Shs 60/- per month. The cash wages themselves came to about Shs 16/- per month.[14] The squatters' real wages, as we saw, did not rise in the years that followed, but declined as a result of restrictions on cultivation and cattle-keeping rights. To most squatters, therefore, the price of admission to settlement was a king's ransom. The colonial authorities were clearly hoping to find a solution to the land issue without making any provision for the problem of landlessness.

Finances. The original plans for the settlement program called for the entire scheme to finance itself. As the plans stood when the LDSB was established in January 1961, the program was to be operated with loan funds from the British government, the World Bank, and the Colonial Development Corporation. Some of the funds would be used to purchase land which would be conveyed to the prospective plot-holders in return for their undertaking to pay for it in instalments. Other loan funds would be re-lent to the plot-holders to help them develop the land. The entire operation, including the board's administrative expenses, would be financed from these funds, so that the project would have paid for itself by the time all the loans were repaid.[15] The board complained that these provisions were 'unrealistic and unworkable,' and the minister of agriculture, in his negotiations, managed to obtain grant funds to help the LDSB in the administration of the peasant scheme and to subsidize the purchase of land for that scheme. The government did not offer to subsidize the yeoman scheme.

By November 1961, when the Kenyan government and the World Bank signed the loan agreement for the program, the finances stood as follows: The British government was committed to a loan of about £2.2 million and a grant of a further £500000 for land purchase. Development loans from the World Bank and the CDC totalled £4.5 million. The British government offered a further £1 million, most of it in grants, to cover the expenses of administering the peasant program and helping the settlers to pay moving expenses.[16]

World Bank controls. Once the colonial authorities had committed Kenya to the project, both the government of the day and any successor regime were subject to rigorous controls over the project's execution. The loan agreement specified that the project be divided into sub-projects, each requiring separate approval from the bank. The bank would not approve a sub-project unless:
- the land purchased for it were 'suitable';
- it had been bought at a 'reasonable' price;
- qualified staff were available to supervise the sub-project;
- prospective settlers with 'adequate' qualifications were available in 'sufficient' numbers and 'suitable' arrangements had been made for establishing them on the land;

– sufficient funds had been shown to be available for the 'proper' execution of the sub-project.[17]

The agreement required the government to furnish the bank with 'plans, specifications and work schedules' for the project 'promptly upon their preparation' and 'in such detail as the Bank shall from time to time request.' The bank was empowered to inspect both the project itself and any documents or records relevant to it, and even to be informed about the financial conditions of the country generally and its international balance of payments position. Finally, the government was required to see to it that the LDSB maintained 'such organization and management as shall be necessary for the efficient carrying out of the Project.' Or, in the more direct language of an internal World Bank document: 'The Bank would be consulted regarding appointments of the Chairman and the Executive officer.'[18] Kenya was being manoeuvred into serious commitments by a fading colonial regime. In chapters 5 and 6, we will see how these commitments later militated against the provision of good agricultural opportunities for landless people.

PROBLEMS OF SETTLEMENT

The IBRD-CDC settlement program, as it came to be known, proved in practice to have a variety of startlingly glaring defects. An analysis of them offers insights into the thinking that underpinned the program. We can begin our examination by looking at some of the problems encountered in the process of the scheme's implementation. They can be divided into two categories: 1) finding suitable land, and 2) winning the participation of suitable prospective settlers.

Suitable land. It will be remembered that the success of these early plans for settlement – especially as long as land remained unsubsidized – hinged on the value that could be added to undeveloped, high-potential land by developing it. The project was supposed to finance itself on the margin between currently low yields and the potentially high yields of the future, a margin that was known to be very substantial, provided the land were carefully selected. According to the LDSB, two different patterns of land purchase were tried. One involved the purchase of existing farms in large blocks of 2000 hectares each – an area suitable for the settlement of some 100 families. The difficulty with that plan, the board maintained, was that the purchase of complete farms meant paying for the buildings on them, including the imposing homes that were a characteristic feature of settler life. The LDSB reported that 'the purchase of a complete farm for sub-division without any grants being available against which unusable permanent improvements could be written off left the yeoman with a debt for unwanted improvements which he could not afford.'[19] An alternative scheme tried by the board was the purchase of smaller blocks of land of 200 hectares or more each. These blocks were to be composed, not of entire existing farms, but of underdeveloped portions of them. The problem with these plans, as the board explained it, was that 'European farmers were generally unable to sell the underdeveloped portions of their farms leaving themselves with the highly capitalized portions as this would have put their farming economy out of balance.'[20]

The board's explanations beg the question of what went wrong with the idea of a scheme that would pay for itself by bringing about the development of underdeveloped land. The idea had received careful consideration. 'The project is economically feasible,' the World Bank's report had stated flatly. 'The land to be purchased would have a high potential for further development and intensification. Farm budget analyses indicate that the annual gross value of production on the land to be settled may be increased from an estimated £900,000 to £3.6 million, or a gain of £2.7 million a year, mostly in export crops ...'[21] Nor had the planning of the project been carried out in ignorance of the fact that the cost of permanent improvements would have to be absorbed in it. Indeed, that problem had been anticipated and provided for. The LDSB had been limited to a maximum valuation of £1300 for a dwelling house, except in cases where the house could be put to immediate use in settlement. The World Bank reported that the LDSB expected to pay less than £15 per acre for land and noted that that figure included an estimate of £2 per acre for buildings.[22]

If the problem of permanent improvements had been anticipated, where did the plan go wrong? Why were the LDSB unable to get the land they needed at acceptable prices? The evidence suggests that European settlers were not prepared to sell high-potential, underdeveloped land at prices that reflected its present worth rather than its ultimate potential, and that those who wanted to do so were able to find buyers at better prices. The LDSB's own policies were offering encouragement to such buyers. The board's valuers were instructed, in the case of people who had bought land since the beginning of 1960, that the owner be offered the price he had paid for the land, plus the value of any permanent improvement he put in, plus 'up to 10 per cent for the risk involved in buying the farm.'[23] The policy meant a guaranteed return for speculators who sold land to the board[24] and Hans Ruthenberg notes that it was taken advantage of. The reason for the policy was to offer incentives that might help to maintain large-scale farms in good order through the transition to independence, when there was a danger that farmers would lose their confidence and allow their land to run down. 'There are even cases,' Ruthenberg said, 'where Europeans have bought derelict farms and developed their production for the sole purpose of selling them, with a substantial bonus for development, to [settlement].'[25]

The development of derelict farms may have been a laudable activity in itself, but it must also have helped to undermine the financial basis for settlement by inflating the price of land being bought for the program. If the LDSB's top priority had been the facilitation of inter-racial land transfer – and not the provision of assistance to large-scale farmers – one would have thought that the board would buy run-down farms itself at bargain prices and use them for settlement, thereby allowing small-holders to have the benefit of the low prices and to reap the profits of redeveloping the land. As it was, the board was offering large-scale farmers an incentive to undertake that development and allowing the cost to fall ultimately on the settlement program in the form of higher land prices.

Another case in which the LDSB permitted the inflation of purchase prices involves land with an undeveloped potential for tea production, one of the types of land which, as we saw, the board needed for the yeoman and peasant programs. In October 1962, a memorandum from the board's acting chief executive officer to the board's valuers gave instruction on how to deal with cases of Europeans who had purchased undeveloped tea land 'at an enhanced price' and were now demanding that the board buy the land at prices that reflected the land's potential, even though the potential remained undeveloped.[26] Arguing on their behalf, board member A.W. Thompson had pointed to government valuations in 1960 in which 'potential tea land' had been assessed at £15 to £30 per acre, 'regardless of the purpose for which the land was to be used then or in the future. These values,' Thompson continued, 'were accepted by most owners in the belief, or hope, that should there be compulsory acquisition of land by a future government, this figure would form the basis of payment.'[27] The idea was vintage colonialism: Europeans should be paid for the potential of their land, although the actual development of that potential might as well be left to Africans.

With some evidence of chagrin, the board yielded to the pressure being applied and created a special status for tea land. But there was evidently concern to keep the precedent from spreading to other types of land. As a result, it became necessary to conceal the concession that had been made. Part of the board's public statement on land valuation policy read as follows: 'Land purchase values should be based on an appreciation of current crop profitability and recent land usage ...' That statement was amended to read 'current crop profitability, *fertility*, and recent land usage.'[28] 'Fertility,' Loggin explained to his valuers, had a 'special meaning assigned to it in connection with "tea potential" ...' A 'special increase in basic land values,' he said, should be permitted for tea land, provided that the potential for tea development could be realized in the near future. 'No mention should be made of this policy in correspondence with the general public,' he admonished, 'because it could easily be misinterpreted ... As you know it is the general rule that we do not value land with regard to its potentiality under any future settlement scheme. I think that this is an occasion in which you might ignore this rule ...'[29]

Another case in which the settlement authorities evidently allowed inflation of land prices is mentioned by Ruthenberg. Not all land bought for settlement was appraised on the basis of 1959 land prices, he maintains. In some cases, land was valued instead 'on the basis of eight times the average annual profit, working on a 12.5 percent return on the capital invested in land, buildings, water supplies, roads, etc.' Ruthenberg does not detail the effect of such a calculation on the ultimate price, but he does say that 'Britain, in paying eight times the average annual profit to out-going European farmers ... is certainly granting one of the most generous compensations for political losses of landownership known in economic history.'[30] Obviously, therefore, part of the LDSB's problem in finding suitable land for its early program stemmed from its own inability to hold the line against pressures to inflate land purchase prices.

After the planning of the settlement program was under way, relief from the problem of purchase prices came in the form of the British government offer, referred to above, to subsidize land purchase in the peasant program. The subsidy helped to save that scheme, a reduced version of which survived in the settlement plans that were ultimately implemented. But the yeoman scheme fell a victim both to the problems of finding land and to other problems, involving the recruitment of prospective settlers.

Suitable settlers. As attempts to implement the yeoman program got under way, its terms proved onerously restrictive. Furthermore, it seems questionable whether the program's administrative set-up was well calculated to attract the people for whom it was designed. Finally, there is evidence that the attitudes toward Africans and the views about nationalist politics manifest in the running of the program created obstacles to effective recruitment of settlers. A look at some of the details of these problems clears the way for a consideration of their significance.

One of the problems encountered in the implementation of the program was its inability to accommodate prospective settlers who wanted to take up farming in their home area rather than in another part of the country. Members of the Kalenjin ethnic groups had shown a considerable amount of interest in buying farms in the highlands, the board reported. They tended to prefer farms in areas adjacent to their 'tribal' reserves in the Rift Valley, but the high-potential, underdeveloped land that was the only kind eligible for inclusion in the program was not available to them there. The board did manage to negotiate the purchase of a number of pieces of land suitable for the program, but they were located in the Dundori area, on the east side of the Rift Valley and much closer to the Kikuyu reserve, where, according to the board, the newly subdivided farms 'proved most difficult to sell.'[31]

In its review of the yeoman debacle, the LDSB tried hard to leave the impression that the recruitment problem was simply the result of the unwillingness of prospective settlers to pull up stakes. In fact, there seems to have been much more to it than that. For one thing, it is doubtful that a closely administered settlement scheme was a suitable vehicle for farmers of proven ability with Shs 10 000/- to invest. Given the rigidity of colonial restrictions on African enterprise, that was a sum of money not ordinarily amassed by someone who did not have considerably more than the usual degree of enterprise and management ability. And yet the provisions for administration of the scheme seemed to suggest that these people would need a great deal of help – and perhaps also that they would bear watching. The program's plan for them included 'on-farm training for the first six months [which] would be followed by close supervision of farmers [under] (a) a Settlement Officer in charge of each [2000 hectare] block ...; (b) an Assistant Agricultural Officer with ancillary staff, for each [200–400 hectares]; and (c) a District Agent of the Settlement Board who would give financial advice and collect loan instalments.'[32] It seems unlikely that many of the people who had enough capital to consider participation in the scheme would have wanted that degree of supervision. Even more important, the costs of administration – since they had to be met from the proceeds of the program – undoubtedly cut back the individual settler's profit margin and reduced the attractiveness of the investment in comparison with other possible investments.

The decision to provide close supervision for people of demonstrated independence and ability suggests that the settlement authorities were underestimating their prospective settlers. Chapters 2 and 3 discussed the European settlers' sense of their own superiority and pointed out that even at the end of the colonial era, the typical European's contact with Africans was restricted for the most part to master-servant relationships, with many Europeans still clinging to the notion of their own superiority. That state of mind would not contribute to an unbiased evaluation of the abilities of Africans – especially Africans who took a jaundiced view of the colonial system. The question arises, therefore, whether the LDSB and its administration had managed, by the time of the yeoman scheme, to adopt a more positive attitude toward Africans than that which prevailed within the European population as a whole. The evidence suggests that it had not and that its failures in this regard had a great deal to do with its recruitment problems.

The experience of Edward Muceru Ayub, one of the first Africans to join the settlement administration, conveys a vivid picture of the milieu within which the program operated until about mid-1962. A graduate of Alliance High School, Muceru was one of the first two Africans to be employed on the board's staff. In an interview,[33] he recalled that his first few months on the job (which began in early 1962) were very difficult. He found his European colleagues slow to accept him and his duties regularly exposed him to the all-too-familiar humiliations of colonialism. One of his duties involved the board's attempts to negotiate the purchase of land for the yeoman scheme. Muceru's job as assistant district agent was to act as the board's liaison with people interested in purchasing land through the program. To this end, his supervisor, a district land agent, took him along on visits to Europeans who were considering selling their land to the board. On these trips, Muceru was to gather the information that he would later convey to prospective purchasers.

In the European settlers' homes, Muceru related, he was not treated as a guest but, in the time-honoured White Highlands style, as his supervisor's African assistant. When they arrived at a home, Muceru would be instructed to wait in the yard while his supervisor and the settler went inside to discuss terms. Before he went in, the settler would order one of his servants to bring a cup of tea for 'the boy' – meaning Muceru. His noon meal would be a sack lunch, while his supervisor and the settler lunched together inside. Later the district land agent, emerging from the settler's home, would give Muceru his first real work assignment of the day: to go out in a Land Rover with some of the settler's employees and check the boundary beacons, verifying their locations.

Looking back on that period, Muceru felt that his presence on these trips had been an exercise in tokenism. He was never allowed to participate in the negotiations and was given no details of how the final price had been arrived at. The only information he was given for his liaison with prospective purchasers was the figure they would have to pay and the terms of payment. The trips, he felt, served no purpose other than to allow the settlement authorities to claim African participation in the negotiations.

These incidents occurred during Muceru's first few months on the job, which, as we will see, was the final period before the initiation of the Million-Acre Scheme and the LDSB's loss of much of its influence over settlement. Later the situation improved drastically for him. He had come to work in March 1962. In July he and the other African staff member were asked to help senior settlement officials screen applicants (including Africans) for the job of settlement officer. Muceru himself became a settlement officer and rose quickly to senior settlement officer, a position of substantial authority. But his first period in the settlement administration was not a good time for an African.

If Muceru's account gives us an indication of the position of African staff members during the yeoman phase of settlement, the question of the settlement administration's approach toward prospective settlers becomes more cogent than ever. What methods were being used to attract settlers? And what criteria were being applied in the selection of suitable participants? These questions are particularly relevant with respect to schemes intended for Kikuyus. The Mau Mau war was still fresh in the minds of Kenyans. Colonial authorities wanted to use emergency regulations to build a new Kikuyu society around government loyalists, 'the salt of the Kikuyu earth, the peers of the Kikuyu realm'[34] (see chapter 3). Attempts had been made to use land consolidation to promote that aim. And agricultural improvements since then had similarly tended to favour loyalists. Yet, as we saw, the loyalists constituted only a small fraction of Kikuyu society. Were the settlement authorities conducting a recruitment campaign that favoured loyalists, or perhaps was pitched to appeal particularly to them? The evidence of the Dundori 'yeomen,' or assisted owners, suggests that the answer is yes.

Rebmann Wambaa, in his account of the period, states flatly that the Dundori settlers were loyalists; he remarks of another scheme that was being implemented at the same time that 'the administration tried hard to make [it] attractive to the revival Christians and the loyalists ...'[35] Documents in the LDSB files show that at least one of the Dundori assisted owners was not only a loyalist, but one who had placed the colonial regime very much in his debt. He had been 'one of the main Crown witnesses at the Kapenguria trial' at which Jomo Kenyatta and five other nationalist leaders were convicted of 'managing Mau Mau.' The documents available for this study do not show whether his past services to the colonial regime were considered in accepting him as a settler, but they do show that he fell far behind in his loan repayments and that when it seemed as if he would be evicted, the director of settlement interceded personally with the chief commissioner to get him placed in a different settlement scheme.[36] Most of the other Dundori yeomen were having serious financial difficulties as well.

The evidence on the board's recruitment policies does not offer a full account of what they were and how they worked in practice. But it does suggest, at least, that the LDSB was not a suitable agent for the recruitment of African candidates into a program that was designed to help bring Kenya's agrarian system into line with the demands of independence. The board sought to suggest that the inadequacies of Africans were at the root of the failure of its recruitment program. 'It has been found,' the board complained, '... that there is at present a very limited number of Africans with sufficient farming and managerial experience as well as capital to support the yeoman farming scheme ...'[37] That explanation subsequently lost its credibility as other land transfer programs attracted numerous African applicants with sufficient capital and ability to operate farms on the scale of those in the yeoman scheme, and larger ones as well. Clearly, it was the program and its administration – not its prospective clients – that were inadequate.

EVALUATION

The yeoman, peasant, and assisted-owner schemes belonged to the colonial phase of the search for a resolution to Kenya's land question. As such, they had all the weaknesses of a system that was itself coming to an end. European domination of the conception, the planning, and the implementation of land transfer was so complete as to exclude the authorities from access to knowledge of the problems with which they were supposedly dealing. At the top level of power, colonialists were clinging to the reins of government with the help of African politicians who, by the most optimistic calculation of their mandate, represented less than one-third of the active electorate. African participation in the LDSB was, as we have seen, even more token than that.

The results were manifest in both the planning and implementation of settlement. The yeoman and peasant scheme fairly bristled with political landmines and the LDSB strolled over them in blissful ignorance. There was, first of all, the spectacle of a land program aimed at a select group of prosperous people, while large numbers of the landless poor were ignored. A sensitive politician would have looked for something more acceptable. A shrewd one would at least have made gestures of sympathy and concern. The LDSB did neither. The board members' sympathy was reserved for European settlers, whose wallets were being filled, in effect, with funds diverted from the coffers of the settlement program. Having once selected, as beneficiaries of a government program, those members of the African rural population who had most clearly demonstrated their ability to fend for themselves (successful farmers and business people), the LDSB proceeded to insult them by requiring them to submit to a novice's regime of supervision and control. The LDSB would surely have been embarrassed to offer successful, upwardly mobile British farmers and business people an 'opportunity' to become 'peasants' and 'yeomen.' They felt no embarrassment in making such an offer to Africans – only irritation at the reluctance of the response they got. Their lack of finesse in dealing with prospective African clients of the settlement program was, as Edward Muceru Ayub's story suggests, matched by their inability to bring settlement's administrative machinery into line with the requirements of majority rule. It appears that the only Africans the LDSB were capable of dealing with were former loyalists, who had been taught to dance to the Europeans' tune. But the loyalists' performance at Dundori made it clear that, though they may have been the salt of the Kikuyu earth, they were not destined, in independent Kenya, to become the peers of the Kikuyu realm.

Not only were the colonial authorities failing to address the concerns of the majority of Africans, they were failing to meet their own objectives. It was time for colonialism to give way to the neo-colonial phase of land transfer.

5

The Million-Acre Scheme:
the neo-colonial phase

While the Land Development and Settlement Board was muddling through with its yeoman and peasant programs, time was running out. By the end of 1961, the colonial authorities had concluded that changes would have to be made. In mid-1962, they introduced the Million-Acre Scheme, a massive program for the settlement of 35000 families on far lower-quality land than that which had been sought in vain for the earlier settlement scheme. It is clear – from the way the scheme was planned and implemented, and from the methods that were used to sell it to Africans – that the authorities had learned a great deal in a year and a half about defending their interests in Africa.

What had they learned? Throughout the yeoman/peasant phase of settlement, they had been operating with a simple, two-class theory of Kenya society. If one had asked them, they would probably have used terms like 'civilization' and 'backwardness' to describe the dichotomy they saw. If we reword their conception in Marxist terms, we can describe it more precisely: They saw the struggle they faced as one that pitted themselves, a bourgeoisie seeking to expand the forces of production and build a modern capitalist system, against a peasantry and a landless class intent on turning the clock back to pre-capitalist modes and relations of production. Given that conception, they sought their allies in the nascent African bourgeoisie, to whom they offered financial and technical assistance in return for protection against peasant political forces. Their concept turned out to be insufficiently sophisticated – too primitive, one might be tempted to say, maliciously – but they did have one other insight that proved itself: They recognized that the preservation of Kenya's agrarian bourgeoisie, and of the neo-colonial economic system, could only be achieved if concessions were made to the peasantry.

That was the first of their important insights, but it was not the last. With the help of experience, they were able to perceive a reality more complicated than their two-class theory. First they learned that the European agrarian bourgeoisie was not monolithic. It included some elements that adapted easily, and profitably, to majority rule, while others – owners of the relatively marginal agricultural enterprises – were in deep trouble. The authorities discovered that they could save these settlers by selling their land to members of the landless class. Thus, they progressed from the idea of peasants and landless people as implacable foes to whom some concessions would have to be made – grudgingly and carefully – to that of peasants and would-be peasants as potential allies who could be manipulated to the advantage of all elements of the European bourgeoisie.

In time, too, it became obvious that the forces favouring the expansion of peasant society were not limited to the peasantry, or even to them and the landless class. They included urban petty bourgeois and bourgeois elements, who would be able to use small-scale agriculture as part of the support system for their primary pursuits. For them, a small farm could serve many purposes: An uneducated wife could live there, raise a family, and produce a surplus for urban consumption; a landless relative could be given building and cultivation rights, in return for which he or she might be expected to offer political or other support; an ageing parent could build a home there that would be appropriate to the status of a person whose child has achieved material success; ultimately, the farm might serve as last-ditch security against the hazards of urban wheeling and dealing. In using land in these ways, Africans were adapting pre-colonial usages to the modern economy (see chapter 2).

The recognition that the *bourgeoisies* were involved in the expansion of *peasant society* rang the death knell for the idea of a simple bourgeois-peasant polarity. For the implication of that recognition was that capitalist and peasant society could exist side by side, indeed intertwined and deeply interpenetrated. Peasant society could be allowed to expand and its very expansion could serve as a bulwark of capitalism. In short, the colonial authorities were abandoning their war on the peasantry and, instead, accepting the reality of Kenya as a peasant society, while seeking ways of allowing capitalism to thrive amid that reality. In doing this, they were laying the rails on which Kenya society would run after independence.

BROADENING THE POLITICAL BASE

In order to implement their more sophisticated strategy, the authorities had to broaden their political base. The first order of business was to find a way of getting KANU to abandon its oppositional stance in favour of co-operation in carrying off the transition to independence. Their strategy was as simple as it was effective: They carried on governing together with KADU, allowed the KANU leadership to taste the fruits of exclusion from power, and gave them time to reflect on the flavour. In short order, the nationalists began to mute the more belligerent noises they had been making and before long they were ready to join the government, largely on the colonial authorities' terms.

Two of the most important issues involved in KANU's capitulation were the land question and regionalism. KANU's position on land was that a settlement should await independence (see chapter 4). That suggestion was anathema to the colonial authorities. The importance of the issue to the British government could be measured in pounds sterling. European settlers had been officially encouraged to come to Kenya and had been led to believe that the White Highlands were a permanent institution. As recently as 1954, Secretary of State A. Lennox-Boyd had declared: 'Her Majesty's Government are not likely to encourage people to come to Kenya if they intend to betray them or their predecessors.'[1] In the wake of that pledge, and many others like it, the United Kingdom could not have evaded its responsibility for compensating the settlers for whatever losses they might suffer as a result of independence. To let independence go by without a settlement of the land question, therefore, would have involved the government in a commitment to compensate European settlers for whatever might happen to them afterwards.

At least one prominent British writer was demanding, in 1963, that the government accept that responsibility. Vividly picturing the anxieties of European settlers – some of them aged and infirm – who waited for independence, uncertain of what the future would bring, Margery Perham declared that the United Kingdom had an 'inescapable responsibility, which cannot be unloaded upon Africans.'[2] At least one of the reasons for the government's failure to accept her view can be deduced from her own figures. She estimated that it would cost £130 million to 'underwrite the settlers' land value.' The government was committed to the settlers, but had no intention of paying out £130 million. That was one reason why a land transfer program was undertaken without KANU.

And that was why, as that program became bogged down, it was so important to the authorities to bring KANU into the government. Judging by the concessions they made, it seems unlikely that the KANU leadership realized how badly the authorities needed them.

The second issue arose in the latter part of 1961, when the KADU-European coalition was cemented by their joint support for the concept of regionalism, a KADU proposal calling for Kenya to be divided into a number of areas demarcated according to ethnic criteria. The regions would have a measure of constitutionally entrenched autonomy and would serve as a base of political power for the minority groups, even if they were unable to command much support at the centre. The idea of regionalism, therefore, appealed both to Europeans and to the African minority groups. Indeed, KANU's Oginga Odinga maintained later that it was settler politicians who had conceived the plan. 'It was no secret,' he said in his memoirs, 'that the authors of KADU's plan for regionalism were Wilfred Havelock, Michael Blundell, R.S. Alexander and their associates, long practised in the art of political survival.'[3] Blundell's own account of the idea's origin is shrouded in discreet ambiguity: 'The members of KANU were in a dictatorial and difficult mood ... As a result KADU turned their minds to a federal type of constitution, with the object of limiting the power of a central government and of the Kikuyu over the remainder of Kenya. Regionalism ... had an immediate and attractive appeal to tribes in all the rural and more remote areas of Kenya ...'[4]

In the meantime, KANU, and the African majority, were excluded from government decision making, while KADU took credit for the programs the government was initiating. Immediately after the coalition government was formed, the British offered a program of grants and loans, including money for land settlement. Bernard Mate of Meru crossed the floor and accepted a portfolio in the new government, a hint that support for KANU was weakening. In August, Jomo Kenyatta, the most important African leader, was released from detention and KADU claimed credit for helping to bring about the release by working within the government. Then came the proposal for regionalism, which was anathema to KANU. It looked as if yet another step toward independence might be taken without the participation of the majority party.

The pressure was too much for KANU's leaders and they capitulated on both the land issue and the issue of regionalism. In January 1962, Kenyatta endorsed the government's plans for land settlement, now thoroughly revised to incorporate a major expansion of peasant society while keeping most of the large-farm sector intact. His endorsement came in the somewhat ambiguous form of a denial that he had earlier expressed a contrary view – a hint that the concession was not made gladly. 'In the allocation of land to the new peasant farmers,' he said, 'we shall bear in mind that our first duty will be to help those poor and landless people who today have no means of livelihood. I did not say – at a recent KANU rally – that such peasant farmers will get land free. I went to great pains to explain that the way our Government would help such peasant farmers would be by giving them loans on easy terms, to be repaid by the farmers in instalments over a period of time.'[5] A few days later he reiterated the principle: 'We do not believe in being given this or that free. I do not want Africans to adopt that attitude. I want them to be able to work with their own hands on a piece of land. I think the landless Africans should be given so many acres on loan for so many years, so they can start farming with the help of the Government, and then when they start earning some money they can start paying the debt back.'[6]

As he spoke, Kenyatta can hardly have suspected how onerous a debt burden many of the peasants would have to bear. But he, and the rest of the KANU leadership, certainly did know that they had left the settlement of the land question in the hands of the colonial authorities.

In February, at a conference at Lancaster House in London for discussion of constitutional change, KANU made its second major concession – an endorsement of the regionalism scheme. The plans for settlement were also ratified at the conference. Accounts written at the time indicate that regionalism was regarded as the biggest issue. It was a major constitutional innovation that was expected to seriously weaken the central government and, with it, the majority party. Settlement, on the other hand, was portrayed simply as a program to benefit peasants – a program controversial only to an extremist minority that demanded free land. In retrospect, however, it is clear that settlement was much more important. Regionalism proved to be short-lived. The regional assemblies never had much power and within a year after independence they had been abolished. Settlement, on the other hand, worked out as intended. It was planned under colonial control – albeit with African participation – and carried out according to plan. It constituted a resolution of the land question that cost Britain £9.6 million in cash – a tidy saving compared with Margery Perham's estimate of £130 million as the cost of Britain's 'inescapable responsibility.' It left both the Kenya government and many individual peasant families with a heavy burden of debt, in return for benefits that were in many instances questionable. And, most important, it had a considerable influence on the shape of Kenya's society after independence.

Could KANU's leaders have driven a harder bargain? In retrospect, it seems clear that the answer is yes. With independence approaching, the White Highlands represented a colonial liability of potentially massive proportions. Britain could escape a significant part of that liability through a program of orderly land transfer, through which African farmers bought land and thereby, in effect, compensated departing Europeans. However, the yeoman and peasant scheme had demonstrated the importance, for the success of such a program, of effective communication with the African population. The participation of KANU's leadership was crucial to the achievement of such communication. In short, KANU's leaders had the political leverage necessary to make demands, but they do not seem to have made much use of that leverage.

Defenders of the settlement program have argued, in effect, that there was no need to make demands, that the Million-Acre Scheme was in the best interests of its African clients, and that the emphasis on the preservation of large-scale mixed agriculture was in the interest of Kenya's economy. A close examination of the Million-Acre Scheme, which we undertake in this chapter and the next, offers plenty of evidence that the interests of African settlers were not being vigorously defended. Nor does the suggestion that large-scale mixed agriculture was crucial to Kenya's economy as a whole withstand careful scrutiny.

The recurrent argument in favour of large-scale agriculture was its importance to Kenya's external balance of trade. But export and production figures (see table 1) show that there were loopholes in the argument. The most important exports were not large-scale farm products per se, but specifically plantation produce, especially coffee and tea. (Sisal, which ranked close to tea in 1959, was soon to lose much of its market to synthetic substitutes.)

Mixed farm production was a different matter. To begin with, it did not include major exports. Furthermore, as Colin Leys has shown, the value to Kenya's economy of the commodities the European mixed farms did produce was largely negated by the foreign exchange they used up and by the cost of the subsidies they needed to remain viable.[7] Finally, the rapid expansion of small-scale African market agriculture (see chapter 3) suggested that it would be possible to offset any decline in large-farm production with small-farm increases. In the long run, there is no reason why there could not have been a similar substitution of

TABLE 1
Source of principal agricultural exports, 1959

Commodity	Domestic exports (percentage of total value)	Production for sale (000 tons)	
		Small farms	Large farms
Coffee	31.8	3.6	19.6
Tea	10.8	0.1	12.3
Sisal	10.4	1.5	53.7
Pyrethrum	6.6	0.6	4.2
Wattle	3.7	18.8	28.3
Corn	3.3	79.7	104.1
Cotton	2.0	10.0	–
Beans, peas, lentils	1.1	12.5	–

NOTE: These figures offer an indication of large-scale agriculture's importance to the Kenya economy at the close of the colonial era. For each of
the agricultural commodities listed, the first column of figures shows
what its share was in Kenya's export market. The second and third
columns compare small-farm with large-farm production for sale for
each of these commodities.
SOURCE: Republic of Kenya, *Statistical Abstract, 1968* (Nairobi: Government Printer) 45, 73, tables 51 (c), 70

small-scale coffee and tea production for plantation agriculture. In
short, KANU leaders had room for manoeuvre. They did not have to pay
lip service to the long-term importance of large-scale agriculture –
although realism would have constrained them to acknowledge the dis-
astrous consequences of a sudden collapse. And they could have demanded a better deal for the Million-Acre Scheme's settlers, confident in
the knowledge that Britain would rather find better land or more
development funds than risk the consequences of trying to force independence without the participation of the party representing the vast
majority of Africans.

In defence of the KANU leadership – or perhaps 'mitigation' is the
appropriate word – it needs to be pointed out that they were at a disad-
vantage in their dealings with the colonial authorities. Although experienced in opposition, the nationalists had no experience of government
and presumably lacked access to much information available to the
authorities – and now available to armchair critics. Nevertheless, they
struck a bargain that was of considerable benefit to themselves, but

unconscionably costly to Kenya, as our examination will show. We begin with a look at the transition from the yeoman and peasant scheme to the Million-Acre Scheme.

TRANSITION

The essential differences between the early plans for settlement and the so-called high-density schemes replacing them were twofold. High-density settlement involved vastly expanded acreages of land that would not have been eligible for inclusion under the standards of the old program. And instead of a relatively small number of carefully selected, successful farmers and businessmen, the new program was designed to accommodate masses of landless families.

As one might well imagine, these changes had very important ramifications. To finance such a program, it was necessary for the British government to greatly increase its support, not only in the form of loans, but also by offering substantial grants. The international aid agencies, on the other hand, were leery of the risks implicit in the program. They were worried that the inclusion of lower-quality land and of settlers who had no credentials might jeopardize the standards set by the World Bank. The bank and the CDC, therefore, reduced their support for the program. It later became obvious that this reduced support seriously undermined high-density settlement and exacerbated the sufferings of the landless people who became owners of high-density plots.

The first plans for high-density settlement were already surfacing in 1961, a year or more before the final abandonment of the yeoman scheme. In its *Review of Activities*, the LDSB notes that during 1961 Kenya authorities began to negotiate with the British for 'a completely new type of settlement scheme, to be financed entirely from British Government funds, for the settlement of 12,000 African families on high-density smallholdings in order to meet the pressing problem of unemployed and landless families especially amongst the Kikuyu tribe ...'[8]

It seems clear that the colonial authorities were not acting primarily out of a concern for 'the pressing problems of unemployed and landless families ...' But it was true that they were launching a new type of scheme, one which would cost considerably more than the IBRD-CDC program would have. In addition to the land-purchase subsidy for peasant settlement referred to in chapter 4, the United Kingdom offered both loan and grant funds for high-density settlement. No IBRD-CDC funds were available for that project, but the West German government offered development loans totalling £1.2 million for high-density settlement. The United Kingdom's total commitment to the settlement program now included grants totalling £3.3 million and loans of £4.1 million (see table 2).

To officials of the World Bank, this turn of events was disturbing, both because the new scheme included low-quality land and because it was open to what the bank evidently regarded as low-quality people. 'The Kenya Government's new smallholder scheme,' a bank report declared, '... involves lower standards for both land and settlers than were considered acceptable for the Bank Project.'[9] At another point, the report said, 'The aims of the new scheme are to settle 12,000 smallholders during the next two years, not necessarily on high potential land. The settlers would not be required to have farming experience and would receive no training ... [The settlement authorities] consider that the new scheme will provide an outlet for less desirable types of settlers ...'[10] The report expressed concern that the new scheme might have an adverse effect on the World Bank program, especially in view of the fact that the LDSB would be administering both schemes. Some reassurance was taken from the fact that the board would keep separate accounts for the two projects and also administer them separately 'insofar as practicable.' In January 1962, the bank sought further reassurance by requiring that the board's Valuations Committee, which had the task of approving all land purchases, be split up into separate committees for high- and low-density land purchases.[11] What remained of the IBRD-CDC program, therefore, would be kept strictly separate from settlement for landless people. In the meantime, the high-density program was due for a drastic expansion.

THE MILLION-ACRE SCHEME

From July to September 1962, colonial authorities were busy flying back and forth between Nairobi and London negotiating terms for the Million-Acre Scheme. The program that emerged involved about £25 million, some 35 000 families of smallholders (most of them landless people), and more than a million acres of largely high-density settlement schemes. It offered a far more realistic approach to the African population – both landless people and more prosperous prospective settlers – than the yeoman and peasant scheme. At the same time, it reflected the continuing primacy of European interests in the resolution of the land question. Following is a sketch of its main features.

TABLE 2
Funding of settlement after introduction of the first high-density program,
November 1961

A. UK FUNDS

	Loans		Grants		
	Low density	High density	Low density	High density	Total £000s
Land purchase	2 201	1 750	438	800	5 189
Administrative and misc. program expenses	120	–	973	1 119	2 212
Total £000s	2 321	1 750	1 411	1 919	7 401

B. OTHER SOURCES

IBRD	Development loans for low-density settlers	3 000
CDC	Development loans for low-density settlers	1 500
West Germany	Development loans for high-density settlers	1 200
Total £000s		5 700

C. TOTAL ALL SOURCES

	Land purchase	Development loans	Administrative and misc. expenses	Total (£000s)
Low density	2 639	4 500	1 093	8 232
High density	2 550	1 200	1 119	4 869
Total £000s	5 189	5 700	2 212	13 101

D. DISTRIBUTION

	Loans	Grants	Total (£000s)
Low density	6 821	1 411	8 232
High density	2 950	1 919	4 869
Total £000s	9 771	3 330	13 101

NOTE: An apparent error in the LDSB's arithmetic had the effect of raising the total of British grants by £80 000. That error has been corrected in the figures shown on this table, with the result that the relevant totals here are £80 000 lower than in the *Review of Activities*.

SOURCE: Calculated from LDSB, *A Review of the Activities of the LDSB (1962)*, para. 7, KNA 3/121, Office of the President

Land purchase. Under the Million-Acre Scheme, the government committed itself to the purchase of about 80 000 hectares of land each year for a period of five years, enough to make a substantial impact on Kenya's land market during the years immediately before and after independence. In addition to offering a market for Europeans who wanted to sell their land, the program also contained a number of other concessions to settler demands, as well as some provisions for tighter budgeting.

One of the new provisions was a change in the pattern of land purchase. Under the original settlement program, land for 'yeomen' was to be bought 'in the interior of the Scheduled Areas ... Solid African "islands" are to be avoided for social reasons ...' Peasant settlement schemes, by contrast, were to be located 'on the periphery of existing African reserves in solid blocks of about [2000 hectares] ...' Yeoman schemes were to be integrated into the highlands, while peasant settlement was to be kept separate.

Now, with the introduction of the Million-Acre Scheme, purchasing for the entire program was to follow the pattern that had originally been applicable to peasant settlement only, although it would take place on a much larger scale. The one million acres (about 400 000 hectares) of land to be included in settlement would be purchased in large blocks located on the periphery of existing African areas. Conversely, the remaining six million acres (about 2.4 million hectares) of highlands not slated for settlement would continue as large blocks of land devoted exclusively to large-scale agriculture. Purchase programs would be published in advance so that farmers living in affected areas could plan ahead. As one might well imagine, these measures were more than simply a convenience for settlers who wanted to plan ahead. We will return to them below.

A second feature of the new program was an offer of more generous terms of payment. From the resumption of land purchase in November 1961 until mid-1962, the terms of payment had been one-half in cash and the remainder in three equal, annual instalments, secured by Kenya government promissory notes bearing 5 per cent interest. In order to avoid the possible hazards of currency controls, payment might be taken in either Nairobi or London. This arrangement had, as we saw in chapter 4, been accepted 'reluctantly and with suspicion' by spokesmen for the settlers. As of 1 July 1962, a new policy was established calling for payment in full in cash at the time of purchase.[12] The seller's right to choose payment in London remained unchanged.

Another change in purchase policy coinciding with the beginning of the Million-Acre Scheme was the introduction of the 'fertility' clause, which was a concession to the demands of speculators in undeveloped tea land (see chapter 4). In other respects, the basis of land valuation remained substantially unaltered: '... the basic value of land is fixed in relation to 1957–1959 (first quarter) open market values, as discovered from actual sales evidence during the period, and then as enhanced or diminished by current crop profitability.'[13]

The purchase program not only affected the market for land, but also had an impact on ancillary agricultural markets as the settlement authorities purchased a wide range of goods and services, both from farmers and from other suppliers. The settlement market appears to have had a particularly strong effect on livestock prices, which were 'being kept very high indeed, largely because the settlement authorities are buying grade stock in order to equip in-going settlers.'[14] Evidently, livestock prices were kept high, not only as an automatic result of the requirements of the settlement program, but also as a conscious policy. In April 1963, the director of settlement told the LDSB that 'the number of cattle held by the Department [of Settlement] were being reduced by sales to settlers. It was intended that herds should be kept at a low level until the commencement of the 1963–64 land purchasing programme, so that the department could enter the livestock market again at that time and so assist in keeping prices stable.'[15] The implication seems to be that the settlement authorities did not simply purchase cattle as they were needed for settlement, but also timed their purchases in such a way as to keep prices up – a boon for large-scale farmers, and one that would inevitably have to be passed on to the smallholders in settlement.

While the Million-Acre Scheme brought a variety of benefits to large-scale farmers, it also heralded closer control on spending. One control measure was a reduction in the degree of latitude that the LDSB was allowed to exercise in its negotiations with individual sellers. Previously, the LDSB's chief executive officer had had the discretion, in negotiations over land purchase, to vary the price by a 25 per cent margin upward or downward. In August 1962, the minister for land settlement and water development, reporting on his negotiations with colonial authorities in London, told the board that henceforth the 25 per cent margin would be reduced to 5 per cent.[16] Another instance of budget tightening applied to so-called compassionate cases. The British government had been supporting the purchase of land owned by aged or disabled people. Now, the board was informed that the United Kingdom 'would give little support to compassionate cases and these would have to be limited to the 63 first priority cases which were being dealt with already.'[17]

There was one other new provision for land purchase that was related to the Million-Acre Scheme, although it was not part of that program. It was the government's offer of increased loan funds to help finance private purchases of large-scale farms. The capital of the Land and Agricultural Bank of Kenya – which had been lending money to European settlers for a generation – was increased by £700 000 in 1963 and again by the same amount in 1964. In addition, the bank was permitted to make loans up to 80 per cent of the value of the land instead of the previous 60 per cent.[18] The money was to be available to both Europeans and Africans who wished to buy land outside the settlement areas. By means of this program, and others discussed further below, the regular market in land was being allowed to become the main vehicle for land transfer to the African bourgeoisie, with government intervening only to supply loan funds where they were not available in the money market. This change in strategy manifested the colonial authorities' recognition that the development of an interest, among the African bourgeoisie, in the maintenance of large-scale agriculture was automatic and did not require the kind of paternalistic government action envisioned under the yeoman scheme. The main problem – and therefore the priority – was the establishment of a workable alliance with the peasantry.

Finance. A look at the financing of the Million-Acre Scheme offers a quantitative measurement of the changes that had taken place in the settlement program. What was left of the IBRD-CDC low-density scheme was now getting short shrift. At the same time, a substantial infusion of funds, in the form of both loans and grants, was redirecting the main thrust of the program into high-density settlement.

Settlement authorities were obviously apprehensive about the reaction of World Bank officials to this bold expansion of a program that the IBRD had viewed with suspicion from the beginning. There were even fears that the money would be cut off. Permanent Secretary N.S. Carey Jones, addressing the director of settlement's planning committee in September, 'stressed that it was imperative to adhere to the terms of the international finance agreements because otherwise there was danger of losing this source of funds.'[19] As it turned out, neither the World Bank nor the CDC cut off the funds, but the amount of money available from these sources was sharply reduced. The IBRD and the CDC agreed to continue to supply development loans for low-density settlement and allowed the acreage involved in the program to remain unchanged. But

TABLE 3

Funding of the Million-Acre Settlement Scheme

A. UK FUNDS

| | Loans | | Grants | | |
	Low density	High density	Low density	High density	Total £000s
Land purchase	1262	6506	632	3478*	11878
Development loans	–	4101	–	–	4101
Administrative and misc. expenses	–	–	1221	4320	5541
Total £000s	1262	10607	1853	7798	21520

B. OTHER SOURCES

IBRD	Development loans for low-density settlers	1647
CDC	Development loans for low-density settlers	824
West Germany	Development loans for high-density settlers	1200
Total £000s		3671

C. TOTAL ALL SOURCES

	Land purchase	Development loans	Administrative and misc. expenses	Total (£000s)
Low density	1894	2471	1221	5586
High density	9984*	5301	4320	19605
Total £000s	11878	7772	5541	25191

D. DISTRIBUTION

	Loans	Grants	Total (£000s)
Low density	3733	1853	5586
High density	11807	7798	19605
Total £000s	15540	9651	25191

*This figure includes £195000 allocated by the British government as a result of its belated recognition that land had been wrongly taken from the Nandi people (see chapter 2). Some 7000 hectares purchased with these funds were returned to the Nandi instead of being included in the settlement program.

SOURCE: Calculated from C.P.R. Nottidge and J.R. Goldsack, *The Million-Acre Settlement Scheme 1962–66* (Nairobi: Department of Settlement) 9–10

the standards of quality applicable to the land being included in the program were lowered, with the result that both the cost of the scheme and its ability to generate income were reduced. The original plans for the IBRD-CDC scheme (see chapter 4) were that some 73 000 hectares would accommodate 1800 'yeomen' earning Shs 5000/- per year each and 6000 'peasants' with annual target incomes of 2000/-, a total of 7800 families. Under the Million-Acre Scheme, the total number of settlers was reduced to 4895 and almost all of them had target incomes of only 2000/-.[20] In the original plans, one-half the land, or 36 500 hectares, was to accommodate 6000 'peasants.' Now, less than 5000 were to be accommodated on the whole 73 000 hectares. Lower-quality land and fewer settlers resulted in lower development costs. The IBRD-CDC contribution was reduced from a projected £4.5 million to less than £2.5 million.[21]

As a result, the British government not only had to finance the program expansion brought about by the advent of the Million-Acre Scheme, but was also obliged, in effect, to cover the deficit left by the cut in development aid. The United Kingdom's financial commitment shot from £7.4 million to £21.5 million, an increase of £14.1 million. Perhaps more significantly, the government now offered £9.6 million in grants, almost triple the previous commitment. The total cost of the Million-Acre Scheme was £25.2 million, and £19.6 million of that total was to go to high-density settlement. This was not a limited project, as the earlier plans for settlement had been, but a major commitment to resolve Kenya's land question.

Management. With the introduction of the Million-Acre Scheme, the government assumed direct control over settlement, shunting the LDSB aside. The authorities were clearly dissatisfied with the way the board had handled the yeoman and peasant schemes. The feeling of disaffection was apparently mutual. Even before the government had openly manifested its loss of confidence in the LDSB, some board members were beginning to demonstrate their dissatisfaction with the direction that policy was taking. A dispute over proposed land purchases on the Kinangop offered a first hint of what was to come.

During 1961, the board had begun to investigate the purchase of some 3200 hectares of land on the Kinangop, which was to become the scene of a massive high-density settlement scheme. The board's appraiser (who perhaps let his empathy for the Kinangop farmers get the better of his professional judgment) valued the land at £192 000, an average price of £24 per acre. As we saw in chapter 4, even the valuable land that would have been used for the yeoman scheme was to be bought at prices averaging less than £15 per acre. The board does not explain how its appraiser came to believe that the government would be prepared to pay a substantially higher price for the much less valuable land that was to be used for high-density schemes. Whatever the reason, it was clear that high-density settlement, even with the help of the British subsidies, could not absorb such a price. The board found itself in the embarrassing position of having to disavow its own valuer's assessment and to retract the offer to purchase land at the price he had named.[22]

The board's decision was 'given much publicity in the press [and] drew a great deal of hostile criticism from political and farming organizations.'[23] The board itself split over the issue. On 24 January 1962, J.A. Seys, a representative of the settlers' Kenya National Farmers' Union (KNFU), resigned from the board 'in protest at the ... decision not to proceed with the South Kinangop smallholder scheme.' Two days later, the board chairman, J.F. Lipscomb, who also served as chairman of the large-scale farmers' Board of Agriculture (Scheduled Areas), likewise resigned.[24] The so-called *cause célèbre* of the Kinangop had become the occasion for an open demonstration of growing disenchantment among board members at the new direction of settlement policy.

The government, for its part, was re-evaluating the LDSB's role in carrying out that policy. In April a reorganization process began that culminated in the removal of the LDSB from its dominant role in the planning and implementation of settlement. Col. B.R. McKenzie – who had excellent contacts with the African nationalist leadership and had been a supporter of the Kenya African National Union for some time – took on the new post of minister of land settlement and water development. The LDSB's staff were placed under the ministry, giving it effective control of the board's operations. Three months later, the board's loss of influence was made official. Carey Jones, the permanent secretary, announced that the task of planning and implementing settlement was to be taken from the LDSB and made a function of the Department of Settlement, leaving the board in control of only the land purchase portion of the settlement program.[25]

Shortly afterwards, at the board's August meeting, McKenzie showed up to give an account of the plans that were then being formulated for the Million-Acre Scheme. He explained that under the new financial arrangements, the United Kingdom would curtail its support for 'compassionate' land purchases. He also told the board that its margin of latitude in negotiating land purchase prices would be reduced (as we have noted already) from 25 per cent to 5 per cent. Consternation undoubtedly reigned. Having just lost its control over settlement, the board was now suffering infringements on its only remaining preserve, land purchase. Later in the meeting, the board chairman noted that, legally, the LDSB still had responsibility for settlement and declared stiffly that he had asked 'for written directions in cases where the Minister wished the law to be ignored.'[26]

It was a nice piece of sarcasm, but it did not amount to any more than a debating point. Although the board was the legal agent for settlement, it had, from the outset, been 'subject to the general and specific directions of the Minister ...'[27] The minister was now taking direct control, and there was more to come. In December, it was announced that the 1963–64 purchasing program would become the responsibility of a subcommittee of the Council of Ministers. Subsequently, it became obvious that the LDSB, far from being responsible for land purchase, could no longer count on even being consulted in the selection of purchase areas. In January,

Members of the Board commented on the fact that the [recently published] 1963–64 purchasing programme ... differed considerably from the draft that had been shown them at their meeting on 12 December 1962 and that it even differed from amended programmes that they had been shown individually subsequent to that meeting ... After a discussion the meeting agreed that a more categorical disclaimer of the Board's responsibility for the selection of areas for the 1962–63 and 1963–64 land purchasing programme was needed.[28]

Even after its demotion, however, the LDSB was by no means a cipher. The government kept it informed on the progress of the settlement program and continued to consult it on a variety of matters, including important policy questions. The board continued to dominate the purchasing program and its chief executive officer acted as a liaison between the government and the settler community.[29] It was still in a position to act as a watchdog over the financial interests of the settlers – and, as we will see, it continued to influence the formulation of government policy – but it had been divested of its power to participate in the management of smallholder settlement.

The settlement bureaucracy. The administration of settlement is worth looking at, because it was the organization used to maintain control over the disaffected class of landless people that had been created by the economic forces of colonialism. Originally designed – wrongheadedly, as we saw – for more prosperous land buyers, it proved readily adaptable to the task of controlling masses of poor people, many of them in desperate straits, some of them seething with resentment. It was so successful that it set a pattern for independent Kenya that, with some variations, was followed in a variety of land settlement programs.

The term 'settlement scheme' – especially when it refers to an accommodation for large numbers of poor people – may evoke the image of a co-operative or communal project. It is necessary to emphasize, therefore, that the settlement program was organized almost entirely on an individualist basis, just as its predecessor program for more prosperous people had been. The Million-Acre Scheme was divided into units which, in one of settlement's terminological oddities, were referred to as 'schemes.' Each unit, or scheme, was made up of some scores or hundreds of individual plots.

The planning of a settlement scheme began with the specification of a target income – meaning the amount of income a plot would be capable of producing after the settler had met all financial obligations and provided for his or her family's subsistence. Equipped with a decision as to what that figure would be, agricultural officials, at the request of the director of settlement, assessed the potential of each tract of land to be included in settlement. They decided what acreage would be required to meet the given income target and then drew up budgets for each plot (see table 4). The budget provided a detailed plan for the management of the plot, specifying what crops and animals would be raised, noting the acreage to be devoted to each activity, and listing anticipated expenses and income.

In return for his or her plot, the incoming settler assumed a debt, which was referred to as the settlement charge, and which covered the expenses incurred by the Kenya government in purchasing the land.[30] The land and the houses, outbuildings, and other permanent improvements had been bought with the help of both loans and grants, as we have seen. The grant element took up about one-third of the total cost and it was presumed to be sufficient to cover the cost of permanent improvements that had been useful for large-scale farms, but which would be of no use to a smallholder – for example, large dwelling houses, trees that would have to be felled, and fencing that demarcated obsolete boundaries. In computing the amount to be charged to the smallholder on account of land, the total cost of land and permanent improvements was divided by the number of plots that would be located on the land. Since that figure included the cost of permanent improvements, the one-third subsidy was deducted from it. The resulting figure was increased by a bad-debt margin of 10 per cent to arrive at the settlement charge.[31]

In addition to the cost of the land, provision had to be made for the expenses involved in developing it. Seed, fertilizer, livestock, fencing, and a host of other items were supplied to the smallholder on credit. That debt and the settlement charge were financed in two interest-bearing loans, a thirty-year land loan and a ten-year development loan,[32] which were assumed by the smallholder upon taking over the plot. The loans were secured through legal documents signed by each settler and the settlement authorities had the right to seize the chattel and repossess the land of loan defaulters.

The rule for settlement, therefore, was individual responsibility. Each settler, in effect, received a small piece of the former White Highlands and it was up to him or her to pay for it and make the most of it. The existence of scheme-level marketing co-operative societies did not do much to qualify the otherwise individualist organization of the program. The co-operatives were little more than service organizations for the administration, designed to facilitate loan repayments and marketing and to supply a limited range of services, such as livestock dipping and artificial insemination.[33] Their effectiveness as purchasing agents for settlers was limited by the fact that they were split up into microcosmic, scheme-level societies instead of being organized into larger co-operative unions, which would have been able to purchase in bulk at reduced prices. Settlement geography and organization offered ideal units for the formation of co-operative unions and the idea of forming such unions was discussed, on one occasion at least, in the planning of settlement,[34] but it was not pursued. Other functions that could have been taken over by co-operatives – such as education, contract ploughing, or the management of trading centres – were, for the most part, left in private hands or given to other agencies.

A slightly more significant exception to the rule of individualism in the organization of settlement is a series of co-operative farms and ranches that were started as part of the settlement program. But their significance is limited as well. At the completion of the Million-Acre Scheme they accommodated only 3800 families, less than one-tenth of the total in the program.[35] Furthermore, they did not constitute a planned, coherent approach to the promotion of co-operative endeavour. Rather, they were ad hoc responses to the fact that some of the land purchased for settlement proved unsuitable for individual small-holdings.[36] Almost half of the non-individualized land in settlement was

TABLE 4
Sample budgets for a high-density scheme (in Shs)

TYPE I BUDGET

10 acres Class I arable
  1/2 acre homestead
  2 acres subsistence
  2 acres pyrethrum
  5-1/2 acres grass

Income
  2 acres pyrethrum @ 300 lb @ 1/80   1 080/-
  2 cows @ 120 lb butterfat @ 2/50 lb   600/-

                              1 680/-

Expenditure
  2 acres pyrethrum @ 75/- per acre   150/-
  2 cows @ 70/-   140/-
  2 acres grass establishment   120/-

                              410/-

Development loan
  housing and fencing   300/-
  2 cows   1 200/-
  cultivation   500/-

                              2 000/-

Loan repayments
  2 000/- development loan   275/-
  5 700/- settlement charge   435/-

                              710/-

Gross expenses   1 120/-
Profit to settler   560/-

TYPE II BUDGET

15 acres Class II arable
  1/2 acre homestead
  2 acres subsistence
  2 acres pyrethrum
  2 acres fodder
  8-1/2 acres grass

Income
  2 acres pyrethrum @ 300 lb @ 1/80   1 080/-
  3 cows @ 120 lb butterfat @ 2/50 per lb   900/-

                              1 980/-

Expenditure
  2 acres pyrethrum @ 75/- per acre   150/-
  3 cows @ 70/-   210/-
  2 acres fodder @ 100/-   200/-

                              560/-

TYPE II BUDGET cont'd
Development loan

housing and fencing	300/-
3 cows	1 560/-
cultivation 2 acres @ 70/-	140/-
	2 000/-

Loan repayments

2 000/- development loan	275/-
5 700/- settlement charge	435/-
	710/-
Gross expenses	1 270/-
Profit to settler	710/-

TYPE III BUDGET
30 acres Class III arable
- 1/2 acre homestead
- 2 acres subsistence
- 2 acres fodder
- 2 acres grass ley
- 23-1/2 acres permanent grass

Estimated income

2 cows @ 120 lb butterfat @ 2/50 per lb	600/-
25 sheep @ 6 lb wool @ 3/- per lb	450/-
20 lambs @ 2 lb wool @ 3/- per lb	120/-
20 sheep sold @ 60/- per sheep	1 200/-
	2 370/-

Estimated expenditure

2 cows @ 70/- each	140/-
25 sheep @ 10/- each	250/-
4 acres fodder grass cultivation @ 100/- per acre	400/-
	790/-

Development loan

housing and fencing	400/-
2 cows	1 020/-
25 ewes @ 60/-	1 500/-
cultivation 1 acre @ 80/-	80/-
	3 000/-

Loan repayment

3 000/- development loan	412/70
6 000/- settlement charge	457/20
	869/90
Gross expenses	1 659/90
Profit to settler	710/10

SOURCE: Ndaragwa Budgets, Scheme 224 (Shamata), KNA 4/97, Agriculture

amalgamated into the Ol'Kalou Salient, which began as an attempted co-operative venture and later became a tightly organized, state-owned farming corporation.[37] The rest were a scattering of co-operative farms and ranches located on low-yield acreages in various parts of settlement. They were a marginal phenomenon, having served only as a last-resort means of organizing farming and ranching operations wherever individual enterprise was not feasible.[38] They represented the kind of poverty-stricken quasi-socialism that inhabits the fringes of most capitalist societies, performing the tasks that private entrepreneurs cannot handle or do not find sufficiently lucrative.

Despite the existence of marketing co-operatives and co-operative farms and ranches, therefore, the real role of collective enterprise in the Million-Acre Scheme was marginal at best. The program was an exercise in the individualist approach to social problems that was to remain a bench-mark of post-independence Kenyan politics.

While the overall organizational scheme of settlement was calculated to favour individual enterprise, the administrative structure was designed for close control. In this regard too the Million-Acre Scheme resembled the earlier settlement program, in which, as we saw, the control was perhaps too close for the comfort of better-off prospective settlers. But in order to achieve that degree of control over a program encompassing 400 000 hectares and 35 000 families, a much larger, more structured bureaucracy was required.

The establishment authorized for the Million-Acre Scheme at the end of 1962 took the form of a four-tiered administration, centred at each level on generalist supervisors in charge of specialist staff. Heading up the Nairobi office was the director of settlement. The top field administrators were two area settlement controllers (ASC), one in charge of settlement east of the Rift Valley and the other supervising the western section of the program. Under the ASCs were senior settlement officers (SSOs), each of whom oversaw the activities of seven to ten settlement officers (SOS). At each of these four levels, seconded agricultural and co-operative staff worked under the supervision of the settlement administrators. Each settlement scheme had at least one SO[39] who was assisted by veterinary, agricultural extension, and co-operative staff, as well as a headman and police officers seconded by the provincial administration.[40]

The various parts of this extensive administrative machinery worked together to produce a combination of assistance and social control designed to create favourable conditions for social stability and for the financial success of the settlement program. The SO functioned, not only as the administrative head of the lowest field-level settlement office, but also, and more importantly, as the overseer of the people in his area, 'responsible for local administration and ... answerable to the District Commissioner of his district for the good administration of his settlement.'[41] As his role developed, he was also to bear a great deal of responsibility for the loan repayment performance of the people in his charge.

The role of agricultural and co-operative specialists, like that of generalists, involved a combination of assistance and control. On the one hand, they were there to help the settlers increase their incomes; on the other, they were watching each settler's performance and trying to ensure that his or her earnings were sufficient to cover loan repayments. From the beginning, the settlement authorities were mindful of the fact that one of the best guarantees of loan repayment was the individual settler's good husbandry. In taking over a plot and accepting the development loan, therefore, each settler assumed legal liability for the proper development of the plot. The liability was enforceable by eviction or seizure of chattels if necessary and ssos were instructed that they had the support of their superiors in 'taking a firm line' in the enforcement of good husbandry.[42]

Settlement administration, therefore, provided a controlled atmosphere within which settlers were given a set of incentives to adjust to the role of a small-scale landowner and agricultural entrepreneur and a complementary set of sanctions against failure to adjust. The control features of settlement worked together with its individualist form of organization to help forge the kind of social and economic institutions that were to characterize post-independence Kenya.

The geography of settlement. The geography of settlement was a reflection of the fact that the land issue had brought ethnic tensions onto the centre stage of Kenya politics. After the agreement in London that there would be a regional form of government, the Regional Boundaries Commission was appointed to hear submissions from local representatives throughout Kenya and to draw boundaries accordingly. The commission reported in December 1962 with recommendations about which 'tribes' should be grouped together within regional boundaries and which should be separated. For example, Kamba and Meru delegations told the commissioners that they did not wish to be included in a region together with the Kikuyus. And a Masai delegation said they did not wish to be placed in a region together with Kamba people. The commission, therefore, recommended the creation of a Central Region, which

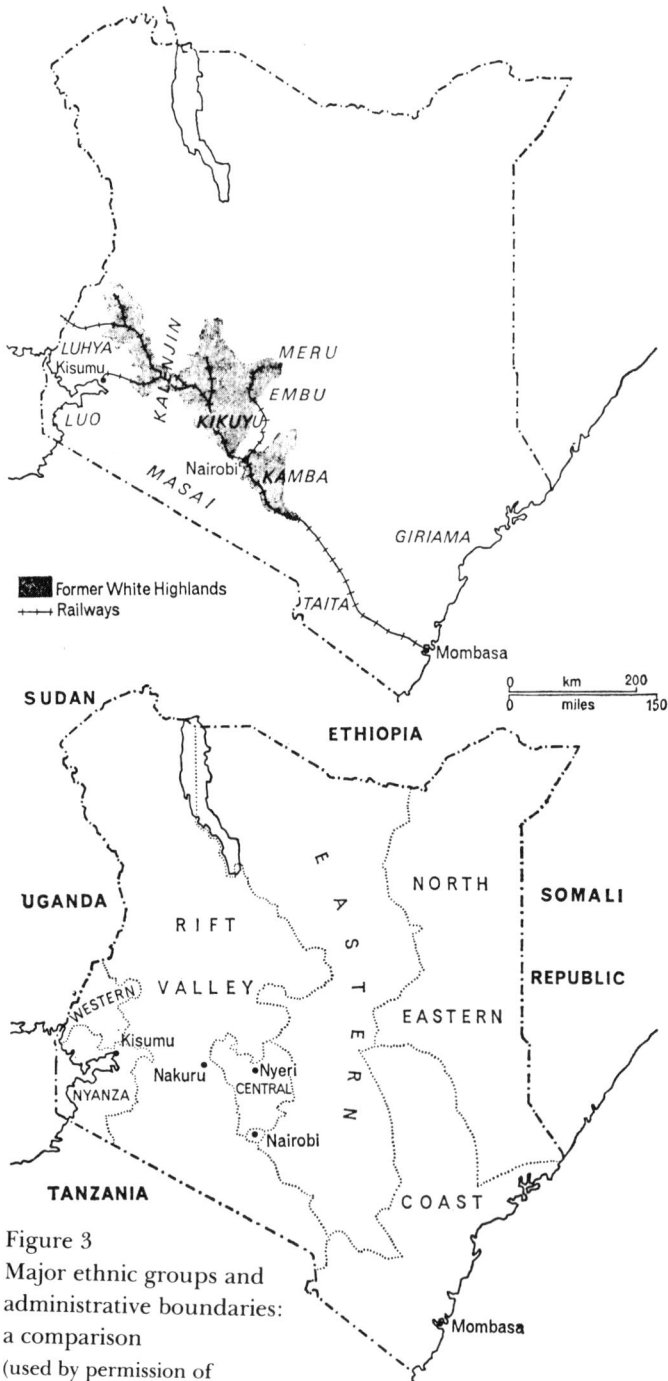

Figure 3
Major ethnic groups and
administrative boundaries:
a comparison

(used by permission of
Heinemann and the
University of California Press)

would include the areas predominantly inhabited by Kikuyus. An Eastern Region grouped Kamba and Meru people together. And the Masai became part of Rift Valley Region, which also included, among others, Kalenjin people and most large-scale farming and ranching areas.[43]

The commission explicitly made provision for the settlement program in drawing its boundaries. And the settlement program, conversely, was planned along ethnic lines. Accordingly, areas of the highlands purchased for settlement were intended to accommodate specific ethnic groups and the commission drew its boundaries to reflect these plans.[44] Thus, for example, the largest single settlement area was the strip of land between the Rift Valley and the western side of the Aberdare Mountains, which was to serve Kikuyus. In drawing its boundaries, the commission excised that area from the Rift Valley, with which it had been associated during colonial history, and included it in the Central Region. On the other side of the Rift Valley, areas marked out for settlement by the Kisii, Luo, and Baluhya people were included in Nyanza and Western regions, while those designated for the various Kalenjin people became part of Rift Valley Region.

The settlement program not only reaffirmed and hardened existing ethnic boundaries, but in fact reintroduced ethnic uniformity in areas where mixing had already taken place spontaneously. Sometimes this was done at the cost of great hardship. For example, at Lugari, in what was to become Western Region, a large number of Kikuyus had to be evicted from land they were occupying in order to make room for the Baluhya people who were to be settled there. The LDSB was told that 900 of the evicted families, who had no clear claim to plots in Kikuyu settlement schemes, would have to be sent to transit farms – refugee areas for homeless people.[45] On the eastern side of the Rift Valley, meanwhile, it was non-Kikuyu who were being evicted to make way for Kikuyus. Chief Commissioner R.E. Wainwright told the LDSB that 'inevitably quite a large number of families who have been working on the farms have to be dismissed and they are replaced by Kikuyu settlers from other areas thus causing what many consider an unnecessary exchange of populations between one area and another. This is of course inevitable to a certain extent in nearly all schemes since they have to be designed on a tribal basis and employees of one tribe have to give place to settlers of another tribe.'[46]

The regional structure of government was also reflected in the provisions for the management of the settlement program that took effect after the advent of internal self-government in mid-1963. After a sweeping victory in general elections, KANU took the helm of the central government, but, as a continuing safeguard for Europeans and the minority ethnic groups, the powers associated with the settlement program were dispersed. The land-purchase program was taken from the LDSB and turned over to the Central Land Board, which included representatives of the prospective sellers of the land and the regional governments as well as the centre. Planning and implementation of the settlement schemes remained a function of the central government, but regional authorities had the power to nominate settlers.[47] In practice, however, these tortuous arrangements had little effect. The central government remained firmly in control of the settlement program, just as it had been ever since the reduction of the LDSB's role.

SETTLEMENT AND LARGE-SCALE AGRICULTURE

Much has been made of the Million-Acre Scheme as a service to the people who became its settlers, and especially to landless people. Indeed, it has been widely criticized for having gone too far in its alleged concessions to the demands of landless people.[48] There has been much less discussion of the scheme as a service to European settlers. In these pages, however, we have seen that its main purpose was not to help landless people, but to preserve large-scale agriculture, and that the settling of smallholders was a means to that end. That point becomes clearer yet if we look at the relationship between large-scale agriculture and settlement – at the interests of the European settler community in relation to land transfer and at how those interests were served by the Million-Acre Scheme and associated programs.

In considering how European settlers stood vis-à-vis land transfer, it is important to remember that different settlers had different interests, especially now that the settler community was on the verge of breaking up. Some, who could not reconcile themselves to majority rule, were determined to liquidate their assets as quickly as possible. But not all settlers were as ill-disposed toward majority rule as were the most vocal of its detractors. A small but influential minority were in fact quite prepared to accept it. Michael Blundell, leader of the multiracial New Kenya Party, and others like him, had been looking ahead to majority rule since the late 1950s and had long since accepted it, albeit with reservations.[49] Furthermore, many settlers less liberal than Blundell had come to think of Kenya as their home and found it hard to contemplate leaving. Then, too, the economic prospects for large-scale agriculture looked good, provided it retained its political support. As we saw in chapter 3, the highlands had been enjoying a period of brisk development since World War II and there remained considerable scope for continued expansion. Given a favourable political climate, there were important economic incentives for staying on. For those who were so inclined and had capital to invest, furthermore, there was the possibility of speculating on future political stability or, alternatively, on a subsidized buy-out of European farms. We saw evidence in chapter 4 that such speculation was taking place.

Finally, there was the fact that for owners of about half of the former White Highlands, early liquidation of assets was all but out of the question. The highlands were divided about equally between ranching areas and arable land (see chapter 2). The arable land consisted mainly of mixed farmland, with a small – but very valuable – portion being devoted to plantations. In the early plans for settlement (described in chapter 4), only certain parts of the mixed farming areas – those which were underdeveloped, but suitable for the establishment of high-value cash crops – were to be subdivided into smallholdings. High-density settlement, by contrast, was to involve a much less discriminating selection of land. But, with a few exceptions, it was still to be restricted to mixed farming areas. Ranching and plantation areas (which included some of the most substantial holdings in Kenya) were still to be excluded from settlement, the former because they were not considered suitable for smaller-scale agricultural enterprise, the latter because they were too expensive. The scale of both ranching and plantation operations was such as to place them out of the reach of most African buyers for some time to come.[50]

In short, while some settlers were obviously determined to get out of Kenya as soon as possible, there were others who were either reluctant, or quite unable, to abandon the country precipitately.[51] For both groups, the most important point about the Million-Acre Scheme was that it entailed a government commitment to purchase some 80 000 hectares of land each year for the next five years. For those who wanted to leave, the government was creating a market through which they might liquidate their assets, in effect compensating them for the losses they would otherwise have suffered as a result of independence.

At the same time, the purchase program was intended to offer interim support for large-scale farming by creating a market in land and thereby restoring or sustaining the confidence of investors. A good deal of confusion – or more accurately, prevarication – has surrounded this point. The official accounts of settlement were at pains to convey the impression that the failure to achieve a quick settlement of the land question would damage Kenya's farming economy. Nottidge and Gold-sack, who helped to plan settlement before assuming the role of analysts of the program, paint a stark picture. By early 1962, they maintain, it had become 'clear that investment by Europeans and Asians had virtually stopped ... and that the economy, still greatly dependent on European farming, might collapse.'[52] That is plainly false – at least as far as investment in the highlands was concerned. Kenya's *Statistical Abstract* shows that capital expenditure on large farms, far from stopping, actually rose slightly in 1960, the year after it was announced that independence would be granted. In 1961, it fell by 13 per cent, still achieving a total of £4.9 million in that year.[53] It certainly did not stop.

The fear that Nottidge and Goldsack were expressing was not that of an economic collapse, but rather of a more subtle political collapse – specifically a loss, by the colonial authorities, of their political leverage. Investment had not come to a stop. What had undoubtedly happened, however, was that a significant number of settlers who wanted to sell were not finding buyers – at least not at prices they were prepared to accept. The Kinangop farmers, referred to above, appear to be a case in point. Although the LDSB retracted its original purchase offer, the farmers later approached the board with offers to sell at lower prices. Obviously, they were anxious to sell. The existence of a significant number of farmers anxious to sell, but unable to find buyers willing to pay good prices, would probably not have seriously damaged the farming economy – not as long as the settlers could count ultimately on British compensation. What it might have done, however, is emboldened the nationalist leaders to escalate their demands in the negotiations over land – by holding out for better financial terms, by taking a more radical stance politically, or both. The European presence, combined with the British commitment to that presence, meant that African politicians were holding a hostage worth £130 million. And time was on their side. The longer negotiations dragged on, and the more European settlers decided to sell their land, the higher the potential cost to the British government. As the financial situation became more bleak for the British, the nationalist leaders would be able to command ever more favourable terms.

The need for a quick settlement of the land question, and for restoration of the confidence of Europeans, was always portrayed officially as a motherhood issue. Kenya's economic health, the propagandists argued, rested on the confidence of Europeans. In retrospect, it seems clear that it was not just Kenya's economic health, but the British government's ability to command favourable political and economic terms, that was at stake. And the cost of those terms, as we will see, fell on the shoulders of Kenya's poor people, while the colonial authorities, their European clients, and better-off Africans reaped the benefits.

Three other provisions of the purchase program worked together to greatly increase the range of options open to settlers who were willing to consider staying in Kenya. One was the undertaking to purchase land for settlements in large blocks and to announce in advance which areas were to be purchased. Under that provision, it was decided that two of the best mixed farming areas – those around Kitale and Nakuru – would remain 'untouched'[54] by the Million-Acre Scheme. A second undertaking was the offer of increased Land Bank loan funds for agricultural investment, to be made available on more liberal terms. Finally, there was the guarantee that payment could be taken abroad, thereby circumventing any exchange controls that might be imposed after independence.

Block purchase and the practice of publicizing purchases in advance meant that settlers could plan ahead. If a settler's land was not slated for purchase, he could continue his farming operations, secure in the knowledge that his area would remain substantially unchanged for the time being. When and if his land was included in the purchase program, he had the option of selling it and using the proceeds (or part of the proceeds) to buy land in one of the remaining large-scale farming areas. Since increased loan funds were available and since they could be had on the basis of a smaller down payment than before, he might be in a position to send a substantial part of his capital abroad and to use the remainder for a fresh investment in the highlands – a speculation on Kenya's future plus some security in case it did not work out as well as anticipated.[55]

The block pattern of settlement, and the fact that remaining large-scale mixed farms would be contiguous and separate from settlement areas, were undoubtedly reassuring to Europeans for more than purely economic reasons. They offered them some assurance that not only the agriculture of the highlands, but also its social milieu, stood a good chance of remaining substantially unchanged for some time to come. That feature of the program, however, had its drawbacks, even from the settler point of view. The problem was that Africans would be able to make the same observation, and after independence African disapproval might well generate a political threat to the security of European large-scale farming. '... It will be quite impracticable, as well as undesirable, to maintain these areas as pockets of exclusively white farming – a reduced White Highlands,' the LDSB observed, a bit wistfully perhaps. 'Already this description has been applied to these areas. This can only transfer the tensions over land to a smaller area.'[56]

Members of the LDSB were concerned with the creation of an alliance between the European and African bourgeoisies. The board, therefore, made it a priority to solicit government support for land transfer schemes designed to integrate Africans into the highlands. Their efforts took on a note of urgency with the introduction of the Million-Acre Scheme, which was accompanied by a decline of government interest in the yeoman and assisted-owner programs for the purchase of land in the areas marked for continuing large-scale agriculture.

In July 1962, in connection with an early discussion of how land transfer would be affected by plans for the Million-Acre Scheme, the board resolved 'that there was a definite need for some form of Assisted Owner Scheme ... and that it ought to continue.' The resolution also called upon the minister of land settlement and water development to 'point out to the U.K. Government that the scheme required an element of subsidy to operate successfully and should be incorporated in the [Million-Acre] Scheme but with better terms.'[57]

In September, members of the board learned what they had undoubtedly already suspected – that the government, having shifted its emphasis to peasant settlement, did not share their sense of urgency about the assisted-owner scheme. The board would not be permitted, in future, to make land purchases outside the areas designated for the Million-Acre Scheme, except under the terms of the yeoman scheme, which – despite its lack of success – was still under consideration at this point.[58] The seventy-six cases already under review for financing through the assisted-owner program were allowed to continue, but no new ones were permitted. Later, even cases that qualified under World Bank criteria for yeoman settlement were ruled out and the board was restricted to land purchase within the areas designated for the Million-Acre Scheme.[59]

Although the LDSB's duties were now clearly restricted to purchase for the Million-Acre Scheme, the board did not lose its interest in land transfer within the large-scale farming sector. With its de facto powers subject to increasing limitations, it began to behave more like a special-interest group than a statutory management board. Accordingly, it turned its attention to the promotion of Land Bank loan programs – a matter well outside the range of its official duties, but which was very important to its settler constituency. The Land Bank's programs were tailor-made for the dual purpose of financing large-scale agriculture and integrating Africans into it because they were available on an inter-racial basis. They could, therefore, finance Africans who wanted to buy large-scale farms as well as Europeans who wanted to stay in Kenya.

In September, therefore, the board resolved that it was 'imperative' for both 'political and economic reasons ... that substantial funds be made available immediately to the Land Bank in order to allow land transactions to take place outside the proposed settlement schemes.'[60] Thereafter, the LDSB solicited regular reports on the progress of nego-tiations, met with the bank's chairman, undertook to discuss the problem with the KNFU, and finally prepared a joint memorandum with the Board of Agriculture, an urgent plea to the British authorities that 'not less than £2 million' be made available to the bank for land purchase and development loans in the highlands. 'It is essential for future stability,' the memo declared

that some parts of these areas be settled with large-scale African farmers. Fortu-nately, there are quite a number who have the resources and capability to run complete European farms or large sub-divisions of them, provided they can receive finance in the first instance for purchase. There are not enough of them to make a change in the racial composition of land-holding, but there are enough to demonstrate that this is no new White Highlands and, by their presence, to give stability to the area.[61]

As we have seen, the British government made an extra £1.4 million available to the Land Bank in 1963 and 1964, in addition to allowing loans to be made on easier terms. The results of the Land Bank's opera-tions during those two years served to affirm the board's prediction: A substantial amount of money was lent to Africans, but the funds served to darken the former White Highlands' hue only slightly. In 1963, the Land Bank approved £1.4 million worth of loans, of which £530000 went to African borrowers. By the end of 1964, the volume of loans had increased to £2.6 million, of which £1.4 million, or 55 per cent, went to Africans in the form of 270 loans. The land purchased by Africans under these loans totalled about 82000 hectares, still only a tiny fraction of the land that remained in European hands.[62]

But it was a substantial amount of land nevertheless, and other pro-grams, more directly associated with settlement, added to the effect of the Land Bank's activities. In addition to the seventy-six assisted-owner cases already referred to and thirty-five yeoman plots that emerged as the net result of that beleaguered program, the compassionate cases also made a contribution to large-scale land transfer. These farm purchases, which were intended as a form of special assistance to aged or disabled landowners, had been limited, as we saw, to a total of sixty-three. Later, however, the British government softened its stand and by mid-1963, £770 000 had been made available for an additional 130 purchases.[63] Some of these farms were included in the Million-Acre Scheme, auctioned off or leased, but a substantial number were sold as farms, 'mostly to Africans.'[64] For administrative purposes, they were categorized with the assisted-owner program. By mid-1963, 102 persons had purchased farms under that program[65] and ultimately the program grew to take in 140 farmers, who among them purchased 229 large-scale farms.[66] The yeoman, assisted-owner, and Land Bank programs helped to lay the basis for the gradual Africanization of large-scale agriculture, which continued into the 1980s, firmly establishing the position of the African agrarian bourgeoisie. However, the intended alliance between African and European agrarian bourgeoises did not hold, as we will see in chapter 8.

6

The Million-Acre Scheme
and landless people

The settlement of Kenya's land question was the kind of political exercise for which British colonial authorities are justly famous: a complex and delicate network of compromises that together managed to satisfy each faction just enough to achieve the maintenance of stability and of the economic status quo. KANU was set on the road to power, but it had to make major concessions to KADU and the Europeans in order to get there. KADU and the Europeans, for their part, got the guarantees concerning land that they demanded, but they ultimately had to accept KANU dominance; and the Europeans had to scale down a few of their more extreme financial demands. Each African ethnic group received land in proportion to its need and/or political clout. Enough landless people got land – as the phrase went – to 'take the steam out of the kettle'; enough experienced farmers and businessmen to ensure social stability; and enough members of the bourgeoisie to reconcile them to the new order.

Viewed in that light, the manoeuvres surrounding the establishment of a land transfer scheme appear as a highly entertaining piece of political action, complete with gaffes, blunders, quick-witted recoveries, fascinating power plays – all spiced with an occasional tinge of unscrupulousness. The story seems entertaining because the rewards are high and the penalties moderate at worst. There is no bloodshed, no imprisonment, and no one is destined to die in poverty. That is how it was for foreigners and better-off Africans. For landless people, however, the political conflicts surrounding the settlement of the land question were not a game, but a deadly serious struggle, and one in which defeat exacted excruciating penalties, while victory brought often dubious benefits.

Settlement involved an accommodation of landless people, but the accommodation was not designed to offer them a serious opportunity for prosperity, even at a peasant level. While the more favoured partici-pants in land transfer – including carefully selected prosperous peasants as well as members of the bourgeoisie – enjoyed top priority in the distri-bution of high-quality land and money, landless people became the objects of a different aspect of the program, one that became more prominent as settlement expanded and the number of poor people in-cluded in it grew: the battle to keep the flames of Mau Mau from reignit-ing, to prevent Kenya's class struggle from exploding again into civil war during the transition to independence. For the landless, therefore, the focus of the program was not on finding a solution to their economic problems, but rather on controlling them and neutralizing the threat they posed to civil order. Throughout the high-density program, as this chapter shows, the demands of European settlers, the desire of the Bri-tish government to save money, and even the financial conditions imposed on the Kenya government by the World Bank took precedence over the needs of landless people. At the same time, the program served as a highly effective tool for controlling, not only those landless people who were settled, but also those who were not. It was Kenya's poorest people who were being made to bear the cost of the gentlemanly chess game at Lancaster House and the compromises it produced.

OPINIONS ABOUT SETTLEMENT

In chapter 1, I noted that this study would address a number of mis-conceptions about Kenya's transition to independence. There is now enough data assembled about the transition to begin to come to terms with these. Briefly stated, they are

1 that the Million-Acre Scheme was a determined attack upon landless-ness;
2 that European settlers were cynically sold out by turncoat European politicians and officials playing demogogic African politics; and
3 that, in order to make a deal with KANU (a multi-ethnic party that has always, to varying degrees, been dominated by Kikuyus), the authori-ties favoured Kikuyus over other ethnic groups.

The first statement represents the official view of the colonial authori-ties who developed the Million-Acre Scheme and is reflected in government documents. The second represents the opinions of disgruntled European settlers, some of whom, after independence, loved to regale anyone who would listen with 'inside' stories of the calumnies, betrayals, and deceptions of *uhuru*. The third view is often expressed by non-Kikuyu Africans as well as Europeans. Until fairly recently, the second and third opinions have remained in the realm of gossip, and were not being treated seriously in the literature.

For example, an early government report on settlement presented the official view when it asserted that high-density schemes were designed 'to meet the pressing problems of landless and unemployed families ...'[1] In a post-independence study of settlement, former colonial civil servants C.P.R. Nottidge and J.R. Goldsack similarly characterized settlement as a response to the problem of 'land hunger.'[2] The views of non-Kikuyu Africans who were dissatisfied with the land settlement were articulated by Gary Wasserman, in a study that is sharply critical of the neo-colonial settlement of the land question. Ironically, the study, which is less clear about its own position than it is about its rejection of the colonial position, also (inadvertently perhaps) lends some weight to the European settler view and to the idea of settlement as an attack upon landlessness. For example, Wasserman states that the location of settlement schemes in Nyandarua District – the largest block of settlement in the Million-Acre Scheme, as we will see – 'was not, in the main, on the basis of which Europeans wished to sell, but rather which tribes were likely to need buying off.'[3] That statement contains the suggestion that the primarily high-density settlement in Nyandarua District was a favour to its recipients and that Kikuyus, who were settled in Nyandarua, were the objects of special treatment. It also implies that 'tribes which were likely to need buying off' were being favoured over Europeans who wished to sell. Although the statement stops short of claiming a sell-out of Europeans, it does suggest that African interests enjoyed a higher priority. None of these opinions – as articulated by Wasserman or otherwise – are supported by the evidence.

A response to landlessness? The colonial authorities always favoured agrarian policies that *explicitly* included the creation of landlessness. The terms of the yeoman and peasant schemes shows that those ideas did not change with the decision to grant Kenya its independence. What *did* change them was recognition of the fact – thrown into sharp relief by the *cause célèbre* of the Kinangop – that much of the European land available for sale was not of sufficient quality to be included in a settlement program attractive to better-off Africans. The colonial authorities then went in search of people who would be willing to pay for land nobody else wanted, and *that* was when they discovered the problem of landlessness. The decision to settle landless people, in turn, spawned a land rush, as we will see in this chapter. After that, settlement of landless people became, in part, a response to the threat implicit in that rush. As a result, the assertion that settlement was a response to landlessness became, in time, a self-fulfilling prophecy. But the documentation is quite clear in showing that the land rush *followed* the decision to settle landless people. The decision came first, and it was motivated by the interests of Europeans. More important, high-density settlement – whether occasioned by European interests or by a threat from landless people – was not designed to offer landless people a chance at prosperity, even on a peasant level. It was designed to control them.

A deal with KANU? *Favouritism for Kikuyus?* For the KANU leaders of the early 1960s, this charge must seem a particularly cruel irony, though they would probably prefer not to talk about it. At that time, at least some KANU leaders were making earnest efforts to maintain a national following and to rise above ethnic politics. The breadth of their support showed that they were enjoying some success in this venture. The irony is that they were fighting a lonely battle. We have seen how the Europeans, with assistance from KADU, played the ethnic game of divide-and-conquer to force KANU to accept, not only the settlement program, but also the regionalism scheme specifically designed to entrench ethnic groups and harden the boundaries between them. We have seen, too, how that regionalism scheme guaranteed that settlement – which would otherwise have been at least somewhat mixed – was carried out along strictly ethnic lines. After all that, an accusation by disgruntled Europeans that KANU's Kikuyu leaders used settlement for ethnic aggrandizement is an irony of Socratic proportions.

It is of course possible that, at some point, some deplorable deals of the ethnic variety were made between colonial authorities and Kikuyu leaders, but in the absence of evidence, there is no reason to take the suggestion seriously. The fact that more settlement land went to Kikuyus than to other groups is in itself unremarkable, since the majority of landless people were Kikuyus, even in the latter part of the colonial era when growing numbers of landless people belonged to other ethnic groups. The fact that Kikuyus got Nyandarua District was a result of the regionalism scheme, a service to KADU and the Europeans – not KANU and not Kikuyus.

To be sure, the Kikuyus have for decades been the most conspicuously expansionist African ethnic group in Kenya. Chapters 2 and 3 indicated the alacrity with which Kikuyu squatters and entrepreneurs fanned out across the country. During the transition to independence and beyond, Kikuyu farmers, entrepreneurs, and job-seekers continued to exhibit the same tendency. In the process, they have stepped on toes and made enemies, both among other African ethnic groups and among Europeans, some of whom must have sensed early on that the Kikuyus would one day be their most powerful competitors for political and economic dominance. That helps to explain why there were dark mutterings of a deal favouring the Kikuyus, but it does not prove that there was such a deal. And the mutterers have yet to produce any evidence.

A sell-out of European settlers? The two assertions previously dealt with are distortions which, until they have been examined, have some colour of plausibility. The present one is a prime example of a Big Lie, an out-and-out falsehood that gains credibility only through constant and vehement repetition. It is understandable that many Europeans were unhappy with the independence settlement, despite the generous terms of the compensation they were offered. No remotely reasonable financial settlement could have compensated them for loss of the power and position they enjoyed in colonial Kenya. From their point of view, majority rule itself could be seen as a betrayal. But there is simply no evidence on the basis of which this sense of grievance can be parlayed into a charge of a sell-out on the land issue. Nor does the evidence support Wasserman's less serious allegation that African ethnic considerations were put ahead of European interests. We have seen how solicitous the authorities were of the settlers: how they changed the terms of payment for land three times, each time making them more favourable to the settlers; how they allowed settler interests to dominate, not only land purchase, but even settlement, until it became obvious that their methods would not work; how various purchase terms – the 'fertility' clause, blanket compensation for development, and more – were skewed to favour the sellers. The settlement of Nyandarua District – which Wasserman offers as the crowning example of how the authorities allegedly bought off Kikuyus at the expense of Europeans – began on the Kinangop where the government bought substandard acreages from Europeans who were manifestly anxious to sell. This chapter describes what happened to buyers of land on the Kinangop, as well as elsewhere, and gives further examples of the treatment Europeans received. It is clear now, and will become clearer yet, that it is not Europeans, but landless people and Kenya's taxpayers who were sold out.

SETTLEMENT AND SQUATTERS

When the colonial authorities introduced the Million-Acre Scheme for landless and unemployed people, they opened the door on a problem that had long been ignored. Landlessness in Kenya originated with European settlement, but was fed by a variety of developments (see chapter 3). In the White Highlands, the expansion of cultivated acreages and the introduction of more capital-intensive forms of agriculture undermined the demand for African resident labourers and turned the presence of their cultivation and livestock into a liability for landowners. In the reserves, the expansion of cash cropping likewise worked against the poorer members of the community and helped to initiate the development of a landless class. Both of these changes particularly affected Kikuyu people, whose location near the administrative and commercial centres of white settlement placed them squarely in its path.

For landless people, the *coup de grâce* was land consolidation and the abolition of the traditional land laws that had favoured the distribution of land to all segments of society. Again it was Kikuyu country where this development unfolded, further accentuating the problem of landlessness. In the late 1950s, as the Mau Mau war ended, many landless Kikuyus who had been consigned to the overcrowded reserve for the duration were being sent back to the Rift Valley.

In 1960, the minister of agriculture acknowledged that Kenya's landless population had grown to an estimated 130 000 families. At that point, the government had not yet grasped the fact that the transition to independence would (as noted in chapter 5) necessitate a realignment of classes. When McKenzie cited the figure of 130 000, he pointed out that most of the landless people had access to some sort of cultivation plots and were eking out a living on them, albeit 'well below the subsistence level.' A European member of the Legislative Council, questioning McKenzie, had asserted that settlement would displace the employers of landless people, leaving them without even the small cultivation plots and low-paying jobs they had then. 'If you introduce peasant farming,' he said, 'you may well find you are introducing one lot of people only to replace another.'[4] He proved to be a good prophet.

But McKenzie did not seem worried. The authorities did not see the problem as a serious one as long as settlement was taking place on a relatively limited scale, especially when perhaps half of it – the yeoman scheme – was to be scattered throughout the highlands. Undoubtedly the labourers who could not be employed by incoming settlers could be absorbed elsewhere. Furthermore, the land being bought for settlement under the old yeoman and peasant schemes was high-quality land, not the type to be housing many squatters. As we saw in chapter 3, it was the better-off farmers with capital to invest who had for a long time been reducing their squatter populations. In most instances, the same people – and not their less affluent fellow settlers – would be the owners of the land being bought for the early settlement program.

Once the decision had been taken to purchase land on a massive scale and to lower the standards of land quality – buying out precisely those settlers who had kept large numbers of squatters – the colonial agrarian class system began to come apart at the seams. Since it was the most marginal European settler farms that had been harbouring landless Africans, the dissolution of the former involved uprooting the latter. Once uprooted, there was nothing left to restrain them from expressing the frustration built up over decades of being denied the land that their forefathers had taken for granted as a birthright. They raised an insistent demand for land and the colonial authorities responded by accelerating the expansion of peasant society while tightening their control of it. Since the problem of landlessness was most acute among Kikuyus, the authorities accelerated Kikuyu settlement during the first year of the Million-Acre Scheme, while letting the settlement program in other areas move ahead more slowly. In 1962–63, more than 2700 Kikuyu families were settled, compared with about 1200 in the entire Rift Valley and all of western Kenya.[5] From the outset, therefore, settlement was generating alarming amounts of landlessness, even while it was trying to cope with it.

Although the authorities had accepted the idea of expanding peasant society, they had not yet understood the power of the social forces they were unleashing, for they seized upon high-density settlement as an opportunity to continue the colonial pursuit (observed in chapter 3) of removing squatters from European farms – an action that was certain to exacerbate the trouble they were getting into. In January 1963, just as settlement under the Million-Acre Scheme was getting well under way, a new Trespass Ordinance came into effect that simplified the procedure of evicting squatters. The law was immediately invoked by European farm owners anxious to clear their land of squatters. At the end of 1962, the LDSB had been informed that 'it was anticipated that farmers in the

[Laikipia-Leshau] area would be discharging a large number of workers in the near future ...' The farmers 'would not be able to get them off their farms,' it was noted, unless the board saw to it that temporary facilities were available for their accommodation.[6] Evidently the LDSB was perceived as an agency that could help large-scale farmers get rid of unwanted squatters.

In early 1963, the labour officer at Thomson's Falls was getting letters from farmers who wanted his advice on the eviction of squatters. 'If you wish them removed,' he replied in one letter, 'this can be done very easily now by the Police under the new Trespass Ordinance which came into force on the 28th January, 1963.'[7] 'May I suggest,' he said in another letter, 'that you hold a *baraza* [meeting] with the ex-employees ... and instruct them to remove themselves from the farm by the end of April 1963. If they do not remove themselves ... then they can be removed by the police under the new Trespass Ordinance ...'[8] The authorities still felt sufficiently in control of events to encourage evictions that added to the numbers of people already being displaced by land purchase for high-density settlement.

But their confidence was misplaced because, with land becoming available and independence on the horizon, landless Africans were now free, for the first time in living memory, to reclaim their pre-colonial birthright of seeking new land for themselves and their families. As a result, the anxiety and frustration built up over two generations of colonial oppression was released in a massive land rush. The news that Nyandurua District, on the west side of the Aberdares Mountains, would be allocated to landless Kikuyus, galvanized the reserves, as well as the Kikuyu diaspora in the Rift Valley. By February 1963, the chief commissioner, who was in charge of land allocation, reported that he had 26 000 written applications for plots from Kikuyu families.[9] Many did not content themselves with writing applications. They went to Nyandurua themselves, moved in with a relative, occupied temporary lodgings in one of the towns, or found a place on an abandoned farm. Then they set about trying to find a way to get themselves enrolled in settlement.[10]

In the year that followed the announcement of the Million-Acre Scheme, the settlement areas in Nyandarua District became inundated with Kikuyus looking for land, some of them having been displaced from the land that was already settled, others having been evicted from large-scale farms or come on their own. The problem was exacerbated by regionalism, which, as noted in chapter 5, necessitated the eviction of Kikuyus from non-Kikuyu areas where settlement was taking place.

Already in December 1962, when the Million-Acre Scheme was just getting under way, the LDSB was being told that the numbers of people to be absorbed by settlement had far exceeded expectations. 'The original target [had] been to accommodate approximately 4,500 evicted squatter families' but now it would be necessary 'to absorb up to 9,000 landless and unemployed Kikuyu ...'[11] That many could not be handled without special accommodation, it was decided. A new type of temporary scheme was created, therefore, consisting simply of ranks of two-acre subsistence plots, each to be settled by one family and cultivated for a slender living. These schemes were initially referred to as 'transit settlement.' But in January 1963, the minister of land settlement and water development – having perhaps had time to reflect on the notoriety of the Emergency transit camps – asked that the name be changed to 'interim settlement.'[12]

In January 1963, the settlement authorities designated seven farms in Nyandarua District as interim settlement schemes and began to move landless families onto them. As they were moved in, they were promised that, within about a year, they would be granted regular plots in high-density settlement.[13] The influx of landless people continued to grow, however, and, by the time another eight months had passed, it looked very much as if the promise were about to be broken. By September 1963, the program had produced more landless people in Nyandarua than settlement plots. The 'crash program' – another plan for Kikuyu settlement even more accelerated than the one that had been under way for the past year – was being formulated. But a Ministry of Lands and Settlement projection noted that some 1000 to 1500 interim settlers would remain without plots and would 'have to be dealt with by other means.'[14] The deluge of landless people had reached flood stage.

LAND AND FREEDOM

As the Million-Acre Scheme got under way, therefore, the settlement authorities found themselves concentrating on Nyandarua District, where they were reaping the harvest of half a century's neglect of the problem of landlessness. Their attempts to deal with the situation, however, involved more than the movement of people and allocation of land. They were also facing the danger that the scramble for land would result in a resurgence of the Land Freedom Army. Although the LFA or KLFA – as it came to be called in the early 1960s – had been defeated in the Mau Mau war and remained a proscribed organization, the bitterness that had spawned it had not died and the dream of driving out the

Europeans and taking their land was still alive. The LFA had no support among the African political leadership, nor did it give any evidence of having either a coherent organization or an ideology. Furthermore, like the Land Freedom Army of the Mau Mau era, it was locked into an ethnic straitjacket – if anything, more so now than before. It was an organization identified only with a segment of the Kikuyu population, unable to draw support outside the tribe. Lacking organization, leadership, an ideology, and a broad base of support, it never posed a real political threat. But during a period of instability and uncertainty, it was capable of serious harassment, or even of creating a real, if temporary, challenge to the authority of the government. In areas marked out for settlement, the interregnum between large-scale agriculture and the Million-Acre Scheme proved to be such a period.

Evidently the talk about driving the Europeans out and taking their land had never come to a stop – even amid military defeat and detention during the Emergency. Rebmann M. Wambaa, one of the small minority of well-educated detainees, who was not released until August 1959, describes how he and people he knew perceived the politics of land in the early 1960s:

... there was tremendous propaganda going around the country that if you were so disloyal as to buy land in the White Highlands you would suffer later. The argument was that the Europeans had been defeated in the Emergency; they would soon all go home and the Rift would be left vacant. Some of the more political people in the camps had told us all about India – how the British had pulled out of there. So for us too, the only question should be: How do we divide up our land? The land would be free for us; after all we don't buy our own land, do we? And yet even while one was immersed in all this propaganda, one saw that the Administration were attracting people to go and buy.[15]

Throughout the early 1960s, there were sporadic incidents. Wambaa relates that his brother was a plot-holder on one of the early settlement schemes. 'These early settlers,' he says, '... were sometimes so afraid of the hostile reaction that they went up to build their new houses and dig their *shambas* during the day, but came back to the Reserves for safety during the night. Even so, many of them found their huts destroyed in the morning.'[16]

In mid-1962, the LDSB reported: 'In certain cases political agitators have dissuaded persons from taking up smallholdings with the story that on the attainment of independence land will fall into their laps free.

Such agitation has been amongst the Kikuyu only and has generally not been supported for long.'[17]

On the Kinangop in Nyandarua, a European settler's wife wrote to the administration to complain. 'In July 1962,' she reported, 'I purchased [a] farm from the Land Bank as an addition and improvement to the farm already owned by my Husband and myself. Since the day of taking over this farm, we have had nothing but trouble from the Labour living on it. The first day the Headman informed me that the farm was not mine as I was not an African, an idea obviously shared by the majority of the labour there ...'[18]

In October, two weeks after the announcement of the Million-Acre Scheme, the temporary minister for defence spoke to the Legislative Council on the question of security:

A good deal has been heard in the last few weeks of the Kenya Land Freedom Army ... From time to time, during the last few years, the Government has been obliged to take action against subversion, action against a very small minority who have sought, and still seek, to achieve domination by illegal means, in the last resort by force if necessary, in order that they can assuage their lust for land. They recruit their numbers from fanatics of the 1950s who do not understand that times have changed ...[19]

A few days later, the minister, in answer to a question, reported that, so far in 1962, the Kenya Police had investigated 450 cases involving the LFA. Convictions had been obtained in 340 cases and 89 were still before the courts.[20]

During the first year of the Million-Acre Scheme, there were repeated complaints, from Nyandarua and other settlement areas where Kikuyu squatters were residing, of illegal squatting, defiance of eviction orders, and theft. In May 1963, the deputy minister of settlement reported to an LDSB committee that Kikuyu squatters in Central Province – and particularly at Kipipiri in Nyandarua – 'were squatting on settled plots and intimidating the owners from taking action against them.'[21] In September, not long before the beginning of the crash program, the General Service Unit, a military force trained to deal with civil disorder, was sent to Nyandarua District 'in order to reinforce the local police in an effort to put a stop to further thieving ...'[22]

People who were living in the Ol'Kalou area of Nyandarua District during this period relate that, among Kikuyus there, the free land movement was referred to by the Kikuyu name of *Kiama kia Hunyu*.

Kiama members were reported to be opposed, in the first instance, to all purchase of formerly European land and, more immediately around Ol'Kalou, to the fact that some of the best land in the area was being sold to 'wealthy people,' i.e. low-density settlers. There was oath-taking and threats that anyone who dared to occupy a low-density plot would be killed. The threats were taken seriously by many people, but no instances were encountered in this study of any attempts to carry them out. Nevertheless, the authorities were taking no chances, and one of their best weapons against subversion was the settlement program.

MAINTAINING STABILITY

From the introduction of the Million-Acre Scheme until after independence, the main objectives of the settlement program were to bring landlessness under control and to restore social stability. In order to meet those objectives, the authorities initiated a substantial expansion of peasant society, while subjecting it to close administrative control. They also took another step in the creation of Kenya's new class system. They took cognizance of the fact (pointed out in chapter 5) that, in African society, there is no rigid separation of the peasantry and the bourgeoisies. On the contrary, many people straddle the two worlds, simultaneously engaging in peasant agriculture and various urban pursuits. Recognizing that, the authorities abandoned the idea (so much in evidence in the yeoman and peasant schemes) that there must be a rigid separation between peasant and non-peasant agricultural areas. In fact, they reversed the idea, because they realized that, by strategically placing members of the bourgeoisie in peasant areas, they could implant capitalism in the heart of peasant society.

Speed. Throughout this period, a heavy emphasis was placed on the achievement of speed in settlement. One obvious reason for the preoccupation with speed was the fact that the sooner purchase areas were settled, the sooner the security situation could be returned to normal. As long as land was in a period of transition – occupied by a settler winding down his affairs or vacant and waiting to be resettled – it was susceptible to occupation by squatters. Vacant land created hopes that could only feed the fires of the Land Freedom Army.

There was probably another reason for speed. Even though the funds for the settlement program had been committed and the basic principles agreed upon, as long as it remained partly unplanned and largely unimplemented, it was vulnerable to a change of political climate. It was important from the viewpoint of all who were interested in its success, therefore, to see to it that the program be firmly established as quickly as possible.

Since land purchase had been halted during the mid-1962 negotiations with Britain over the Million-Acre Scheme, the first order of business, once the scheme had been agreed upon, was to get the purchase program going again. In November, the LDSB was told that the Department of Settlement was 'acutely embarrassed by shortage of land due to the unavoidable hiatus in the purchasing programme which occurred while the five-year scheme was being planned. The purchase programme was now accelerating and it was hoped that approximately 150,000 acres would have been purchased by February 1963 ...'[23] In the meantime, settlement officials had been directed to settle 400 families per month, a rate which, it was noted, 'is difficult to implement ...'[24]

By December, land purchase had moved well ahead of settlement and the director of settlement was telling his Planning Committee that settlement east of the Rift Valley, most of which was for Kikuyus, 'must be speeded up.' He was 'perturbed at the buildup of unoccupied plots. These must be settled earliest despite the difficulties of which he was aware.'[25]

During the first half of 1963, the LDSB were getting monthly reports on the progress of settlement, which went from a total of 2500 families on the ground in January to 'just short of 5,000' at the end of April, on the eve of internal self-government.[26] At the April meeting, the minister of land settlement and water development, Mr McKenzie, told the LDSB that the planning of the entire settlement program would be completed by the end of May, i.e. before internal self-government. He noted reassuringly that 'although it would be within the power of the Central Land Board [which was taking over the purchasing program] to alter subsequent years of the plan it would be virtually impossible for them to alter the 1963–64 programme.'[27] The terms of land transfer were set, and independence was not going to interfere with them.

By that time, there seems to have been very little for the colonial authorities to worry about on that score, for it was clear that the African leadership were prepared to carry out the program as it had been planned, whatever may have been their misgivings about some aspects of it. But the push to resolve the squatter issue was far from over. From May to November, 2000 settlement plots were allocated and in the crash program on the eve of independence some 3000 smallholders were settled in twenty-one days. By the end of 1963, the population of the

Million-Acre Scheme had reached 11 400 families and some further plots were ready for settlement.[28]

Selection as a system of rewards and punishments. In order to serve the ends of security, however, the program was designed to do more than simply settle a large number of people in a hurry – especially since the total number of landless people was far too large to be accommodated by the Million-Acre Scheme. Selection of high-density settlers was in the hands of the Provincial Administration, the branch of the colonial civil service in charge of overseeing local government in African areas and maintaining security there.[29] The administration used its network of chiefs and headmen – which gave it a pipeline into every African community – to assure that those selected for high-density settlement were genuinely landless and unemployed. It also designed a selection process calculated to make the most of the settlement program's potential as a tool for the punishment of subversive activity and a reward for those who shunned such activity.

Concurrently with the implementation of settlement, the police and courts were taking what the chief commissioner (the head of the administration) referred to as 'severe punitive measures' against the LFA. Once people had been convicted of LFA offences, both they and their families were declared ineligible for settlement. In short, anyone who became involved in oath-taking or other suspect activities risked severe trouble with the law and loss of a chance for land.[30]

In the system of incentives supporting civil order, the stick, therefore, was relatively simple to administer. The administration of the carrot, on the other hand, posed a more complicated problem because any given landless person's statistical chances of getting a plot in Kikuyu settlement areas were poor. Even on a superficial analysis of the landless population, that point was abundantly clear. For administrative purposes, the population living on farms that were being taken over for settlement were divided into two categories: 1) 'legal labour,' meaning anyone who was certified as having been in the employment of the departing European owner of the land on which he resided; and 2) 'illegal squatters,' those who had been evicted from other farms or had arrived on their own in search of land.

Legal labour were, under the colonial regime, further subdivided into two categories: 1) those who had been employed for more than four years on a farm bought for settlement; and 2) those who had been there for less time. The landless people living on farms that were being bought for settlement, therefore, were of three types: 1) four-year qualifiers, 2)

legal labour, and 3) illegal squatters. In addition to these, there were
landless people living in the reserves and in other parts of the highlands.

In February 1963, the chief commissioner, R.E. Wainwright, estimated that the total number of legal labourers in Kikuyu settlement
areas was roughly equivalent to the number of plots available for
settlement.[31] Thus legal labourers alone could have filled up Kikuyu
settlement schemes, leaving no provision for illegal squatters or the untold numbers of landless Kikuyus in the reserves and in non-settlement
areas of the highlands – including, as we saw, 26 000 people who had
applied in writing for plots.

From the viewpoint of the authorities, it was important, in Wainwright's words, to give 'some hope to all classes of landless Kikuyu wherever they are that eventually they have some chance, albeit a small one,
of obtaining a plot of land.'[32] The policy, therefore, was to settle some
people from each of the landless categories. As long as there was some
hope for land, the threat of losing eligibility for settlement was a real one
and constituted a genuine incentive to landless people to refrain from
subversive activities. If any of the groups of landless Kikuyus had lost all
hope of being included in settlement, the sanction would have lost its
force for them. It was a cruel manipulation of the hopes of people who
had already suffered greatly, but it was very effective.

In the early months of the Million-Acre Scheme, preference was given
to four-year qualifiers.[33] The significance of that category becomes clear
if we look at it in the context of recent Kenyan history. A four-year
qualifier would have been a labourer who had been working in the
highlands since late 1958 or early 1959. Since Kikuyus were evicted from
the highlands to the reserves early in the Emergency and were not
allowed back without a pass until 1960, a record of four years' service in
the highlands meant that the labourer had either been spared eviction
by the intervention of his employer or been given a pass by the administration to return to the highlands. Either employer intervention or a
pass amounted to a certificate of political orthodoxy. Preference, therefore, was being given to people who were regarded as politically safe
from the colonial point of view.

Since a significant number of plots remained available for settlement
after the four-year qualifiers had been given their plots, it was possible
to cast widely among the rest of the population – among shorter-term
legal labourers, illegal squatters, and landless people from the reserves
and the highlands – for the rest of the settlers. These remaining selec-
tions were carried out at least in part through the use of lotteries,[34]

which served as dramatic demonstrations of the government's power. Throughout Nyandarua (and presumably elsewhere in Kenya as well) landless people desperately travelled from one lottery to another, each time seeing a handful of their number strike it lucky, while the rest went home, their hopes crushed once again, to face a future of poverty for themselves and their children.

In search of social stability. Once landless people were settled, the fact that they were landowners should serve as a strong incentive for them to reject subversive political ideas. Happy with their own good fortune, envied by those who were less lucky, and saddled with a heavy burden of debt, they would undoubtedly have every reason to concentrate on farming and stay out of politics. Still, the expansion of peasant society was worrying to the authorities and they believed that it would be prudent to include a 'socially stabilizing' element in the high-density farming areas. It was decided, therefore, that 'a small proportion of Civil Servants, Soldiers and employed persons should be allocated plots on each settlement scheme since they tended to provide stability and leadership.' In order to ensure that such people would not pursue their other activities to the neglect of their settlement plots, it was stipulated that absentee settlers should hire 'capable managers' to supervise agricultural operations.[35]

The means used to implement this policy varied with circumstances. In some cases, more prosperous people were allowed to take up ordinary plots. Among the high-density settlers interviewed for the present study, a few reported that they had achieved a modicum of prosperity before coming to settlement. Some of them had plots that appeared to resemble those of their neighbours. In other areas, the plots were larger or were more valuable. One of the better-off settlers reported that his was one of seven plots in Ol'Kalou West Scheme that had been sold together with milk quotas (contracts to deliver milk to Kenya Co-operative Creameries) to people who had a down payment to offer.[36]

Settlement documents refer to such farms as 'special plots,' which, it was noted at one point, 'should be open to I.B.R.D. type applicants who had limited capital ...' Area settlement controllers were instructed 'to make special note of plots which would suit this type of settler.'[37] One example of a special plot cited in the documents is a parcel of land in Mweiga Settlement Scheme that includes, in addition to the usual land and development loans, a charge of Shs 12 650/- for grapevines,[38] which presumably would allow the plot to produce a higher income. In July 1963, settlement officials were instructed that 'a maximum of five per cent of the total [high-density] plots may be large plots with target incomes of Shs. 1,500/- to 2,000/- ...'[39] Another method of accommodating prospective members of the bourgeoisies was to sell them two adjacent plots. 'Under no circumstances can two plots be given for the price of one,' it was noted, 'but smallholders may have two plots on paying for both.'[40]

From the viewpoint of landless people, the presence of a 'stabilizing element' meant that land supposedly earmarked for them was being diverted into the hands of people who did not need it. Settlement authorities, meanwhile, confronted a rather different problem. They found that more prosperous settlers were prone to absentee ownership. With independence on the horizon, numerous career and business opportunities were suddenly materializing for Africans who had skills to offer or capital to invest. A piece of land in settlement was only one of these and it was easy to see that, although many other opportunities might well disappear in time, the land would always be there. Already in May 1963, the director of settlement was reporting to the LDSB that some relatively well-off settlers had taken up their plots and accepted development loans, but were doing no cultivation.[41] It was a problem the settlement authorities were to see more of in the coming years, not only on the 'special plots' in high-density settlement, but also in low-density schemes. We will return both to the problem of absentee ownership and to that of diverted resources in the final section of this study.

DISTRIBUTION OF RESOURCES

Objectives. If the Million-Acre Scheme was designed as a means of compensating European settlers, preserving large-scale agriculture through an expansion of peasant society, and maintaining social stability, what were its aims vis-à-vis the landless people who were to be settled? The answer seems self-evident. The program was designed to settle some 30 000 landless and unemployed families and each plot was carefully budgeted to allow the settler to earn a specified cash income – Shs 500/-, 800/-, or 1400/- per year. Its purpose, therefore, was to solve the economic problems of the people who were to be settled – to bring them back into agriculture and to give them an opportunity to make a living as peasants producing for their own consumption and for a capitalist commodity market.

Surely that would be a minimal objective for such a program – and a realistic one as well. The prospective clients of the high-density settlement program were products of a rural society, accustomed to agriculture as a way of life and eager for an opportunity to continue that life. The motivation was there. All they lacked was land and some of the necessary skills. The program would convey the land to them and teach them how to make a living from it.

That, at least, was the impression the settlement authorities sought to convey. The truth, unfortunately, is more sombre. An examination of the program's terms shows that the problems of landless people were among the least important considerations in the design and implementation of high-density settlement. At every stage of the program, from land purchase to settlement and beyond, it is clear that the aspirations of poor people were being sacrificed to the demands of large-scale farmers, to restrictions imposed by the World Bank, and, last but not least, to the British government's desire to save money on compensation of settlers. The aim, clearly, was less to help the poor become peasant producers than to get them to help pay for the land. It was left to the government of independent Kenya to figure out how the peasants would find the money for their payments.

Choice of land. In choosing the land to be bought for high-density settlement, it was quite obvious that one of the least important considerations was its suitability to the purpose for which it was intended. Certainly this was true of a substantial proportion of the land in Nyandarua District. Document after document confirms that much of the land on the high plateau called the Kinangop was waterlogged, frost-prone, and relatively infertile; agricultural advisers were pessimistic about the prospects for successful high-density settlement there. Leslie Brown, a former agricultural official, commented in 1965:

I have never been able to understand why anyone ever regarded the Kinangop as high-potential land. There is a narrow strip of good red soil at the foot of the Aberdare slope, but even here the prevailing low temperatures severely limit the variety of crops that can be grown. Most of the rest of the plateau is sour, badly-drained and often shallow soil supporting poor, coarse herbage, exposed to sweeping winds and rain. In the old days Africans avoided it except as a seasonal grazing ground, and they were right.[42]

Farther north in Nyandarua is the Ol'Kalou Salient, 'an area known to be agriculturally difficult,'[43] which was taken over by the government in 1965, after '40 or 50' farms there had been abandoned.[44] There, and in other areas of the country, landless people were settled on co-operative farms, not because that form of organization was preferred as a means of settling smallholders, but because the land was regarded as unsuitable for any form of small-scale agriculture. Here, as on the Kinangop, it is clear that land bought for the settlement of landless people was chosen with a view to finding hapless buyers for difficult agricultural areas.

Pricing. If the choice of areas to be used for high-density settlement was influenced by considerations other than the effectiveness of the settlement program, the pricing of the land was even more divorced from the interests of landless people. Land purchase, and with it the negotiation of prices, was the one function that remained under the supervision of the Land Development and Settlement Board after the introduction of the Million-Acre Scheme. Chapter 4 described how the LDSB yielded to settler pressures for the inflation of prices for tea land. Even though it was clear that the board was making some attempt to hold the line on prices,[45] it was nevertheless a body representative of the interests of land sellers rather than those of purchasers. There is no question where its sympathies lay and there is other evidence, besides the case of tea land, to suggest that it was lenient in its negotiations with sellers. In May 1963, a settlement official wrote to the acting provincial agricultural officer (PAO) for Central Province to familiarize him with land valuation procedures. The official told the PAO that he would send a summary of the land valuations affecting his province. 'It should be borne in mind,' he commented, 'that for planning purposes these are the initial offers made to the farmer and are likely to be revised and it would be wise when planning to consider valuations as the minimum price, and that in general if any variation occurs it is one in favour of the farmer.'[46]

In at least two instances, settlement officials had occasion to complain about the LDSB's open-handedness. In December 1963, the director of settlement's Planning Committee, considering land purchases in the Ol' Kalou area, declared the valuations there 'altogether too high, but noted that owing to pressure of work [the LDSB's chief executive officer] had had to go ahead with making these offers.' Turning to the buying program at Bamboo Forest, another scheme, the Planning Committee 're-solved that the valuations here must be carefully watched ...'[47]

Nevertheless, four months later, the Planning Committee again found itself sanctioning what it regarded as excessive purchase prices. In April 1963, the committee approved *pro formae* for Cheplelwa Scheme in the Sotik area, 'although concern was expressed at the high cost of the land.'[48] An apparent irregularity in the purchase program was un-covered that same month by Walter Keir, the district agricultural officer

for South Kinangop, when he visited three farms recently taken over by
the LDSB and found 290 acres of pyrethrum instead of the 500 acres that
were supposed to be there.[49]

It is impossible to estimate the extent of such questionable or irregular
occurrences. What we do know, is that, whatever their costs, two-thirds
of it had to be borne by the smallholders who were to purchase the land,
but whose interests were not represented in the determination of the
prices they were to pay.

Budget manipulations. Theoretically, all of this should not have affected
the financial situation of the individual settler. Each plot, after all, had a
budget detailing the agricultural activities to be pursued, specifying the
expected income from each form of produce, and showing how that
income would provide for expenses, loan repayments, and subsistence
requirements, plus the target income of Shs 500/-, 800/-, 1400/- or, for
low-density settlers, 2000/-. (See table 4 in chapter 5.) The budget should
have stood as a guarantee to the settler that, whatever else might happen, his or her plot would be capable of meeting the targets set out for it.

In practice, no such guarantee existed. The budget was susceptible to
any number of manipulations – involving the acreages of the plots, the
setting of predicted market prices for produce, the calculation of subsistence requirements, and so forth. For example, in low-density settlement, the value of the settler's subsistence was set at Shs 800/- per family,
'a figure given by the Kenya National Advisory Council on Nutrition as
being sufficient to supply the basic nutritional and material requirements.'[50] In other words, the gross income of a low-density settlement
plot had to be large enough to allow for expenses and loan repayments,
plus Shs 800/- for the settler's subsistence, and to yield, beyond those
figures, Shs 2000/- in cash income. On high-density settlement, there
was no such calculation. Instead of allowing for extra gross income to
cover subsistence costs, the settlement authorities simply added two
acres to the plot. The term 'target income' therefore had a different
meaning in high-density settlement than it did in low-density, and it
seems certain that the difference was usually, if not always, to the dis-
advantage of the former.[51]

Another example of how budget figures could be – and were –
manipulated is in the so-called acreage conversion scale. Since soils vary
in fertility, two plots of the same acreage would not necessarily have the
same value. For example, a plot of ten arable acres might be worth more
than another plot several times its size, but capable only of supporting
scanty grazing. In setting standards for the sizes of different types of

plots, therefore, the soils were classified and equivalency scales were set up. Thus, in July 1963, officials in Nyandarua had agreed on a soil classification of five categories, with Class I representing good arable soil and Class v, at the other extreme, denoting completely waterlogged soil. One acre of Class I soil, it was agreed, would be regarded as equivalent to two acres of Class II soil, and so forth, as follows: Class I, 1:1; Class II, 1:2; Class III, 1:3; Class IV, 1:5; Class V, 1:7.[52]

Less than two months later, when settlement officials were preparing for the crash program, in which a large amount of relatively low-quality land was to be settled at great speed, the conversion scale had changed:[53] Class I, 1:1; Class II, 1:1.5; Class III, 1:2.5; Class IV, 1:4; Class V, 1:5 or 1:7. It had been shifted so that in all but Class I soil, smaller plots than before would be permissible – presumably for the same price and at the same target incomes.

A system of exploitation. Settlement, therefore, had many hazards: the selection of unsuitable land, the inflation of purchase prices, and myriad possible manipulations of budget figures. High-density settlers were particularly vulnerable to all of these because they lacked the protection of World Bank requirements. Bank officials were anxious to ensure that projects funded by the bank be capable of meeting the targets set out for them. As we saw in chapter 4, the loan agreement for the IBRD scheme contained extensive legal safeguards designed to ensure that the choice of land, the selection of settlers, and the process of implementation would all meet the bank's criteria. Later, when high-density settlement was introduced, the bank viewed the program with a jaundiced eye and expressed concern that the finance for the two schemes be kept separate. Settlement officials, for their part, were worried that the bank would withdraw its support for settlement. I noted in chapter 5 that the permanent secretary for land settlement and water development, addressing settlement planners, 'stressed that it was imperative to adhere to the terms of the international finance agreements because otherwise there was danger of losing this source of funds.'

Although low-density and high-density settlement were being administered together, the former was the subject of extensive legal safeguards (covering land quality, pricing, and all aspects of administration), while the latter enjoyed no such protection. That meant that low-density settlers got the best program inputs available, at prices which – by means of a budget backed by the World Bank – were related to the productive potential of their smallholdings. Landless people, meanwhile, got the land that was left over after the demands of low-density settlement had been met. And – thanks to the manipulation of budgets, against which they enjoyed no protection – the prices they paid might or might not be related to the value of the plots they were buying. It was a system of exploitation in the most literal sense of that phrase: A series of administrative mechanisms operating automatically to ensure material advantages for the better-off at the expense of the poor.

That, at least, is how the situation appears in theory. How did it work out in practice? L.H. Brown, acting director of agriculture, toured selected areas of settlement in mid-1963 and reported on his observations. The difficulty with the Lugari high-density scheme west of the Rift Valley, he said, 'is basically that the charges per plot are so large in relation to the productive capacity that doubts must be felt that the average settler will meet his commitments ...' Turning to Nyandarua District he said the South Kinangop settlement 'is likely to be a good deal more problematical economically than some other schemes. I would have been inclined to say that except for a proportion of favoured, well-drained plots even Lugari had a better chance of success ... much of the land ... is quite plainly unsuitable to high density settlements in its present conditions ...'

At Ndalat high-density scheme, on the other hand, Brown found land of better potential. The picture, therefore, was not one of unrelieved gloom. Nevertheless, he concluded that a major problem of settlement generally was the 'difficulty that is going to be experienced in maintaining loan repayments by settlers on high density schemes ... This difficulty stems from the large loan commitments which have to be met in relation to the productive capacity of the land ...' At two low-density schemes that Brown visited on the same tour, by contrast, he found a different situation. He pronounced Lessos Scheme in the Rift Valley and Gelegele in the Sotik area economically 'sound' and 'viable.'[54] The system of exploitation was doing its work. But Brown's findings fall short of revealing its full extent (see chapter 7).

Education and assistance. In a sense, the most revealing characteristic of high-density settlement was not its material deprivation, but the inadequacy of its education and assistance program. A person of saintly temperament might argue that the material deprivations were all results of bad planning, hasty implementation, and unfortunate combinations of circumstances. But the terms of the education and assistance program clearly indicate that the scheme was never seriously intended to meet its own ostensible objectives. Considering the fact that the high-density settlers' biggest liability was their lack of skill in modern agriculture – while low-density settlers, on the contrary, were selected for their skill – one might have thought that extension services would have concentrated heavily on the former and assumed that the latter would require much less help. If a program designed to make unskilled people capable of fending for themselves in a modern economy were to be successful, the key to it had to be the development of the participants' potential. Surely the most important factor in its success or failure would be the quality of its facilities for education and assistance.

Apparently the settlement authorities thought otherwise. For planning purposes, each 5000-acre unit of low-density settlement was allocated virtually the same staff as a 10 000-acre unit of high-density settlement – despite the fact that the latter might have several times the population of the former. Each unit was allotted two agricultural instructors, two assistant agricultural instructors, and two veterinary assistants. A low-density unit was given two veterinary scouts, compared with a high-density unit's three – still, in most if not all cases, a substantial disparity in favour of those who needed the least help.[55] The failure to allocate adequate extension services to high-density settlement made a sham of the program's pretensions of offering landless people a chance to succeed as cash farmers.

CONTINUITY AND CHANGE AFTER INDEPENDENCE

So far we have been looking at how settlement for landless people developed up to the end of the crash program and the end of colonial rule in December 1963. By the beginning of 1964, the planning of settlement had been complete for some time, nearly 14 000 plots were ready for settlement, and the program was well on its way to completion. It is not surprising, therefore, to find that very little changed after independence, either in the high-density scheme or indeed in any aspect of the settlement program. To be sure, a 1965 white paper grumbled that 'the settlement process was inherited from the British and was designed more to aid those Europeans who wanted to leave than the Africans who received the land.'[56] And in 1966, the settlement authorities appeared chagrined over the currency drain caused by the purchase program. 'It might be of interest to note,' the Department of Settlement declared acidly, 'that over 90 per cent of the total purchase price of the farms during the year was either paid or committed to be paid in sterling currency in Britain.'[57] But it was clear that the government had accepted settlement as its own policy and was committed to carrying it through to completion. In 1964, the process of settlement went forward without a pause. By mid-year, 16700 plots had been allocated.[58] Within another two years, the total had reached 28800[59] and the bulk of the program was completed. The changes that did take place after independence involved further developments or relatively minor adjustments of the existing policy rather than a shift in its direction.

One of these changes affected the four-year rule giving preference for plots to anyone who had spent four years as a legal labourer on a farm being taken for settlement. Kikuyu political leaders had opposed that rule, presumably because, as we noted, it favoured loyalists. KANU leaders were now as interested as had been the colonial authorities in preventing civil unrest, but that objective could presumably be achieved without giving special favours to people who were likely to have been supporters of the colonial regime that KANU fought to bring to an end. As a result, even before independence, 'Kikuyu political leaders' asked for a reduction of the qualifying period from four years to one year.[60]

After internal self-government, they got their way. The preference that had previously gone to four-year qualifiers was now extended to all legal labourers. Since there were not enough plots to settle all legal labourers, lotteries continued to be used to decide among eligible applicants.[61]

The government also continued the policy of selecting landless people in other areas of the country and bringing them to Nyandarua to be settled. Again, there were indications that nationalist supporters were now being favoured, undoubtedly to compensate for favouritism extended to loyalists before internal self-government. For example, the chairman of the Nyandarua District Agricultural Committee complained in April 1964 that one of Nyandarua's new settlement schemes was being used to settle 'former freedom fighters.' The regional government agent replied: 'The people who are going to be settled ... are not freedom fighters. They are ordinary landless people coming from Njiru near Kahawa ...'[62] Whether or not the settlers were former freedom fighters, the selection policy was substantially unchanged. Lotteries were still used and landless people were still selected from various parts of the country, presumably so that no one would lose hope of eventually being settled.

The biggest problem facing the settlement authorities after independence was the sombre fact that landlessness was far from eliminated. This had been clear on the eve of the crash program, when the settlement authorities had been forced to acknowledge that they would find it difficult to settle all the landless people who had been sent to transit schemes to await settlement.

In 1964, Nyandarua District authorities were reaping the whirlwind. At the end of the year, the district commissioner reported that there were almost 18000 landless people in the district: 'In North and South Kinangop [the areas that had been under settlement for the longest time] there are still almost 6,000 landless adults and 8,000 children in the category of destitute landless squatters.' Some 6800 families had received famine relief.[63] Landless people – even legal labourers, not to speak of illegal squatters – continued to outnumber the plots available for settlement.[64] 'The re-settlement programme will not absorb even half the legal labour ...,' the district commissioner said.[65]

Despite these figures, and the misery they revealed, the settlement program's objective of maintaining social stability appeared to be well on the way to realization. In September 1963, the General Service Unit had been sent to Nyandarua to reinforce the police. Since then, settlement had moved forward rapidly, visible evidence to free-land advocates that their cause was being lost. At the end of 1964, the district commissioner was able to report that the incidence of crime in the district had decreased sharply, from 104 incidents in January 1964 to 'just about 30' in December.[66]

Even if calm was being restored, the problem of landlessness was well out of control. Settlement schemes were not absorbing nearly all the landless people. And the settlement program itself was suffering as a result. In 1964, newly settled smallholders were complaining to the authorities that they were unable to develop their land because squatters were living on it and refusing to move.[67] Large-scale landowners were registering similar complaints.[68] In reply to one of the letters, the district commissioner commented that the problem was 'spread all over the district.'[69]

The government responded by expanding existing settlement policies or developing variations of them. To accommodate illegal squatters in Nyandarua – and presumably elsewhere as well – trading centres in settlement schemes were planned to include squatter villages consisting of residential plots with some minimal space available for cultivation. The residents could cultivate some subsistence crops and earn wages as labourers in the settlement scheme. Such villages had been part of the original plans for the Million-Acre Scheme, but the building of them did not start in Nyandarua District until mid-1964. By the end of that year, nine villages had been established[70] and the government was planning to close the transit farms that had been accommodating squatters on a temporary basis.[71] These villages were by no means capable of accommodating all the landless people. As chapter 7 will show, small, unofficial squatter villages dotted the settlement area sampled in this study, eight years after independence, despite the existence of regular villages in the trading centres.

On the national level, the government undertook to assess the proportions of the problem of landlessness and to devise further programs to deal with it. In 1965, a squatter registration program was launched to identify all landless people who were not employed as resident labourers and to check with their home district to ensure that they were genuinely landless. Under the program, 46000 families were registered.[72] By the end of the 1960s, the government had initiated a series of new programs designed to settle some of the many Kenyans who remained landless. The expansion of peasant society, which had been held in check by the colonial system and which had at first been so fiercely resisted by the settlement authorities, was now becoming a regular feature of Kenya politics.

CONCLUSION

It was landless people on the one hand and Kenya's taxpayers on the other who bore the brunt of the neo-colonial solution to Kenya's land question. All the other groups concerned with the settlement program did well by it. European settlers received 1959 prices – and sometimes more – for their land and they were given the right to take their money out of the country. The British government won a land settlement at a price that was ludicrously low considering the obligations it had accumulated, not only to European settlers, but also to landless people, whose misery was a result of the colonial enterprise. More prosperous Africans – from ambitious peasants to the emerging bourgeoisie – gained a variety of lucrative opportunities in agriculture and associated enterprises. Landless people, meanwhile, got a program that was grossly inadequate to their numbers, that loaded them with unconscionable burdens of debt (often in return for substandard land), and that was patently incapable of meeting its distinctly modest objectives. Taxpayers picked up the tab for the ongoing administrative costs of settlement and for loan arrears, including those of settlers who were predictably unable to scratch a living from the land they had been sold.

For the people who had been made landless by colonialism, and by the economic changes it brought, the reality of *uhuru* fell far short of its promise. That does not mean it was worthless – at least not to those who got land. Some of the land in the Million-Acre Scheme had good potential, and – from the viewpoint of a former squatter – even poor land may be better than no land at all. But *uhuru* might have brought much better opportunities to a larger number of poor people – and enhanced their contribution to Kenya's economy – had the Million-Acre Scheme lived up to its pretensions of making a serious attack on the problem of landlessness.

Part III

Land and class in independent Kenya

In chapter 1, I undertook to make a case for Kenya as both a peasant and a capitalist society, with a peasantry and capitalist classes developing side by side and in a relationship of mutual support. My thesis was put forward as a refutation of the assumption that the persistence of the peasant mode of production acts as a block to capitalist development and that, obversely, capitalist development involves the expropriation of the peasantry. We have now reached the point where I can begin to marshal evidence in support of the thesis.

The review of the existing literature on Kenya's political economy in chapter 1 enabled us to visualize two possible futures for that country: 1) a peasant/petty-bourgeois society, involving a series of class alliances that had the net effect of allowing peasant society to flourish, or even expand; and 2) a society with a dominant bourgeoisie, which, by gradual and progressive expropriation of peasant and petty-bourgeois elements, built a base of wealth from which to launch Kenya's industrialization. The former scenario had a number of elements in common with Langdon and Kaplinsky's preferred future, while the latter approximated the development path that Leys, in his writings of the late 1970s, saw as the only possible route to prosperity for Kenya.

What is apparent so far suggests that the first scenario is the one materializing in Kenya; but it also raises questions about whether the second scenario is as clearly distinguishable from the first as one might have thought. Chapters 2 through 6 have done much to buttress and elaborate Leys' earlier work on 'peasantization,' and this, as we will see, operates to the detriment of his more recent work.

Chapter 2 looked at pre-colonial land usages, noting that they were neither individualist nor communal in the Western senses of those words. The usages featured a mixture of the personal and familial with the economic – a mixture in which land served as a way of simultaneously building economic fortunes and personal relationships. Thus, for example, a man who controlled land would allow a relative or a friend to use it and in return would gain the use of livestock or a share of the harvest. Chapter 5 showed that these usages proved adaptable to the capitalist/peasant economy that was evolving in the transition to independence. Members of the petty and upper bourgeoisies – as well as peasants – were able to meet family obligations and at the same time increase their own power and prosperity through the acquisition of peasant holdings.

Therefore, the impetus toward the expansion of peasant society came, not only from landless people scrambling for smallholdings, but also from members of the African bourgeoisies who saw the ownership of peasant holdings as integral to their careers in the capitalist economy. The colonial authorities initiated the expansion of peasant society for quite different reasons (they were, it will be remembered, seeking buyers for substandard European land) but once the trend had been set in motion, it proved irresistible. Soon the colonial authorities themselves were actively promoting it, and hedging their bets (chapter 6) by ensuring that the new peasant schemes would be 'stabilized' through the presence of selected petty- or upper-bourgeois settlers.

All of this looks very different from the notion of two dichotomous development paths, a petty-bourgeois/peasant one and a bourgeois one, each able to advance only at the expense of othe other. Instead we find peasant and capitalist classes thoroughly interpenetrated, with many an individual merging the two class identities in his or her person. Cowen recognized the existence of dual occupations with his concept of 'straddling' (see chapter 1), but it does not seem to have occurred to him to generalize it. On the contrary, although he observes individuals 'straddling' the bourgeoisie and the peasantry, he argues that, for the society as a whole, a peasantry that achieves stability will block the expansion of the bourgeoisie.[1]

On reflection, it is not clear why the stability of a peasantry will prevent bourgeois aggrandizement or, obversely, why a bourgeoisie must necessarily expropriate a peasantry in order to bring about industrialization. In the first place, a bourgeoisie can generate a surplus from a large-farm sector that exists side by side with a peasantry. We have already seen that land settlement at independence combined the preservation of the most productive large-farm areas with the expansion of peasant society. Furthermore, on the face of it, there is no reason why a peasantry cannot generate a surplus for industrialization, especially if what we have in mind is the Danish or Australian development model rather than the British one (see chapter 1). In many agricultural pursuits, Kenya's peasants have proved their ability to match, and even outstrip, the productiveness of large-scale farmers (see chapter 8). The capturing of a surplus, therefore, is a matter of amassing the profits of a large number of smallholdings into a single investment fund. This can be done through companies, co-operatives, or by taxation. In short, there seems to be no support for Leys' suggestion (chapter 1) that industrialization must entail a struggle pitting the bourgeoisie against petty bourgeois and peasant elements. In the long run – if capitalist development continues – peasants will be replaced by capitalist farmers, large or small, either in a head-to-head class struggle, or by some other, more complex, process of evolution. For the time being, however, such a development is not in evidence, and our understanding of Kenya today, or in the foreseeable future, is not enhanced by assuming it.

If it is true that the peasant/bourgeois contradiction is a chimera, what kind of a society does that leave us with? A land of stability and calm, with hard-handed peasants and smiling business people working in harmony to build a better future? A static society, conservative, rigid, and tradition-bound? By no means. The agrarian society I observed in the research for this book was bursting with activity and rife with conflict, caught in the grip of continuing change and the continuing formation of classes and class alliances. Some peasants were trying to work their way into large-scale agriculture or commerce; others were expanding their holdings on a more modest scale or acquiring multiple holdings and making familial arrangements to have them farmed, all as peasant farms; members of the bourgeoisies were doing the same thing, and finding numerous other, more spectacular ways of building their fortunes, while marginal peasants were being forced to sell off some of their land as they were squeezed closer to proletarianization; other peasant families found that the process of inheritance was fragmenting their holdings and pushing them as well toward proletarianization. But the formation of a large proletariat is not inevitable as long as there remains a frontier of unoccupied or underutilized land, and such a frontier still existed in the early 1980s.

Chapter 7 undertakes a close examination of the peasant society that developed out of the settlement of the land question at independence. It is very much a class society, even though it does not conform to the preconceptions of Western Marxists. Chapter 8 deals more discursively with the development of Kenya's agrarian system into the 1980s, examining fresh class formation and new class alignments, considering their implications for the future, and addressing the political and policy questions they raise.

7

Hakuna cha bure:
the Million-Acre Scheme
at the grass roots, 1971–72

Hakuna cha bure is the Swahili equivalent of 'you can't get something for nothing.' Jomo Kenyatta expressed that sentiment when he was explaining his reasons for accepting a colonial settlement of the land question. 'We do not believe in being given this or that free,' he said. 'I do not want Africans to adopt that attitude. I want them to work with their own hands on a piece of land.' Throughout the 1960s and the early 1970s, *hakuna cha bure* was repeated again and again on political platforms across Kenya. It became a central proposition in the individualist ideology underpinning Kenya's political and economic system.

For ordinary people in Kenya in the early 1970s, the truth of that phrase had been amply borne out in experience. Again and again, the government – in its policies relating to land, education, health care, and many other areas – had served notice that people must be prepared to work for the benefits and amenities they hoped to enjoy. That, undoubtedly, is as it should be. Unfortunately, the rule did not apply equally to everyone, as ordinary people were able to observe every day. While the poor were required to work hard for whatever slender rewards were available to them, Kenya's new bourgeoisie were offered privileged access to land and were able to use franchises, directorships, and trading licences as avenues to wealth easily earned – or not earned at all. *Mwenye nguvu mpishe* – Power will have its way.

Individualism? A privileged bourgeoisie? In an expanding peasant society? Although Marxist (and much non-Marxist) orthodoxy treats peasant predominance and bourgeois dominance as successive phases in the development of society, it was already quite clear in Kenya in the early 1970s that the two phenomena were flourishing side by side, with no signs that either one was pre-empting the other.

NYANDARUA DISTRICT

When Kenya's regional boundaries were established on the eve of independence,[1] Nyandarua District was designated as an expansion area for
Kikuyu people into the former White Highlands. A strip of land extending from Kiambu District in the south to the town of Nyahururu in the
north, Nyandarua was bounded on the west by the Rift Valley escarp-
ment and on the east by the Aberdares Mountains (which were called
Nyandarua by Kikuyus). From the early 1960s onward – beginning with
the Kinangop scheme described in chapter 5 – one area of Nyandarua
after another was converted to settlement schemes, until large-scale
farms had virtually disappeared.

By 1970, the sixty-four settlement units of the Nyandarua area –
including a handful of schemes in areas adjacent to Nyandarua District – were home to more than 15 000 of the roughly 37 000 families
who by then had joined the settlement. The hectarage of Nyandarua
area settlement had grown to about 240 000, not much less than half of
the 540 000 hectares in settlement as a whole.[2]

Near the centre of Nyandarua District, the town of Ol'Kalou lies at the
foot of a range of hills lining the district's western boundary. To the
north and east, away from the hills, extends the high plateau called the
Ol'Kalou Salient and beyond it the blue Aberdare Mountains over-
shadow the eastern part of the district. On a clear day, it is possible, from
some points near Ol'Kalou, to see the tip of the traditionally sacred
Kirinyaga – Mt Kenya – located in the heart of Kikuyu country on the
far side of the Aberdares. It was from the foot of Mt Kenya that Kikuyu
traders used to set out for what is now Nyandarua District to trade with
the Masai. In 1904, Europeans induced the Masai to vacate the area and
took it over themselves (chapter 2). At independence the Europeans left
in their turn and Nyandarua became Kikuyu country.

Vestiges of ubeberu. Although the area around Ol'Kalou had been in
African hands since the mid-1960s, the memory of *ubeberu* – colonial
oppression – was still very much alive in the early 1970s. Its direct influence over people's lives had vanished, but there remained numerous
signs of its former presence. Dotting the hills and the salient were the
grand stone houses that had belonged to European settlers. Some of
them had become offices and housing for settlement administrators. A
few – especially the less ostentatious, more functional ones – had been
taken over by some of the better-off settlement farmers. Some of the
best houses, together with 100-acre tracts of land, had become the prop-

erty of prominent politicians and other leaders of national stature. But most people did not care to maintain the expensive pretensions of the would-be English and Afrikaans country gentlemen who had lived there before. Cows were turned out to pasture on former croquet lawns and goats nibbled delicately on what had once been manicured hedges.

Although the Europeans were gone, some of their names remained. The small town of Matura was still often referred to as Major's, after a European whose former home was located there. And the name Rurii – a town a few miles north of Ol'Kalou – is an African version of the name Luies.

More interesting than the real names, however, were the nicknames. One former settler, for example, was still referred to as 'Major Bado' – *bado* being the Swahili word for 'not yet' – because that was reportedly his stock answer when he was asked to pay wages. Another had been nicknamed 'Kiongo' – the Kikuyu word for 'head' – after his most prominent and conspicuous physical feature; the small trading centre of Gwa Kiongo, in northwestern Nyandarua District, enshrines his memory. Under colonial oppression, African squatters had found some refuge from their sense of grievance in ironical humour. Now, all that remained of some of the more detested former settlers were the grim jokes that had become their secret nicknames.

The physical layout of the major towns – the ones that had served as shopping centres for the former settlers – also bore memories of colonialism. Typically, the focal point of a town was what was coloquially called *Barabara ya Bwana Mkubwa*, 'the boss's street,' or – to translate it into the more appropriate idiom of the southern United States – 'Mr Charley's street.' In colonial times, it had been lined with banks, retail stores carrying imported goods, auto showrooms, and other commercial establishments catering to Europeans. In a different part of the town-site – often at some remove from the *Barabara ya Bwana Mkubwa* – was a more down-at-the heels district, called 'the location,' the area where Africans had been allowed to live and ply their trades. In the early 1970s, it was still easy to identify the two sections. 'The location' was still the less elegant of the two districts, but often it was busier. Some of the formerly European stores retained a bit of their old flavour by catering to the tastes of remaining Europeans and the African bourgeoisie, but for the most part they had either adapted to the service of a broader section of the population or were being deserted.

Perhaps the most poignant vestiges of colonialism were its visible effects on people's behaviour – a hint of the personal toll taken by a system of racial discrimination. For example, Africans related that during the colonial era it had been *de rigueur* to tip one's hat when encountering a European. Failure to do so might result in a beating, they said. With the coming of *uhuru*,[3] most people had been delighted to doff the habits and mannerisms of obeisance. But occasionally one still encountered an old man who, upon meeting a European, stopped dead in his tracks and involuntarily lifted his hat.

The psychological scars people had suffered in the colonial era stemmed, not only from racial discrimination, but also from the class conflict spawned by the colonial economic system. The memories of the Mau Mau war were still vivid in the early 1970s. Many of the wrongs individuals suffered in that war as a result of bitter family feuds, as well as the horrors of armed conflict and detention, had been painful beyond description. The bitterness of the memories of the Emergency were recognized in the official ideology, and the official answer was that they must be put aside. 'We must forgive,' Jomo Kenyatta was often quoted as saying, 'although we cannot forget.'[4] The importance of forgiving seemed to be widely accepted in principle, but in practice many people clearly found it difficult. Both former loyalists and their former adversaries lived in Nyandarua and each was reminded of the past by the presence of the other. Furthermore, the causes of the conflict had not been eliminated. We return to that point below.

Fruits of uhuru. Despite the bitterness that *uhuru* had failed to erase, independence was almost universally regarded – by the people contacted in the course of the present study – as a marvellous achievement and a major historical turning-point. To be sure, the systematic surveys conducted in the course of this study did not sample landless people, or even – as it turned out – the poorest high-density settlers. Perhaps a sample of settlers in such notoriously impoverished areas as the Kinangop or the Ol'Kalou Salient, or of people living in squatter villages, would have yielded a different result. Still, the Ol'Kalou area surveys included many settlers who were poor by any standard. And even in their eyes *uhuru* remained a great boon.

Interestingly, settlers were not asked in the survey how they felt about *uhuru*. The subject came up because, again and again, they found occasion to bring it up of their own accord. Most commonly it was raised in connection with a pair of questions intended as a means of probing the settlers' changing perceptions of the economic possibilities available to them. The questions read: 'Have new opportunities for advancement arisen since the Emergency? How are they different from the old ones?'

Invariably, however, it was not the Emergency, but *uhuru*, that settlers perceived as the watershed.

Clearly, the most important material benefit of *uhuru* was land. This was especially true of the high-density settlers who – as we saw in chapter 6 and as they confirmed in their own accounts – had had good reason to fear that they would be passed over by settlement. For most of them, winning a plot in settlement was a fantastic piece of good luck and a turning-point in their lives. It is not surprising, therefore, that they – as well as their better-off fellow settlers – perceived the lowering of the colour bar to landownership that came with independence as a major advance for Africans.

But most respondents volunteered at least two or three major benefits that they attributed to the achievement of independence. Education was frequently mentioned. Under the British, one smallholder said, the only schools in the area for Africans were the ones in the three towns of Nyahururu, Ol'Joro Orok, and Ol'Kalou. The Europeans, another declared, were trying to keep Africans ignorant so that they could be used as farm labourers. Since *uhuru*, respondents emphasized again and again, education had become widely available to Africans from all walks of life. Another benefit often referred to was access to extension services, and to the skills and technology of modern agriculture. Some respondents mentioned new roads, which have eased farmers' access to produce markets. Others mentioned the availability of new opportunities in trade and commerce. Some recalled that the approach of independence had coincided with the lifting of the Emergency pass regulations that had greatly restricted their mobility. New job opportunities, improved health care, and greater personal prosperity were also mentioned. Throughout, the recurrent theme was the sense of relief in having been freed from the indignities of a system in which Europeans took for granted rights and privileges that were denied to Africans.

Economic insecurity. Despite widespread satisfaction with the benefits of *uhuru*, there was – implicitly at least – a sense of uncertainty about economic prospects for the future. Among the poorer respondents, the uncertainty manifested itself in an often-expressed scepticism about the permanence of opportunities in trade and in white-collar occupations. Such opportunities might be very lucrative, they acknowledged, but businesses can go bankrupt, while graduates and school-leavers are finding more and more difficulty in getting employment. At the same time, most of them expressed considerable confidence in the security of a future in agriculture, although they did not perceive it as financially rewarding.

Some of the better-off settlement farmers appeared not to share the confidence of the poorer smallholders. Indeed, in Passenga – the low-density scheme surveyed in this study – there was a considerable amount of anxiety in 1971 about the security of their position as landowners. The anxiety had been triggered by reports that one or two Passenga farmers had paid off their loans, but had not been granted title to the land.[5] Reassurances to the effect that the deeds would be supplied as soon as land surveys had been completed were greeted with scepticism. A few farmers openly expressed the fear that, in the event of a change of government, they might yet lose their rights to the land. In the mean-time, several farmers said, the lack of a title would make it impossible for them to take out loans to develop their land.

If some of the more prosperous settlers felt unsure about the security of their position in agriculture, they did not always seem sanguine about other aspects of the economy either. The evidence of that sentiment was less in what they said than in their behaviour. As we will see in more detail below, they – like many other better-off peasants and members of the nascent bourgeoisies – often sought to pursue a number of economic opportunities simultaneously. Thus a low-density settler might retain his interest in his smallholding while at the same time investing in a series of hotels, or a sawmill and a town trading plot, or another farm and a butcher shop. In part, this apparent frenzy of economic activity was simply a reflection of the fact that Africanization of the economy and the growth of many Africans' purchasing power had very rapidly opened up a whole range of new business opportunities. But something else also seemed to be implicit in the activities and in the way people talked about them: the fear that the scope for economic expansion was narrow, that new opportunities would not continue to arise in the future, and, there-fore, that if one wished to secure one's own position and that of one's children, one had better move quickly.

Political discontents. The undercurrent of unease about the economic future was accompanied by a somewhat more pronounced sense of dis-quiet about politics. In the Ol'Kalou area, as in rural areas everywhere, conversation was a much-favoured pastime. Many of the interviews con-ducted for this study lasted for hours and ranged freely over a wide variety of topics. But one question that almost invariably drew a mono-syllabic response was a seemingly innocent inquiry about the respon-dent's KANU activities. It was obviously a subject that most people did not like to talk about.

The reasons were not far to seek. Despite *uhuru*, some of Kenya's most deeply rooted political conflicts remained unresolved. It was a widely accepted part of Kenya's political lore – and is undoubtedly true – that the Mau Mau war was an important influence in the British decision to end their colonial enterprise in Kenya. As a result, members of the Land Freedom Army – or freedom fighters, as they were commonly called – were credited with having been the foot-soldiers in Kenya's struggle for independence. Since independence, a very visible minority of Kenyans had become wealthy, and a much larger minority had become prosperous but, as a rule, former freedom fighters were conspicuously absent from their ranks. It followed, therefore, that many of those who had fought the hardest for *uhuru* had benefited least from it. Conversely, a goodly number of its biggest beneficiaries had remained clear of the military action, or – as it was sometimes alleged – had been loyalists. In short, there was a glaring disparity in the distribution of the fruits of *uhuru*. The existence of that disparity was widely accepted as one of the hard facts of life in an imperfect world, but it was a fact that few people were comfortable with.

Meanwhile, the conflict – or rather, Kenya's various interrelated political conflicts – continued to simmer under the surface. In 1969, in the wake of the assassination of Tom Mboya, KANU, in order to solidify its political support, resorted to a campaign of compulsory oath-taking across Kikuyu country.[6] In Nyandarua, people who expressed their reluctance to take the oath were harassed and threatened. The government also had more drastic ways of commanding support. The General Service Unit – which, as we saw in chapter 6, was sent into Nyandarua in 1963 – remained active. They were neither numerous nor highly visible, but their appearance and bearing, when they did present themselves, seemed well calculated to inspire fear. Occasionally they were reported or rumoured to have been sent to quell an outbreak of sedition or disorder. Their presence – in the 1970s, as in 1963 – served as a reminder that the safest course for a citizen was that of political orthodoxy.

Other conflicts, which surfaced in the day-to-day administration of the settlement program, made it clear that a significant number of settlers remained dissatisfied with Kenya's land policies. Several schemes in central and northern Nyandarua were widely assumed to have been settled entirely by former freedom fighters, i.e. 'Mau Mau.' It was clear, however, that many settlers identified, not only with the anti-colonial insurgency of the 1950s, but also with the free-land movement of the early 1960s. Administrators involved with such schemes reported that many of its settlers were 'political' – occasionally they were referred to as 'bush politicians.' Agricultural extension officers found them unco-operative and suspicious, still insisting on the injustice of having to pay for former European land and unwilling to believe in the goodwill of government administrators. Like the Land Freedom Army of 1963, they were unreconciled to Kenya's land policies, but lacked the resources to pose an alternative to them.

THE SETTLEMENT SCHEMES

Chapter 6 reveals that the terms of the settlement program had built into them a systematic bias favouring low-density settlement at the expense of high density. The bias affected the choice of land, the pricing of the land, the establishment of plot budgets, and the allocation of extension personnel – in other words, virtually every aspect of the program. In a spot survey of a number of settlement schemes, a colonial agricultural official passed a favourable judgment about the economic prospects of two low-density schemes, while expressing pessimism about the viability of two out of three high-density schemes he visited. Taken together, the evidence seemed to suggest that, as a whole, high-density settlement had been seriously short-changed in relation to low-density, but that some high-density schemes had fared better than others.

Subsequent evidence on the comparative condition of high- and low-density settlement suggests a similar mixture of outcomes. In 1964, for example, a district agricultural officer made a series of visits to high-density plots on the Kinangop in response to complaints from their owners. In plot after plot on Kipipiri, Muruaki, and Nandarasi schemes, he found poorly drained, infertile soil. More significantly, he rejected a number of complaints, not on the grounds that they were unfounded, but on the grounds that the plots in question – however bad they might be – were no worse than other plots in the scheme. On Kipipiri, for example, he said of one smallholding: 'I do not consider that this farm is bad enough to warrant another plot for the settler. It is very much like the plots around it and although water-logging continues impeding cultivations in the wet seasons this is no condition of one man or one plot, but of all the area round.'[7] A plot on Muruaki drew the following judgment: 'The farmer is complaining that the drainage is very poor and that there is murram [i.e. rock] very near the surface. I consider this not to be a genuine case where special consideration should be given. It is just like any other plot around, and unless all the plots around are to be given the same consideration, I would recommend that this complaint should be slighted off, and should not be entertained.'[8]

The Ol'Kalou Salient, likewise, was 'known to be agriculturally difficult' (see chapter 6) when it was taken over in 1965 for the settlement of landless people. Adjacent to the salient is a high-density scheme called Ol'Kalou Central. Administrative officers concerned with it reported that it contained plots that were hopeless from an agricultural point of view. In Sotik, in western Kenya, a settlement officer reported that low-density settlement in that area took in noticeably better-quality land than did high density.[9] A senior agricultural field officer in the Turbo area, to the north of Sotik, observed, similarly, that low-density land in his area was generally the more fertile settlement land.[10] In northern Nyandarua District, an agricultural official offered a rather different judgment on his area. Low-density schemes, he said, were intended to receive higher-quality soil than high density, but it did not work out that way in practice.[11] A government economic appraisal of settlement offers a more generalized judgment: '... some areas which were known to be of poor potential had to be chosen for settlement. This was particularly so in the case of certain High Density schemes.'[12] We can accept the government's acknowledgment that land of poor potential *was* chosen for settlement without necessarily giving credence to the assertion that it *had to be* chosen. The available evidence, then, supports the conclusion that high-density settlers got the worst of settlement, without necessarily having come off badly everywhere, or in all cases.

But what does that mean in practice? What is the difference between living in high- and low-density settlement? The differences were, in fact, enormous, for reasons that went far beyond the relatively simple matter of land quality. Although the two types of schemes often bordered on each other, they were separated by an invisible wall, consisting of the social, economic, and personal distinctions of class. Colin Leys' failure to recognize this was one of the weaknesses in his otherwise very perceptive article on the development of peasant society, which is discussed in chapter 1 and in the introduction to this part. 'The distinction between the low and high density settlement schemes,' he maintained, 'is in reality a narrow one ...' He built that conclusion on the quicksand of a comparison of average acreages that ignores land quality, and which failed him, as we will see. This was one of the elements contributing to the fallacious impression left by the article that the development of peasant society would herald an era of stability and limited change.

In fact, the contrast between high- and low-density settlement in the early 1970s was stark. Typically, settlers in the two kinds of land units had different personal histories, different sets of economic problems and prospects, and – as a result – different life-styles and different hopes and fears for the future. Anyone who was familiar with rural Kenya in the early 1970s could usually tell at a glance whether a given settlement area was high density or low density. A low-density scheme, as a rule, had an abundance of all the status symbols and signs of prosperity of the countryside: *mabati* (corrugated iron) roofs, houses of wood and sometimes stone, and, occasionally, a tractor, a pick-up truck, or even a sedan. In high-density areas one could see the evidence of a poor peasant's life-style: mud houses with thatched roofs and extensive areas of uncleared bush and wild grass. Such a life-style is not necessarily an indicator of inferior husbandry (as we will see) or of lives hard-pressed by want. The rural status symbols, by the same token, may often be expensive fripperies that add little to the quality of life or of agriculture. Nevertheless, the presence of the symbols, or the degree to which they were absent, offered reliable indicators of an area's overall level of prosperity.

In the case of Passenga and Ol'Kalou West, two adjacent settlement schemes located near the town of Ol'Kalou, which were the subject of a systematic survey for the present study, these impressions were amply borne out by data. They were also qualified in some interesting ways. The surveys consisted of interviews with a 40 per cent random sample of plot-holders or managers and the results showed that, although formerly landless people and more prosperous settlers did indeed live in different worlds, the boundaries separating those worlds were not entirely congruous with those separating high- and low-density settlement from each other. The incongruities confirm some of the data discussed in chapter 6 and extend them further.

Origins. As the settlement authorities had intended, most of the people in Passenga, a low-density scheme, had been prosperous peasants or members of the petty bourgeoisie before coming to settlement. Of thirty-six plot-holders who reported their occupations before coming to settlement, fourteen said they had been businessmen or farmers. Four had been employed as overseers on European, large-scale farms; eight as teachers or civil servants (including a court assessor, a health inspector, an education officer, a settlement officer, and a chief). A further three had been clerks or typists and four had been skilled tradesmen (mechanics and a carpenter).

In Ol'Kalou West, a high-density scheme, most settlers came from very different origins, although there was a significant minority of better-off people among them. Fifty-one out of seventy-five respondents had been squatters (i.e. farm labourers, forest squatters, or herdsmen); eight had been either tractor drivers or cooks on large-scale farms; and one had been a turn-boy (a helper on a bus or truck). Sixty of the respondents, or 80 per cent, therefore, had been unskilled labourers, while four people reported that they had been skilled workers – a truck driver, a mechanic, a carpenter, and a shoemaker – and one gave his former occupation as an overseer. The remaining ten residents reported that they had held white-collar positions before coming to settlement: four had been clerks, three civil servants, two businessmen, and one a teacher.

The skilled workers constituted 6.7 per cent of the total population and the white-collar workers a further 13.3 per cent – all of them people whose occupations did not fit into an otherwise uniform pattern. Obviously they were among the 'civil servants, soldiers, and employed people' who, as we saw in chapter 6, were included in the high-density program in order to help promote 'social stability.' Indeed, three of the former white-collar workers had plots of between thirty-five and forty hectares of apparently high-quality farmland – obviously 'special plots' of the kind that the settlement authorities had been reserving for 'I.B.R.D. type applicants ...'

The petty-bourgeois presence within Ol'Kalou West is a significant one, and its significance appears to be heightened if we look at it in a historical perspective. The scheme was settled near the end of 1963 – just before independence and at the height of the 'crash program,' when the settlement authorities were at their most desperate to settle landless people, whose unrest had reached dangerous proportions. If, at a time like that, the authorities were able to divert 13 per cent or more of the plots available for high-density settlement into petty-bourgeois hands, it is clear that they had found their way to a whole-hearted acceptance of the idea of mixing peasant and bourgeois society together. The same action throws a glaring light on the insincerity of the commitment to resolve the problems of landless people.

Indeed, the results of the random sample substantially understate the diversion of resources from landless people to the bourgeoisies, for two reasons. In the first place, the thirty-five to forty-hectare special plots were between three and four times the size of the average plot in Ol'Kalou West.[13] Thirteen per cent of the plots, therefore, took in substantially more than 13 per cent of the land area. A second bourgeois – in this case upper bourgeois – element in Ol'Kalou West not accounted for in the random sample was that represented by Z-plots – holdings consisting of a former settler home, together with forty hectares of land each. During 1963–64, Z-plots had been laid out around 'the better class houses' bought for settlement and sold to 'a leader of the community such as a member of the Central Assembly or a Senator, etc.'[14] Seven Z-plots were located within the boundaries of Ol'Kalou West.

If calculations are adjusted to take account of the size of the special plots and the hectarage represented by Z-plots, it is apparent that the bourgeois presence in Ol'Kalou West encompassed, not 13 per cent, but more than one-third of the scheme's total land area.[15] In chapter 6, we came to the conclusion that low-density settlement, thanks to its more favourable terms and to the protection afforded by the World Bank, had systematically diverted settlement resources out of the hands of poor people and into those of better-off settlers. An examination of the situation within Ol'Kalou West suggests that a significant process of diversion was taking place within high-density settlement as well.

Population. It remains true, therefore, that settlement encompassed two different worlds, although that truth is complicated by the fact that one of the worlds had spilled over into the area supposedly reserved for the other. But the two worlds were very real nevertheless, and the differences between them were manifest, not only in the origins of the settlers, but also in the patterns of population that characterized each world. Those patterns also offer an insight into the social distribution of the burdens resulting from the problem of landlessness.

Once settlement got under way, it proved quite incapable of offering plots to the masses of people in need of them, whose numbers were swelled, not only by evictions from large-scale farms, but also by the process of settlement itself (see chapter 6). The government built a series of squatter villages to accommodate some of the many people who remained landless while, at the same time, continuing and extending the policy of selective settlement that had been established in the Million-Acre Scheme.

Some people, therefore, were living in squatter villages built by the government while they waited for the settlement plot that they hoped to win one day. But the villages could not begin to accommodate all the landless people. Furthermore, the government did not intend to accept permanent responsibility for the maintenance of squatter housing. In September 1965, as the settlement of Nyandarua neared completion, the special commissioner for squatters wrote to the Nyandarua district commissioner:

In my opinion, there is a great danger of allowing the [squatter] villages to continue as this will mean, among other things, that there will be a continued inflow of squatters from the neighbouring farms into the villages ... when these people move into the villages they become a government liability, leaving everything on their future squarely on the government's shoulders.

To avoid these unnecessary responsibilities on the part of the government, I feel that every effort should be made to induce the squatters to remain in the farms where they are currently residing. This can be done in two ways: firstly, by making the squatters realize that not everyone will get land and that as many of them as possible should try and be ready to be employed as farm workers, preferably in the farms in which they are already squatting. Secondly, by persuading the farm owners and particularly the new African settlers to allow the squatters to stay in the parts of the farms which they may not be using at the moment. It should be pointed out to the new African farmers that by keeping them that way, they would indeed be keeping a reservoir of labour for the time when their economic position improves to enable them to employ some labour. While this would initially be resisted by the farmers, it should not prove to be an impossible job to convince them of the wisdom of it ...[16]

In central Nyandarua District in the early 1970s – and presumably elsewhere in Kenya as well – the commissioner's suggestions had become a reality. The district officer in charge of Ol'Kalou Division said it was government policy to phase out squatter villages. Residents of the villages, he said, were being settled as plots for them became available. After each family left, the hut it had occupied was pulled down and the land made available for regular commercial or residential use.[17] The chief of Ol'Kalou Location confirmed that the policy was being implemented in his area. In the town of Passenga, for example, a village that had accommodated 110 families in 1965 had shrunk to about 50 by 1971.[18]

The government, then, was trying to reduce its responsibility for offering plots to people who had found no place in settlement. That responsibility was being left in private hands, as the commissioner for squatters had suggested. Who were the private individuals upon whom the burden of accommodating landless people had devolved? The ran-

TABLE 5
Comparison of high- and low-density population patterns (average population)

	Passenga (low density)		Ol'Kalou West
	Per unit	Per plot	(high density)
Total population	12.1	9.3	13.3
Nuclear family	8.6	6.6	8.5
Labourers and members of their families	2.1	1.6	0.7
Relatives	1.1	0.9	1.9
Others (squatters)	0.3	0.2	2.2

dom sample survey of Ol'Kalou West and Passenga shows that, in those two schemes, it was high-density settlers who had inherited the bulk of it.

The average population per farming unit was slightly higher in Ol'Kalou West, the high-density scheme, than in Passenga (see table 5), even though the resources available for the maintenance of those people were far greater in the latter. Passenga's annual target income was Shs 2000/-, compared with Ol'Kalou West's 800/-; and those figures, as noted earlier, substantially understate the real differences between the two types of plots. But that is only the beginning. The survey revealed that 12 of the 45 respondents in the Passenga sample (26.6 per cent) owned, not one, but two or three plots. The 45 respondents, among them, owned 59 plots. Table 5, therefore, has two columns for Passenga – one giving the averages per farming unit, regardless of whether that unit includes one, two, or three plots; and another for the averages per plot. (The Ol'Kalou West sample revealed no multiple units.) Although the average population per unit in Passenga was 12.1 – compared with 13.3 in Ol'Kalou West – the average per plot was only 9.3.

The sizes of nuclear families were similar for the two classes of settlers, with the result that, in this category too, the per-plot averages were lower in Passenga than in Ol'Kalou West. It is the other three categories, however, that reveal the most about the differences between high- and low-density schemes. If, for the sake of convenience, we multiply the per-plot averages in table 5 by 100, we find that 100 high-density plots supported 70 labourers, 190 relatives, and 200 squatters; the same number of low-density plots supported 160 labourers, 90 relatives, and only 20 squatters. Low-density settlers employed more than twice as many labourers as high-density plot-holders, while the latter were offering refuge to more than twice as many relatives as the former. At the same time, high-density settlers were supporting eleven times as many squatters as their low-density counterparts.

It comes as no surprise that better-off farmers with larger farms employ more labour than do poorer farmers. Nor are the relatively low numbers of relatives and squatters in low-density settlement hard to explain. Additional people, not working for the plot-holder, but sharing the space available to him or her for cultivation and husbandry, are an economic liability. But the same is also true for high-density settlers. Indeed, it is the more true because their chances of economic success are less to begin with, and can only be worsened by the presence of additional, non-productive residents. Why, therefore, would such settlers allow large numbers of relatives, and even of squatters who are not related to them, to live on their property?

Observations made in the course of this study – not only in the Ol'Kalou area, but also in other areas of the country[19] – suggest that the uneven distribution of obligation for the care of kin was a direct result of the uneven distribution of wealth. Kinship obligations, although they had lost some of their traditional force, continued to be taken very seriously. To be sure, better-off people were often accused of neglecting their kin, and there was undoubtedly some truth in that accusation. On the other hand, it was also clear that large numbers of better-off people took their obligations to kin very seriously. In discharging those obligations, however, they enjoyed considerable advantages over poor people. A high-density settler whose kin were landless might have no way of helping them other than to invite them to come and live with him. A more prosperous settler had a wide variety of options: He could buy a home and a cultivation plot for his parents; buy a share in a co-operative farm for one brother and use his political connections to get a settlement plot for another; he could pay school fees for a third until that brother was able to get a job and help support the rest of the family. In short, instead of having to care for his kin, he could use his resources to help them achieve independence. While better-off people, therefore, were able to create further wealth by sharing with their kin, the poor had nothing to share but their poverty.

That undoubtedly explains why high-density settlers had more kin to support than did low-density farmers. But what is the reason for the even more lopsided distribution of responsibility for squatters who were not relatives of the plot-holders? Here, too, it appears that we have a case of poverty – and powerlessness – begetting more poverty still. To begin with, the government had obviously been anxious, in so far as possible, to divest itself of its share of the responsibility. That point had been made explicit in the letter from the commissioner for squatters, quoted above, telling the district commissioner (hence the Nyandarua District administration) that the government should avoid 'unnecessary' responsibilities for squatters by 'persuading' farmers, 'particularly the new African settlers,' to accommodate them.

In Ol'Kalou West, the commissioner's suggestions were implemented, and the comments of settlers suggest that the tactics used were rather stronger than persuasion. Among the people interviewed for the present study, two were accommodating more than forty squatters each on their plots and neither thought he was at liberty to evict them, although both were annoyed at their presence and felt it interfered with their own husbandry. They, as well as others, said they had found squatters living on their plots when they first arrived in settlement. At least two plot-holders agreed that, in their view, it was not permissible to evict squatters from one's plot. One said explicitly that it was against settlement regulations to evict squatters and another – who was accommodating five families of squatters, numbering forty-three people – said that if he evicted them they could report him to the authorities. It seems clear, therefore, that high-density settlers were not persuaded, but told, to accommodate landless people.

In Passenga, matters stood differently. There, only three families of squatters, totalling twelve persons, were reported in the survey for the present study. They were living on two of Passenga's farming units, and both plot-holders gave every indication of having decided of their own free will to accommodate them. One plot-holder, indeed, reported that he was engaged in a business enterprise in partnership with the head of the squatter family. There were no reports of squatters residing on the scheme when plot-holders arrived.[20] The government's apparent policy of discouraging the eviction of squatters, therefore, had had the effect of unloading the bulk of the burden of landlessness upon the shoulders of high-density settlers. If the case of Ol'Kalou West and Passenga is typical, the poor people in the Million-Acre Scheme were being given the primary responsibility for the maintenance of those who had been passed over by settlement.

Economic activity. While high-density settlers were burdened with relatives and squatters, as well as substandard land and unconscionable debts, low-density plot-holders were free, not only to devote their re-

TABLE 6
Proportion of plot-holders engaged in non-agricultural pursuits (percentages)

| | Passenga plot-holders | Ol'Kalou West plot-holders | Ol'Kalou West | |
			Plot-holders with white-collar backgrounds	Plot-holders with non-white-collar backgrounds
Commercial enterprise or investment	40.5	6.8	50.0	1.5
Paid employment	31.8	12.3	57.1	7.6
Ownership of or interest in other land	25.6	9.5	25.0	7.6

sources and energies to agriculture, but also to seek a variety of other economic opportunities. The results of our survey in Passenga show that many of them preferred the latter.

For people who had skills that were usable in the modern economy, or who had money to invest, independence opened a wide variety of new opportunities. These included many kinds of employment, in business or the civil service, as well as investments in land, or in a multitude of commercial ventures, including retail stores, pubs and hotels, service stations and auto repair shops, town real estate, construction, flour mills, sawmills, and many more. It is not surprising that these opportunities were not equally available to everyone in the Million-Acre Scheme. Landless people, as a rule, had no skills to offer and no money to invest. As a result, only a small number of the settlers in Ol'Kalou West scheme had become involved in other areas of the economy: 7 per cent had made business investments, 12 per cent had found employment, and less than 10 per cent had invested in land (see table 6). Furthermore, a substantial proportion of these ventures had been undertaken by the handful of settlers in the sample who were not former members of the landless class but rather had held white-collar jobs before coming to settlement. Among the rest of the settlers, economic activity outside of their plots was minimal.

Passenga settlers were in a very different position than the poor people in Ol'Kalou West. Their personal resources – which had given most of them entrée to a favoured position within settlement – also opened many other opportunities to them, as table 6 shows. Of the settlers in the Passenga sample, more than 40 per cent had made commercial investments, almost one-third had jobs, and about 25 per cent owned other land. Only 25.9 per cent reported that they had no employment or economic interests outside of their plots. Twenty-five per cent said they were engaged in at least two of the areas of economic activity set out in table 6.

One result of this flurry of disparate economic activities was that many low-density farming units were being neglected. In more than half the Passenga sample, the owners of the plots were either absentees or were engaged in a full-time activity elsewhere (see table 7). Among the non-white-collar people in Ol'Kalou West, the rate was less than 6 per cent. Comments of settlement administrators in Nyandarua, as well as in other areas of settlement, suggested, on the one hand, that the situation in Passenga was a common one, and, on the other, that agricultural production in the Million-Acre Scheme suffered as a result of it. An agricultural official in the Turbo area, for example, said that, in his experience, the best farmers in settlement were those in low-density schemes who concentrated on agriculture and the next best were the more enterprising high-density farmers. Among the worst, he declared, were low-density absentee owners, whom he referred to as 'telephone farmers.' He estimated the absentee ownership rate on Turbo-area low-density plots at 10 to 20 per cent.[21] A settlement official directly in charge of the Turbo area's two low-density schemes offered a much gloomier assessment yet. He estimated the absentee ownership rate in the low-density schemes at two-thirds.

In the Sotik area, an agricultural official estimated the low-density absentee ownership rate at about 40 per cent. Some people, he said, had taken low-density plots 'for prestige' and farmed 'over the weekend and by telephone.' Others, who were not absentees, neglected their plots in favour of business enterprises in town.[22] An agricultural official in Nyandarua observed that low-density absentee owners often failed to give their managers sufficient authority to allow them to farm properly and that settlers with economic interests outside of their plots tended to neglect agriculture.[23]

AGRARIAN CLASSES AND ECONOMIC DEVELOPMENT

It is more than clear, from all this information, that peasant predominance in Kenya is combined with sharp class differentiation and ongoing

TABLE 7
Proportion of farming units lacking owners' full-time supervision (percentages)

| | | | Ol'Kalou West | |
| | | | Plots whose owners have white-collar backgrounds[1] | Plots whose owners have non-white-collar backgrounds |
	Passenga	Ol'Kalou West		
Absentee ownership: plot(s) not managed by owner	33.3	7.9	40.0	2.6
Owner manages plot(s), but has other, full-time[2] activity	17.8	8.1	50.0	3.0
Owner manages plot(s), but has other, part-time activity	4.4	5.3	11.1	4.6

[1]This column adds up to more than 100 per cent because the only three plot-holders who did not respond to the questions represented on this table happened to fall within the small group of white-collar people in Ol'Kalou West. All ten of the white-collar people responded to the first question and four, or 40 per cent, reported that they were absentees. Of eight responses to the second question, four, or 50 per cent, said they had other full-time activity. Nine responded to the third question and one (11.1 per cent) said he was engaged in part-time work away from the plot.
[2]A 'full-time' activity was defined as one that required at least several hours of the owner's time each working day throughout the year. Thus, for example, a plot-holder who also managed a store would be classified as having other full-time activity. Contract ploughing in the immediate vicinity would, however, be counted as part-time work because of its seasonal nature.

class formation. The point does not need to be stressed further, but it is time now to take the next step. It should be remembered that the real point of our discussion is not classes, but forces of production. In the passages cited in chapter 1, Leys was extolling the progressive qualities of the bourgeoisie, not in recognition of their sterling moral character – he acknowledged that they left something to be desired in that department – but because he believed they would expand the forces of production, that their dominance, and the eclipse of the peasantry and the petty bourgeoisie, would result in industrialization and ultimately prosperity for Kenya.

In these pages, I am arguing a contrary thesis: that it is technological advancement in agriculture rather than the establishment of industry which is likely to be at the heart of Kenya's development; that an expanding peasantry is a political fact of life in Kenya; and that this political fact need not stand as a block to Kenya's economic development, partly because small-scale agriculture is an efficient way of producing many commodities, and partly because it is clear that a peasant sector is capable of thriving alongside urban and rural bourgeoisies. These classes, along with the forces of production that each of them is expanding, are capable of coexisting.

But that does not mean that Kenyans are all one big, happy family, that each class and class fraction may go about the business it chooses confident that it is contributing to the nation's growing prosperity. No nation has ever achieved prosperity without conflict, without some groups gaining ascendence over others, and Kenya is unlikely to be an exception to that sombre rule. Nor is any country safe from the hazards of perverse development, of economic dominance by groups that enrich themselves without enriching the country – and indeed may impoverish it. Where then is the class struggle for Kenya's agricultural development located? Which classes are progressive and which ones are promoting perverse development? The final chapter of this study looks at Kenya in 1983 and addresses those questions.

8

Land and class in Kenya, 1972–83

The Kenya of 1983 had changed since the early 1970s, but the change did not seem discontinuous. It seemed rather to consist of further movement in a familiar direction. The expansion of peasant society, the intense and universal preoccupation with land, combined with an ongoing frenzy of capitalist wheeling and dealing were all still very much in evidence. Kenyans seemed more untroubled and self-confident in asserting their identity, and the last vestiges of colonialism had all but disappeared. A government campaign to promote Swahili – the only language virtually everyone in Kenya speaks – as *lugha ya taifa*, the national language, had done much to remove the stigma of inferiority that the colonial European community had sought to attach to it. In 1983, Swahili was spoken more and better than it had been a decade earlier. The final retreat of colonialism manifested itself in small but significant ways: 'Beware of the Dog' signs in Swahili only – a signal that the dogs were trained to attack Africans, but not Europeans – had become a rarity; gone, too, were the merchants who used to insist that their European customers jump queues while requiring Africans to wait their turn. Expatriate hostility had subsided. In 1973, a substantial section of the European community in Kenya had consisted of fiercely clannish little groups, frequenting their own clubs and each others' homes, full of a sense of their own superiority and of disdain for Kenya's independence and the changes it had brought. In 1983, those groups were no longer in evidence.

Up-country, agricultural centres like Nyahururu and Eldoret had boomed. Scores of new buildings had mushroomed, extending the cities beyond their old limits and giving them a more uniform appearance, so that the old *Barabara za Bwana Mkubwa*, referred to in the previous chapter, were no longer distinguishable from the former 'locations.' The word 'location,' as a way of designating a section of town, seemed to have lost its currency. Other name changes, too, were signs of the times. The small town of Hoey's Bridge, named after a former European settler, had been renamed Moi's Bridge by Kalenjin people in the Rift Valley who were visibly bursting with pride that one of their own, *Mtukufu Rais* Daniel arap Moi, had broken the Kikuyu monopoly at the centre of power to become president of Kenya. In Nyahururu, the local tourist hotel, the Thomson's Falls Lodge, retained its colonial name, but it had become Africanized. The dinner menu was bravely manning the last bastions of colonialism in the form of three-course breakfasts and five-course dinners, but the *à la carte* menu in the pub had yielded to the chips, grills, and fresh vegetables of majority rule.

The development of agrarian society in the 1970s and 1980s was characterized by a similar steady progress along predictable lines. The basic elements of the neo-colonial formula for the expansion of peasant society and the preservation of selected large-scale farming areas (described in chapter 5) proved remarkably durable. Landless people continued to be given modest peasant holdings in return for minimal down-payments; members of the bourgeoisies were also allowed, as before, to acquire such holdings, or to buy bigger ones at correspondingly higher prices; and the prospective landed upper bourgeoisie continued to purchase large-scale farms without the benefit of a settlement administration but with the help of government loans. If all that seems sane, rational, and well planned, the appearance is deceptive, for concealed beneath the apparent continuity were some very significant policy changes. And the continuities as well as the changes were powered by a massive scramble for land – the heaviest demand being for smallholdings – which placed the settlement authorities under intense political pressure. In the grip of the pressure, they gradually lost control of policy and were reduced to a purely reactive role, while peasant society expanded powerfully on all sides of them.

POLICY ISSUES

The settlement authorities, in adapting to the political realities of Kenya's transition to independence, were forced to change some of their major premises (see part II). Thus, after initially rejecting the idea of any settlement schemes for landless people, they reversed themselves and introduced a massive high-density scheme, primarily for landless people. In the process, they abandoned their initial resistance to a substantial expansion of peasant society. Likewise, they gave up their idea of maintaining a strict separation between peasant and bourgeois society, deciding, on the contrary, that a 'stabilizing' bourgeois presence within peasant society would work to their advantage.

Amid all that back-pedalling, one idea remained unchanged: Even if they had to make 'political' concessions to high-density settlement, 'economics' was on the side of the low-density settlers. Low-density settlement would be capable of meeting its objectives because it was aimed at farmers and business people who had proved their capabilities. High-density settlement, although it served a regrettably necessary political purpose, could not possibly be successful in economic terms because it was designed to accommodate people who were – as Hans Ruthenberg put it – 'poor or landless and who, more often than not, had failed somewhere else ...'[1] Opinions like these reflected the World Bank's policies of the 1960s – they were later changed to emphasize assistance to the rural poor[2] – and the bank was as alarmed by high-density settlement as it was supportive of low density (see chapter 5). The settlement authorities, fearful that they would lose the support of the bank, were therefore anxious to ensure that the privileged position of the more affluent settlers was in no way infringed.

The bank's views were shared by top levels of the settlement administration. A. Storrar, the colonial director of settlement, felt strongly enough about the issue to use his 1962–63 *Annual Report* as an occasion to lobby for low-density settlement and against the settlement of landless people.

Kenya's main national asset is the land, and its overall economy must, therefore, rest on reasonable use of this land provided subdivision does not become too small. It is, therefore, incumbent on the Government to recognize the fact that in order to achieve this, it would be much wiser to select smallholders and not to draw from a cadre of landless and unemployed ... experience is showing that resettlement in units of not less than subsistence plus Shs. 2,000/- [the low-density income target] ... is perfectly sound from the economic viewpoint, in that an increase in productivity can result and, at the same time, political aspirations can be reasonably satisfied.[3]

The settlement authorities bent every effort to make sure that the realities of settlement confirmed their views (see chapter 6). At every stage of the planning and implementation of settlement – in the choice of land and the setting of prices for it, through the manipulation of plot budgets, and in the allocation of technical assistance – they saw to it that high-density settlement was given short shrift, while low-density settlers got the best inputs available. One would have thought that those efforts, by themselves, would have been enough to ensure the failure of high-density settlement, even if the theory favouring more affluent settlers had been misconceived.

It was not enough, however. The theory proved to be so thoroughly misconceived that a pair of economic studies done in the late 1960s concluded that high-density settlement was, if anything, doing somewhat better than low density, despite the administration's systematic bolstering of the latter at the expense of the former. The government's *Economic Appraisal of the Settlement Schemes* showed that, from 1964 to 1968, farm profits per acre grew considerably faster on high-density schemes than on low-density schemes, and that, although the high-density schemes began the period with lower profits, they ended with higher ones (see table 8A). The return on capital invested in settlement schemes followed a similar pattern: high-density settlement began the period at a lower level, but ended higher (table 8B). The comparison of cash surpluses on the two types of schemes was less clear-cut, but not noticeably to the advantage of low-density settlement (table 8C) – despite the fact that high-density plots were budgeted for substantially lower incomes. The results in two further categories of comparison – the proportion of farms achieving a positive cash surplus (table 8D) and the proportion reaching the target income (table 9) – also failed to reveal any superiority in the performance of low-density settlement. In output per acre (table 10), low-density settlers did come off better, but even here the results were not uniformly favourable to them. The report said: 'Although output grew more quickly on the High Density schemes (with the exception of 1967–68), the level of output was substantially greater on the Low Density schemes ... Nevertheless ... in 1966–67 output per acre on the High Density farms exceeded that on the Low Density farms.'[4]

In another extensive economic survey of the settlement program, comparisons of high-density and low-density schemes yielded similarly mixed results. The author concluded: 'A comparison between high and low-density farms does not show any clear superiority of one or the other settlement type. At low altitudes the low-density farms gained better results, at high altitudes the exact opposite was true.'[5] In a sober

TABLE 8
The profitability of Kenya settlement schemes, 1964–68

Survey year	High-density schemes	Low-density schemes
A *Growth of farm profits: net profit in Shs per acre*		
1964–65	−1	39
1965–66	32	35
1966–67	73	30
1967–68	90	73
B *Return on capital invested: percentages*		
1964–65	5.4	15.3
1965–66	15.5	13.5
1966–67	20.8	12.8
1967–68	29.6	18.9
C *Cash surplus: Shs per farm*		
1964–65	−308	−529
1965–66	−56	193
1966–67	414	−25
1967–68	30	355
D *Positive cash surplus: percentage of farms*		
1964–65	33.5	44.1
1965–66	42.1	42.3
1966–67	48.6	42.0
1967–68	41.8	45.1

SOURCE: Statistics Division, Ministry of Finance and Economic Planning, *An Economic Appraisal of the Settlement Schemes 1964–5 to 1967–8*, Farm Economic Survey Report No. 27 (Nairobi 1971), 39–42

second look, therefore, it became questionable whether the substantial loan funds and administrative resources that had been pumped into low-density settlement were a justifiable use of public funds. High-density settlement, by the same token, began to look like a much better investment than it had at first.

The relative value of high- and low-density settlement was not the only shibboleth of the early 1960s that came to be regarded as dubious in the 1970s. An article of faith even more fervently professed by the settlement authorities during the transition to independence was the belief in

TABLE 9
Performance of settlement schemes in relation to target income, 1964–68

Target income group (Shs per farm)	Proportion of farms reaching target income (%)			
	1964–65	1965–66	1966–67	1967–68
500	6.3	20.8	17.1	69.2
800	13.6	14.7	27.1	21.1
1400	5.7	6.2	13.2	14.5
2000	7.5	15.8	12.5	19.8

SOURCE: Statistics Division, Ministry of Finance and Economic Planning, *An Economic Appraisal of the Settlement Schemes 1964–65 to 1967–68*, Farm Economic Survey Report No. 27 (Nairobi 1971), 45

TABLE 10
Growth of output on settlement schemes, 1964–68

Scheme group	Survey year	Output per acre (Shs)	Annual growth rate (%)
High density	1964–65	53	–
	1965–66	88	66.0
	1966–67	135	53.4
	1967–68	149	10.4
Low density	1964–65	131	–
	1965–66	134	2.3
	1966–67	116	–13.4
	1967–68	182	56.9

SOURCE: Statistics Division, Ministry of Finance and Economic Planning, *An Economic Appraisal of the Settlement Schemes 1964–65 to 1967–68*, Farm Economic Survey Report No. 27 (Nairobi 1971), 31

the importance of preserving as much as possible of Kenya's large-scale agriculture. Large farms were extolled as essential to the maintenance of agricultural export markets and domestic food supplies and as indispensable in the maintenance of employment. In chapter 5, we saw that these arguments were questionable, especially in regard to the productive capacity of large-scale mixed farming, which was so dependent on government subsidies as to constitute no asset at all, and perhaps a net liability. By the 1970s, a significant body of expert opinion was raising ever more serious questions about large farms. Their importance as employers proved a chimera,[6] while, at the same time, the growing successes of small farmers in an ever-wider variety of agricultural pursuits strengthened the case for small-scale agriculture as an alternative.[7] The position of large-scale agriculture was further weakened by the fact that many of the Africans who bought large-scale farms soon found themselves in financial difficulties and needed government assistance to bail them out.[8] By 1974, the government was officially taking the position that large-scale agriculture – although it was still welcome – was necessary only in a limited number of pursuits, including the production of wheat and hybrid seed maize and the maintenance of breeding herds of livestock. In the long run, smallholder production would grow in importance while, by implication, the relative importance of large farms would decline.[9] Once again, the conventional wisdom had taken an about-face since the mid-1960s.

POLITICAL PRESSURES

It is difficult for the non-agriculturalist to judge the extent to which these conclusions represent agricultural science and to what degree they reflect politics – if indeed the two can be separated. What is clear is that the conclusions are well in line with the trends developing in Kenya's agrarian system in the 1970s. These trends, we must emphasize again, were not limited to 'peasantization:' They involved the development of peasant society in concert with capitalism and alongside a flourishing bourgeoisie. Despite the potential for clash among them, these tendencies were able to develop simultaneously because their development did not take place primarily at each others' expense. The peasants and the bourgeoisies who invested in peasant holdings continued to expand into unoccupied or underutilized areas. In many cases, members of the bourgeoisie were able to play intermediary roles in the provision of small-holdings for landless people and peasants and to profit personally from that activity. The landed bourgeoisie expanded, and in the 1970s they were able, with state assistance, to play the same dominant role in setting the terms and conditions of land transfer that European settlers had played vis-à-vis peasant settlement in the 1960s.

Africanization of large farms. One of the main purposes of the Million-Acre Settlement Scheme and associated land transfer program was to ensure the stability of Kenya's market in land. Despite many other changes in the program, that objective remained a constant throughout the transition to independence, and it was achieved. Indeed, the authorities overshot their objective. They went beyond the achievement of stability to the creation of an investment climate that proved highly attractive to foreign and expatriate capital. By 1967, non-citizen individuals and companies had bought up almost as much land as had been earmarked for smallholder settlement,[10] and it became obvious that the Africanization of the former White Highlands could be thwarted by the operation of market forces. Prospective African land buyers, finding themselves outbid by foreign money, secured the passage of the Land Control Act, whereby district-level boards were given the power to vet land transactions.[11]

The operation of the land divisional boards created the opening that the prospective landed bourgeoisie were looking for. Apollo Njonjo, in a meticulous study of land transactions in Kiambu and Nakuru districts in the late 1960s and early 1970s, found that the boards acted forcefully in the interests of prospective African land buyers. In Kiambu, which had been particularly heavily infiltrated by foreign capital during the 1960s, he found that 'the upsurge of foreign capital ... came suddenly to a halt in 1972 ...'[12] Not only foreign individuals and companies, but also non-African Kenyan citizens preparing to sell land to other non-Africans, found their proposed transactions coming under the close scrutiny of the boards. Njonjo cites a number of examples in which boards refused to permit sales of land to non-Africans, forcing prospective sellers to deal with Africans instead, and one in which a company that tried to circumvent the Kiambu Land Board was later refused a mortgage and forced into receivership.[13] In another case, a European preparing to sell land to a group of African buyers at what the Nakuru Land Board considered an excessive price was required to submit his land to valuation and then forced to sell at the valuer's price, even though he did not wish to sell at that price.[14]

Obviously, the land boards had taken their gloves off, and their rough treatment of foreign capital provoked angry reactions in the British press.[15] But if we judge the boards' actions by the standards of probity in the acquisition of land that the British themselves established in Kenya in the colonial era (see chapter 2), we would have to characterize them as remarkably restrained. The pity is that, although the government was able to act vigorously in defence of Africans who had managed to prosper in the colonial era, it never summoned up a similar determination to take action on behalf of colonialism's most abused victims.

Whatever judgments one may make about them, the facts are clear. Even as peasant society continued to expand, a significant landed bourgeoisie established itself in the former White Highlands. In 1977, a report to the Ministry of Agriculture declared: 'The process of transfer of ownership of land to Kenyan citizens is now well advanced. In the mixed farming sub-sector it is almost complete.'[16] A substantial expatriate presence remained, and seemed to be entirely welcome, in the highly capitalized plantation and ranch sectors, but the highlands could no longer be called white.

Continued expansion of smallholder settlement. The Million-Acre Settlement Scheme (long since grown beyond a million acres) continued to expand, though at a much reduced rate, throughout the 1970s and into the 1980s. The policies that were followed reflected above all a continued intense pressure, both from landless people and from the bourgeoisies, for the multiplication of smallholdings. Indeed they were less policies than a series of expedients, each one designed under pressure to come to terms with a particular set of circumstances.

The pattern of ad hoc responses to unforeseen circumstances was already being established in the late 1960s, as the high- and low-density schemes described in chapter 5 were in the process of being completed. At the same time, the Department of Settlement planned a program (dubbed Harambee settlement), the rationale for which was that settlers were to be carefully selected, as in the World Bank-financed low-density program, but that they were to be given more modest plots, with projected target incomes of Shs 800/- to 1200/- in place of the World Bank's 2000/-. However, only two Harambee schemes were established, after which the program was quietly dropped for reasons which are undoubtedly related to the failure (discussed above) of the theory on which they were based.

In the meantime, other agencies besides the Department of Settlement were becoming involved in settlement. The Provincial Administration instituted a series of settlements for landless people called Jet schemes. A series of irrigation schemes, begun in the colonial period, were eventually taken over by the National Irrigation Board. Another settlement program grew out of the abandonment of some farms by European owners who fled the country during the transition to independence, either because they misunderstood the character of the transition or because they had special reasons of their own – debts they had incurred or enemies they had made – for fearing majority rule. The government, anxious to avoid anything that smacked of expropriation, was unwilling to make a final disposition of such cases without consulting the former owners. But because of the intensity of pressure from landless people, the land was made available to the commissioner for squatters (see chapter 7) for schemes that could provide a temporary accommodation while the government traced former owners and negotiated clear title to the land.

Eventually clear titles were obtained and the temporary schemes, having been taken over by the Department of Settlement, were established as a permanent part of its program, called Haraka schemes, after the Swahili word for 'haste.' Another scheme, begun in the mid-1970s as high-potential land began to be harder to obtain, involved the identification of state-owned land (remote areas or more arid land not previously considered for smallholder settlement), which could now be made available. By the end of 1982, according to the Department of Settlement, its Million-Acre, Harambee, Haraka, and Stateland schemes together comprised more than 670 000 hectares and accommodated almost 64 000 families.

These figures should be regarded with caution, for they have been generated in an atmosphere of permanent crisis. In truth, the department was less in charge of settlement than being dragged along by it, and barely managing to hold on. In the process, its affairs had fallen into disarray. For example, the figure for the number of families settled is not, strictly speaking, based on fact, because it actually refers to the number of plots demarcated and – as we have seen already – many people own more than one plot, while many plots accommodate more than one family. Perhaps the two phenomena balance each other out, but there is no way of knowing that.

More significantly, the hectarage figure may not be reliable either. A few random calculations have revealed that there is no stable relationship between the department's figures for the total number of plots, on the one hand, and the average plot size, on the other. For example Sabharwal scheme in Kwale District and Mtwapa in Kilifi were both listed as having average plot sizes of 4.85 hectares. However, according to the department, Sabharwal had 20 plots on 202 hectares, which works out to an average size of 10.1 and Mtwapa had 607 plots on 1369 hectares, an average of 2.26.[17] One might try to explain the former discrepancy in terms of allowances for roads or other public facilities, were it a more modest one; the latter defies any explanation at all that would preserve the integrity of the figures. More likely the discrepancies arose when officials were forced to make concessions to political pressures they did not dare acknowledge. For example one scheme might prove attractive to members of the bourgeoisies, who would mobilize their political connections to secure plots bigger than those called for in the policy, while another might be under pressure from landless people who would lack the down payment for standard-sized plots or from politicians who would want to take credit for settling their landless constituents.

If those were the explanations, there would be nothing unusual about them. Land is Kenya's obsession, as order is Germany's and self-sufficiency is Israel's. In 1983, the obsession was palpable everywhere. Settlement officers and administrative officers were besieged by land seekers. People at all levels of society, from shanty dwellers to high officials, wrote letters to the Department of Settlement claiming to be landless and asking to be awarded a settlement plot. According to one well-placed source, the department had to abandon the use of hectarage conversions (the adjustment of a plot's size to take account of its fertility) because the field officials responsible for making the conversions were being bribed to 'adjust' their figures to favour some plot-holders over others. As a result, the department was placed in the ludicrous position of awarding uniform-sized plots regardless of fertility, so that one plot-holder might get 4.85 hectares of good topsoil while another got the same amount of stony or waterlogged land. In short, the pressure for the expansion of peasant society was far more intense than the pressure from prospective buyers of large farms. It is small wonder that the settlement authorities have been unable to maintain control of the situation. Not even in a police state would it be possible to control Kenya's groundswell of land hunger, and Kenya is decidedly not a police state.

Although they lacked control over the settlement process, the authorities had every intention of allowing it to continue. In early 1983, settlement planners were mooting agricultural development programs for some 13 000 Haraka plots in Kilifi, Kwale, Murang'a, and Kiambu districts and at Yatta. New settlement was being planned as well. German funds had been obtained for some 5000 new plots in Stateland schemes in Kilifi and Lamu districts. Locations had been identified for further state land programs in Lamu and Tana River districts, while less definite plans were under development for small-scale ranches and for thousands of new plots in Kilifi, Kwale, and Taita-Taveta districts.

Peasantization of group-owned farms. Africanization of the highlands meant the establishment of an African landed bourgeoisie, while expansion of smallholder settlement illustrated two other themes: the expansion of peasant society and the authorities' loss of control over policy in the face of intense political pressure. A third subject, the fate of group-owned farms, illustrates all three themes, for such farms have served as a vehicle for the establishment of new peasant holdings while figuring prominently in various schemes of bourgeois aggrandizement, including some of the most reckless in the nation's recent history. Through it all, the government has failed to maintain firm control over policy and, indeed, has been just able to prevent chaos.

From early in the settlement program, the plans for land transfer included provision for co-operative farms. In the beginning, they were conceived of as a desperate last resort for such land as the Ol'Kalou Salient, which not only failed to meet the standards for inclusion in low-density settlement, but was too marginal even to be usable in the high-density program (see chapter 5). Since the Salient and similar areas were just barely suitable for certain large-scale agricultural pursuits, such as the growing of wheat, it was hoped to salvage them by giving small subsistence plots to the settlers and then hiring professional management to work the rest of the land as a large farm.

The Salient did not work out as a co-operative farm and was converted to a large state farm, but in the early 1970s, the idea of co-operative farms as a vehicle for smallholder settlement was revived in a new context. At that time, the settlement authorities were still working under the influence of the idea that it was essential to preserve much of Kenya's large-scale farming sector intact – an idea later revised. As the Million-Acre Scheme wound down, while the pressure for the multiplication of peasant holdings continued unabated, the authorities decided to convert co-operatives from a desperate last resort for the settlement of hopeless areas to a positive policy instrument. The government would purchase large farms which, according to the reasoning of the time, should be preserved as such, and allocate them to groups of smallholders, each of whom would receive a subsistence plot and a share in the professionally managed farm. The program was named Shirika.

But the plan did not work, partly because the authorities changed their minds about the importance of preserving large-scale farms, but much more fundamentally because they found that Kenyan society was a rocky soil on which to plant the seeds of collective enterprise. It became clear that most farmers – whether peasants, urban dwellers interested in part-time agriculture, or prospective members of the agrarian bourgeoisie – were not interested in sharing landownership with others. They wanted their own farms, small or large. Already in 1973, a survey of large-scale co-operative farms identified inadequate management as the main problem of the co-operative farms it studied and attributed the problem, in some cases, to the fact that 'the attitude of the members is towards the individual ownership of plots and cattle ... Those members see the co-operative only as a means to get their own private land, and as soon as the loans are repaid they want to split the farm.'[18] In a similar vein, the report said: 'Members tend on several farming societies to put their houses and select the best fields for their subsistence plots ... with the result that the farms are left with the poorer areas for farming and have difficulties in operating as profitable farming units.'[19]

A 1977 consultants' report to the Ministry of Agriculture reached similar conclusions, but stated them more emphatically and carried the reasoning a step farther to project, and to commend, a long-term trend toward subdivision of large-scale farms into smallholdings. The report found 'poor performance' in group-owned coffee estates, and particularly in mixed farms.[20] It noted that 'up to 35 per cent of the total land area of mixed farms' – and 56 per cent of those owned by large groups – had been subdivided into smallholdings.[21] 'Group farming,' the consultants stated flatly, 'is alien to the traditions and aspirations of most group farm members. Their primary concern is to own and operate their own individual holding.' And time could only make matters worse.

Kenya's population will at least double over the next 25 years. Given the limited availability of cultivable land and the dominance of the agricultural sector as a source of employment, the resultant increase in land pressure is the most serious problem facing Kenya today and increasingly so in the future. The population densities in the main large farm districts are much lower than those in neighbouring small scale areas of similar agricultural potential ... It is therefore inevitable that the increase in land pressure will be directed increasingly towards the large farms and their continued existence ... will become increasingly difficult to defend ...[22]

Furthermore, in a comparison of large-scale farms with units of twenty hectares or less, the consultants concluded that the latter had substantial advantages. Their intensity of land use and gross input were as high or higher and they generated more employment, while their production costs per unit of output were lower. Nor were their high production figures being negated by high consumption, as one might assume of peasant holdings. The consultants found that even marketed output per hectare was at least as high as on larger farms. Finally, they pointed out that the government would find development programs for smallholders easier to staff than large-scale programs.[23] They recommended that the government permit subdivision of group farms wherever the carrying capacity of the land and the company or co-operative membership was such as to make for commercially viable smallholdings.[24]

At the same time, the report implicitly sounded a warning. It pointed out that there were group farms 'on which the number of members is greater than the area could support as individual commercial small-holders or sometimes even as subsistence farmers.'[25] But it made no recommendations as to what to do about such cases, saying only that subdivision should be permitted 'provided that the individual's holding size would be large enough to allow a balanced farming system to be practised.'[26] That recommendation begged the question for which, as it turned out, no one else had an answer either.

But by this time events were already running ahead of the authorities. They once again lost control over policy as the poor and the more affluent alike exerted intense political pressure for the breakup of Shirika farms into different-sized peasant holdings to suit different thicknesses of wallets. In 1978, the Department of Settlement was ordered to increase the size of the standard one-hectare subsistence plot on Shirika farms to two hectares. Next, according to well-placed officials, more affluent land seekers secured larger holdings, sometimes with buildings, thereby undermining the viability of the large-scale farming operations. Thus the authorities were forced to undertake an across-the-board program of subdivision. In 1979, the Ministry of Lands and Settlement was reorganized, with the Department of Settlement coming under the direct control of the Office of the President, presumably to bring the subdivision process under close political control. Until 1982, when the department was released from the supervision of the Office of the President, settlement officials were preoccupied with the subdivision of Shirika farms. The task was said to be nearing completion in early 1983. According to the department's 1982 figures, Shirika farms – including those already subdivided together with those awaiting subdivision – comprised more than 100 000 hectares and accommodated more than 15 000 families. These figures should be treated with the same caution accorded the figures for the rest of the settlement program, and for the same reasons. For what they are worth, however, they suggest that the amount of land included in the settlement program as a whole was nearing 800 000 hectares (the million acres of the 1960s were not far from becoming a million hectares) and that almost 80 000 families had been settled.

The headlong rush into peasantization that was dragging the Department of Settlement along with it was also occurring in the private sector. Indeed, it had been going on since the beginning of land transfer; and from 1963 until 1983, 24 000 private land-buying firms were registered in Kenya.[27] That figure includes companies that had failed to obtain land, as well as upper-bourgeois companies, and is therefore not a reliable indicator of the extent of peasantization, but it does give some sense of the magnitude and intensity of the phenomenon of group land buying. The procedures followed were not unlike those that had produced Shirika farms. An individual or group would form a co-operative society or a company and offer to sell memberships or shares, often thousands of them, in order to raise the funds for purchase of a large-scale farm or ranchland. Normally, members – like Shirika settlers – would be offered a piece of land, together with a share in the proceeds of the farm's operation. Different land-buying groups included people from different levels of society: Some groups consisted of landless people; other co-operatives and companies – by virtue of higher share prices – were open only to the affluent.

The organization of land buying became a focus for bourgeois aggrandizement. Political careers were built on the management of companies and co-operative societies as directors went on to stand for public office, using society members as part of their political base. In time, too, it became obvious that personal fortunes had been built in the same way, especially as reports of mismanagement of funds began to circulate. One of the most spectacular cases – illustrative of the whole course of events – was that of Kihika Kimani, who rose to fame and fortune as founder and chairman of the 55 000-member Ngwataniro Mutukanio Farmers' Company. He went on to become MP for Nakuru North and a director of Gema Holdings Corporation, which, according to Nicola Swainson, 'has acted to link up capital raised in the agricultural and merchant sectors with industry – it is the clearest instance of the large-scale *concentration* of indigenous capital.'[28] In February 1983, Kihika was reported to have fled the country amid charges that he had misappropriated nearly Shs 50 million belonging to the company.

Even more than Shirika farms, the private-sector land-buying organizations manifested the raw power of the social forces engaged in the scramble for land. Chaos was never far from the surface and the government was always hard put to keep it from erupting. One of the most famous, or notorious, of the land-buying companies was NDEFFO, which consisted of squatters who were ex-members of the Land Freedom Army. NDEFFO began its colourful career in agriculture by seizing a farm and forcing the government to negotiate transfer of the land. The squatters got their land but, significantly, ended up paying double the price at which the land had earlier been offered for sale.[29]

According to Robert Buijtenhuijs, the government dealt with the threat of further land seizures by lionizing NDEFFO, raising it to the status of the only legitimate Mau Mau land claimant, and then dealing harshly with other groups that had similar ambitions.[30] When NDEFFO's financial difficulties caught up with it, its potential for violence turned in on itself as five leaders who were accused of mismanagement were massacred by their members. In the early 1980s, another farm company leader, Moses Kamau Mbogo, was hacked to death after a heated company meeting in which some 200 members demanded subdivision of their 300-hectare farm. In February 1983, with land scandal headlines filling the press, the Rift Valley provincial commissioner, Hezekiah Oyugi, ordered all land-buying companies in the province to subdivide their land and allocate it to shareholders. The Kiambu District commissioner in Central Province followed suit with an order to companies in the district to allocate plots to their shareholders or refund their money. It appeared as if the private-sector organizations were becoming unravelled in much the same way as the Shirika farms had. Once again the power of an expanding peasant society was crushing the organizations that stood in its way – but not before the bourgeoisie had had time to skim off some profit.

Many of the policy calculations of the 1960s, and even the 1970s, had been brusquely swept aside. And it was not just a matter of abandoning the idea of maintaining much of Kenya's large-scale agriculture intact. By all appearances, that was no great loss, indeed very likely a net gain. But even the strongest supporters of smallholder agriculture have acknowledged that there are some agricultural activities (the growing of wheat, for example) whose viability on a small scale is questionable and that in lower-potential areas a family cannot support itself on a tiny hectarage. One of the most worrying aspects of the inexorable expansion of peasant society is that it has taken place regardless of even such minimal, common-sense strictures. Chapters 5 and 6 deal with many examples of unviable plots allocated through the Million-Acre Scheme. In the more recent fragmentation of companies and co-operatives, it is clear that there have been similar casualties, though their extent has not yet been recorded.

One example, however, is the Ol'Kalou Salient. We have already seen that it was considered a difficult agricultural area, even for the growing of wheat on a large scale, and that it was never considered suitable for smallholder settlement. In order to be able to use it anyway, the government made it a co-operative farm in the transition to independence. When that organization did not produce satisfactory results, it was converted into a state farm, which was not successful either. All of these problems did not prevent the Salient from being subjected to the ubiquitous pressures for peasantization. In 1973, in the circumspect wording of the Department of Settlement's *Annual Report*, 'approval was given for the number of settlers to be increased from 1,808 to 2,500 and each was allocated five acres [about two hectares], unlike the previous years when each family was allocated with only two-acre non-permanent subsistence plots.'[31]

In 1975, department officials were still protesting that the area, because of its 'marginal soil, topography and climate ... was ... uneconomical if subdivided into small plots.'[32] In 1976, the customary section on the Salient was quietly dropped from the annual report, perhaps because the area, in violation of all expert opinion, was on the way to being subdivided. In 1983, the subdivision was complete, with much of the area – and especially the poorer land – subdivided into two-hectare plots. Officials were desperately searching for an agricultural system that would make those plots viable and were declaring, with an optimism that was as unconvincing as it was dogged, that they would find one. Meanwhile, according to officials, plots of up to forty hectares had been allocated in the Salient's Malewa River Valley – an area visibly more fertile than the surrounding land – to settlers who had larger down payments to offer.

THE AGRARIAN SYSTEM: A CLASS ANALYSIS

This chapter confirms the main conclusions to be drawn from the material in previous chapters: Kenya society is marked by a powerful expansion of its peasant sector. That expansion is not an alternative to capitalist development; on the contrary, the development of the capitalist classes and of capitalism is intertwined with, and heavily dependent upon, a thriving peasantry, which is so important a part of the nation's productive capacity. Nor does it imply, as some commentators seem to suggest, a static or stable society. The expansion itself is highly dynamic, as has been demonstrated in these chapters, and it spawns conflict on all sides. Both the settlement schemes and the breakup of group-owned farms have entailed struggles of landless people against the landed classes; exploitation of small landowners by various sections of the bourgeoisie; and struggles among the various landed classes for the best benefits land has to offer.

But conflict over the best benefits a system has to offer is one thing. Conflict over the survival of the system itself is quite another. What are the limits of Kenya's present agrarian system? I have argued that it can continue to expand along current lines as long as there is unoccupied or underutilized land available. How long will that be, and what will happen when all the land is taken up? Another set of questions suggests itself as well. A thriving peasantry, far from being an obstacle that must be eliminated by an industrializing bourgeoisie, can be a mainstay of Kenya's development, a development that would be centred on agriculture, although it would necessarily include industry as well. If that is true, then how can it become a reality? Is Kenya's agrarian system evolving along a path that can lead to prosperity? Or are there signs in the agrarian system of the perverse development (referred to in chapter 1) feared by dependency theorists? These questions cannot be answered definitively, of course, but some greater understanding of them can be provided by a class analysis of Kenya's agrarian system. Drawing on propositions put forward in the preceding pages, the following analysis divides Kenya's agrarian society into five categories.

1 *Landless people.* The effort to count landless people is one of Kenya's longest-running exercises in futility. Chapter 3 showed that the Kenya Land Commission, the East African Royal Commission, and M.P.K. Sorrenson stumbled over the question of how to conceptualize the different categories of Africans resident outside their reserves. If the task was difficult in the 1930s, it seems impossible in the 1980s. For one thing, with smallholdings available in different parts of the country through different channels – including, among others, the Department of Settlement, the provincial administrations, and private land-buying companies – there is no way of knowing who has land and who has none. For another, the phenomenon of people from all walks of life using every conceivable strategem to get themselves declared landless so that they may be awarded a settlement plot, combined with that of an administration anxious to take credit for settling landless people, is more than enough to undermine the credibility of any official information on landlessness.

But even if the numbers of landless people cannot be determined, the problem of landlessness remains real and acute. Although the settlement of landless people is an ongoing process, it will not result in the settlement of all landless people, for at least three reasons: because a significant proportion of settlement plots are being diverted into the hands of people who are not landless; because the ethnic rigidities observed in chapter 5 (under the heading 'Geography of Settlement') leave some areas of the country overpopulated while others still have an excess of land; and because one of the highest population growth rates in the world[33] is creating landlessness faster than it can be eliminated. A peasant family on a small hectarage will not be able to provide for its heirs on the same hectarage. The children who cannot be provided for on the family plot will either become poverty-stricken, in which case they will become eligible for the plots being allocated to landless people, or they will prosper, in which case they will join the ranks of petty bourgeois and bourgeois contenders for land, who necessarily will be in competition with future generations of landless people for a dwindling supply of land. By virtue of Kenya's current social dynamic, therefore, landlessness is a revolving door: the forces that place some people on the land push others off it. But as long as new land is available, the door can keep turning, and peasant society can continue to expand. Only when all available land is taken up does the revolving door become a passage market 'Exit Only.' Then the expansion of peasant society must cease and Kenya's development will enter a new phase.

2 *Uncaptured peasants.* This subclass, drawn from the analysis of Goran Hyden (see chapter 1), consists of people who can and do produce for the market, but who do not feel compelled to do so on a regular basis and are therefore free to withdraw into subsistence agriculture whenever market strictures, taxes, or government regulations become too onerous. 'Compelled' is the appropriate word, for few subsistence farmers who have not already formed the habit of producing regularly for the market will take up doing so without some strong extrinsic motivation. The ordinary life of a peasant family – farming with hand implements, building and maintaining housing by hand, fetching and carrying heavy loads on foot – is quite hard enough without adding to it the quantity and quality controls and the demanding schedules that go with regular production for the market. Peasants can be forced into the pressure cooker of the capitalist market through taxation, through land shortages, and through the threat that their children will not prosper if

they do not get an expensive education; or they can be lured by the enticing proximity of consumer goods and machinery. But as long as they can separate themselves, physically and/or psychologically, from such pressures, few will take them on voluntarily.

In Kenya, because of taxation, land shortages in some areas, and the longstanding proximity of a capitalist economy, a substantial proportion of the peasantry have long been captured. But, even in the 1980s, there remains a diminishing minority of uncaptured peasants, generally older people no longer able to adapt to new ways or people in more remote areas of the country. Early in the 1970s, it had become obvious that the Million-Acre Scheme included a proportion of uncaptured peasants. Throughout settlement in 1971, administrative officers complained about settlers who would not, or could not, develop their plots. Many of them had concluded on their own that a settlement plot, with a debt burden that forced production for the market, was not for them, and by that year, in the Uasin Gishu and Trans Nzoia districts of the Rift Valley, hundreds had sold their plots and left.[34] In the years that followed, there was a steady stream of such sales. Many of the sellers moved on to Shirika farms, where they were able to get subsistence plots and to leave the burden of market agriculture primarily on the shoulders of the co-operative farm manager. To a significant degree, therefore, Shirika farms, as well as a proportion of group-owned farms in the private sector, functioned as a welfare program for uncaptured peasants. The breakup of group-owned farms, by the same token, has thrown many of them back on their own resources, often with a piece of land that is inadequate for market agriculture.

From the viewpoint of settlement officials under pressure to collect loan repayments, the loss of uncaptured peasants was their gain, for it generally meant an exchange of farmers unmotivated to engage in cash agriculture and sluggish in meeting their payments for others better able to pay. Later, the settlement authorities developed another technique to achieve similar objectives. As it became obvious that uncaptured peasants were, on the one hand, not making full use of their land from a market perspective and, on the other, not meeting their payments, it was decided that they could get along with less land. Thus they were pressured to make their payments and, if they could not, were 'allowed' to subdivide their land, selling off part of it. Since land prices were rising, it was possible to arrange deals in which an uncaptured peasant would sell part of his land, realizing enough money to pay off the loan while retaining enough land for subsistence. In the early 1980s, subdivisions had become a common phenomenon in settlement, and administrative officers reported that agriculture was much improved as a result. It would be pleasant to report that the same is true of the lives of the people forced to subdivide, but that is unlikely to be the case.

Some of the more remote areas of the country – parts of the coast, for example – are primarily populated by uncaptured peasants, and such areas are visibly developing far more slowly than other regions. It might be argued, as Hyden did in Tanzania's case, that the uncaptured peasant is one of the blocks to development, one of the factors that could contribute to perverse development or stagnation rather than to development for prosperity. Hyden gave qualified support to some of the Tanzanian government's more coercive agricultural policies on the grounds that these would help to capture peasants and thereby promote agricultural development. In Kenya, such policies are not in the cards. There, economic pressure is politically acceptable, but administrative coercion is not. The subdivision and sale of the lands of peasants in debt has not raised political storms, especially since the government appears to have been scrupulous in ensuring that no one was left landless by such transactions. But the idea of the government using taxation or regulations to force agricultural improvement is anathema. Although most Kenyans in the 1980s are too young to have a personal recollection of the forced labour and the coercive agricultural improvement campaigns of the colonial era, 'remembering,' in the collective sense, is a serious preoccupation, in line with Kenyatta's powerful dictum: We will forgive, but we cannot forget. Accordingly, no politician would dare to make proposals smacking of the coercive measures of the colonial era.

In the more remote areas, therefore, where uncaptured peasants are still able to insulate themselves to some degree from the market, they will probably be allowed to continue in that way until demographic and market pressures catch up with them. That, undoubtedly, is as it should be, since it seems doubtful whether coercion would be successful in any case, and there are potentially more fruitful and politically more acceptable avenues for the pursuit of agricultural improvements.

3 *Captured peasants.* This category includes people who are full-fledged, full-time peasants in the sense that they must rely on small-scale agriculture for their living. They are captured in the sense that they are committed to regular production for the market. It seems likely that it was their presence in high-density schemes that was largely responsible for the fact that that part of the program out-performed low-density settlement. During the transition to independence, both settlement offi-

cials and international aid agencies seriously underestimated these people, assuming that their lack of financial resources was a sign of their lack of ability as farmers. Since then, both the Kenya government and the World Bank have changed their attitudes, as is evidenced by the belated recognition of the importance of giving support to small-scale agriculture.

But the policy-makers' re-evaluation of their position has not been precise enough, for in fact a policy of support for small-scale agriculture is not the same as one of support for captured peasants. Small-scale agriculture includes petty bourgeois and bourgeois owners of peasant holdings, many of whom may not – as was evident in the disappointing performance of low-density schemes – be serious about agricultural production. It can also include uncaptured peasants, who are deserving of sympathy and support, but who – since they have relatively little interest in market agriculture – would be poorly chosen as recipients of resources designed to bolster commodity production. In a country whose future prosperity depends as heavily upon small-scale agriculture as Kenya's does, it is critically important to make the most of the human resource represented by captured peasants. This point will be developed further.

4 *Prosperous peasants and telephone farmers.* This category includes two groups of people who are economically similar, but who have made different choices. What both have in common is that they are engaged in peasant agriculture, but that they have the option, if they wish, to engage in other pursuits as well: the necessary education and experience for an attractive employment opportunity or money to invest in an enterprise – in short, a chance to become a member of the petty or upper bourgeoisie. Chapter 7 described many such people in the Passenga Settlement Scheme, and they are representative of large numbers of others like them throughout the country. A proportion of them – prosperous peasants – have decided to concentrate on farming. Administrators in peasant areas again and again characterize them as the best farmers they know, because they are motivated to concentrate on agriculture while enjoying personal and material resources superior to those of the average smallholder. They constitute the idealized image on which the World Bank based its plans for low-density settlement.

To a significant degree, however, reality failed to measure up to the World Bank's image. The majority of Passenga farmers, although relatively prosperous, did not turn out to be real peasants. They – and many others like them elsewhere in Kenya – became what some administrative officials referred to as telephone farmers, people who concentrate on more lucrative activities while farming 'over the week end and by telephone.' They were the cause of low-density settlement's unexpectedly poor performance, and it is clear that their ownership of land, as long as they are neglecting it, represents an obstacle to the full development of Kenya's agriculture. In 1983, Passenga looked less well developed than it had in 1972, and at least a couple of the most committed farmers of a decade earlier had cooled toward small-scale agriculture, discouraged by its difficulties and drawn by more attractive opportunities elsewhere. A tour of a number of Kenya's agricultural areas, and conversations with farmers, agriculturalists, and settlement officials confirmed that the underutilization of prime smallholder areas was a continuing and perhaps worsening problem.

In one respect, it was certainly worsening. Chapter 5 looked at the various motives a member of the petty or upper bourgeoisie might have for owning a peasant holding: personal security, the discharge of family obligations, and the building of influence. Depending on circumstances, any of these objectives might be met without full utilization of the plot's potential. In the 1980s, a further motive had arisen: land speculation. Throughout Kenya, the price of agricultural land was rising steeply. An agricultural official in Kitale, for example, reported that land that could be had for less than Shs 10000/- per hectare in 1980 was fetching in excess of 17000/- by early 1983.[35] A Kenyan, therefore, could now hope to turn a substantial profit from the ownership of land without making any use at all of it. If such a pattern became widespread, it would constitute perverse development writ large.

5 *The landed bourgeoisie.* Despite the expansion of peasant society, and despite the fact that members of the bourgeoisies were involved in that expansion, there was also a landed bourgeoisie proper, a group of people whose landholdings, activities, and aspirations were comparable to those of the former European settlers. Available evidence suggests that they are subject to generalizations much like ones made about prosperous peasants and telephone farmers: some are serious about agriculture, and concentrate on the management of their farms or hire capable managers, while others concentrate on their urban activities, allowing the management of their land to fall into a state of disarray. However, precise information on the management of large farms owned by partnerships, small groups, or individuals – in short, the agrarian bourgeoisie – is hard to come by. For example, the *Large Farm Sector Study*, which was done for the Ministry of Agriculture,[36] contains a substantial

volume of information on the management of large-scale farms, but the authors seem consciously to be wording their way around a clear statement on bourgeois farm management – at least as far as the African bourgeoisie are concerned.

The reasons are not far to seek. The agrarian bourgeoisie have a great deal of political clout. Included among their numbers are many of the most powerful people in the country, and a significant number of their farms are not well managed, as we can gather from the informal statements of officials, as well as from such hints as the *Large Farm Sector Study's* recommendation that the Group Farm Rehabilitation Project be extended to include large farms with few owners.[37] However, officials have been loath to make clear and unequivocal statements on a subject that is likely to offend sensibilities in very high places. Here, as in the case of telephone farmers, we have a problem that combines great political sensitivity with serious significance for Kenya's prosperity. Indeed, it is undoubtedly one of the knottiest political problems facing Kenya today.

ECONOMIC DEVELOPMENT AND THE AGRARIAN SYSTEM

Given the class system outlined above, what is Kenya's agrarian future and how can it be enhanced? Peasant society is continuing to expand, and there is some room for further expansion. As of early 1983, the subdivision of large-scale farms was not complete, and it remained possible that this process might yield some further smallholdings. More significantly, the Department of Settlement's plans, discussed above, held out the hope of tens of thousands of new plots. In addition, there was potential for further expansion of peasant society through irrigation schemes.

Even taken together, however, all of these sources of land are insignificant when measured against an average annual population growth rate in excess of 4 per cent. In any event, the most important question for the future is not how long peasant society can continue to expand, but what kind of a contribution it can make to Kenya's economic development. In answering both questions, the most significant data have to do with the *use* of agricultural land rather than its *extent*: Which segments of the population will have access to agricultural land and which ones will be barred? What can be accomplished in the way of further subdivision and intensification of underutilized land? These are the most important questions for the future of Kenya's agrarian system.

Three problem areas stand out in looking at the future and confronting some of the hard political questions it poses: 1) landlessness, 2) the fate of uncaptured peasants and the land they occupy, and 3) underutilized land.

1 *Landlessness.* I have argued that this problem, because of the nature of Kenya's social dynamic, cannot be finally resolved. But that does not mean it cannot be dealt with more or less well. The colonial authorities dealt with it as badly as possible, through repression. Their policies caused landless people untold misery and deprived Kenya of the valuable production that – as became clear later – can be achieved by those landless people who become captured peasants once they have land. In addition, the authorities, because of their failure to understand the significance of land – and the social dynamics surrounding land – in an African peasant society, reaped the whirlwind of a revolt by landless people against colonial rule. In the end they were forced to back down.

Once they changed their approach, things improved considerably. Large numbers of landless people got land, in some cases good land, in many cases usable land, and they vindicated the new policy direction by producing far better (in comparison with low-density settlement) than the authorities had expected them to. On the other hand, many got substandard land, some got worthless land, and the resources made available to all formerly landless people were greatly inferior to the resources that went to the low-density settlers who in the end disappointed the authorities with their performance. Although we have no subsequent studies as detailed as the ones from the late 1960s and early 1970s, it appears that government policies toward the settlement of landless people have continued to produce mixed results. For example, when the Ol'Kalou Salient was subdivided, it seems clear that many of the plots given out were as bad as any distributed in the transition to independence. But at Lake Kenyatta, a new settlement in a relatively remote area of the coast, some of the plots apparently went to landless people, and that scheme, located on land with a good potential, has, by all accounts, been a striking success.

Landless people have never been able to count on favours from the government. What they have won has been a result of direct political pressure, or even the threat of force; of the fact that others – for example European owners of substandard land and, more recently, organizers of land-buying companies – have found ways of benefiting from their settlement; and of the widespread sympathy their cause still commands in Kenya, even in the 1980s. The only thing we can add to those factors is the observation that it pays, in policy terms, to settle landless people who, once settled, will become captured peasants. They have proved to be capable, given half a chance, of making an important contribution to commodity production and therefore to Kenya's future prosperity. Policy-makers who have advocated their cause have not been disappointed, as have many who have advocated the causes of other classes.

2 *Uncaptured peasants.* The problems of uncaptured peasants, like those of landless people, are not susceptible to a final resolution. But unlike the latter, their problems will, in the long run, resolve themselves, assuming continued economic development. These are, for the most part, older people or people who live in remote areas, and in future generations, with the continued penetration of capitalist development into the countryside, they will become absorbed into the rest of the population. But that is cold comfort for uncaptured peasants. Their problems and those of their families remain very real, and a long histori-cal perspective will not fatten their cows.

In the settlement schemes, in cases where settlers are not able to de-velop their land or meet their loan repayments, they are being pressured to subdivide, and sell off part of their land. There is probably no alterna-tive to this, as wrenching as it must be for the people experiencing it. In the face of continued landlessness, and given the importance of agricul-tural production to Kenya's economy, it would be cant to advocate that good land be left, at public expense, in the hands of people who are not developing it. It is possible, of course, to minimize hardships, and the government deserves credit for its apparent scrupulousness in assuring that the process of subdivision and sale of the land of uncaptured peas-ants does not create new landlessness. The authorities would deserve even more commendation if they could apply the same standards of toughness and scrupulousness to their management of the problem of underutilized land in the hands of the bourgeoisies.

3 *Underutilized land.* The government is well aware of the fact that telephone farmers and upper bourgeois weekend farmers pose a first-order policy problem – politically because of landlessness and of the subdivision of the land of uncaptured peasants and economically be-cause of the importance of agricultural production. However, the authorities have not been able to see their way clear to addressing it. In the end, it seems likely that they will have to, for, given the expansive thrust of peasant society, the problem clearly has a life of its own.

The government's awareness of the problem was officially documented in the late 1970s and its inability to come to terms with it was manifested in the action, or rather inaction, that followed. The 1979–83 *Development Plan* contains a provision for the establishment of a National Land Commission, to examine, among other things, 'ending speculation in the purchase and holding of land ...' and 'penalizing absentee landlords who permit high potential land to sit idle ...'[38] The commission was not appointed, and a 1982 white paper explained, somewhat lamely, that such issues as 'land speculation [and] idle land ... will be examined by Sectoral Planning Groups during the course of preparing the next Development Plan.'[39] Translated, that seems to mean: 'We dare not be perceived as trying to avoid this issue, but something with as high a profile as a Land Commission is too dangerous.'

Indeed, the issue cannot be avoided. Already in 1983, there were tantalizing hints of the forms that future action might take – hints suggesting that if the government did not take the initiative, it would be dragged into action, as it was in the expansion of settlement and the subdivision of group-owned farms. The hints:

– A Rift Valley agricultural official reported that, a year earlier, local administrators in Uasin Gishu and Trans Nzoia districts had launched a campaign of pressure on owners of larger farms that were being left underdeveloped. The official noted that the pressure had a salutary effect and resulted in improved agricultural development.
– Another official, highly placed, recalled an incident near Nakuru in which an owner of underdeveloped land was pressured into selling off part of it.
– In Mombasa, Shariff Nassir, assistant minister for labour and head of the local KANU branch – who is of Arab descent – incurred the wrath of a number of prominent African political personalities in one of Kenya's ubiquitous political disputes. One of Nassir's antagonists, Juma Boy, secretary general of the Central Organization of Trade Unions, referred to a large tract of land, which he said Nassir owned on the coast. Placing that ownership in the context of poor Africans squatting on Arab-owned land, Boy invited Nassir to subdivide the land and give it to landless squatters.[40]

The hints offer a range of the permutations of possible action: administrative initiatives under government control, as occurred in Uasin

Gishu and Trans Nzoia at the local level; political initiatives responding to the pressure of a combination of rational and irrational impulses, as in Mombasa; or some combination of the two. If the government can find a way of tackling this issue, it can reduce the risk of irrational action, of violence, and of rents in the fragile fabric of mutual trust.

In a legal sense, the authorities have more than enough power to act. The Agriculture Act gives the minister for agriculture the power to seize inadequately managed land and manage it, sell it, or lease it, with net proceeds going to the owner.[41] It would not be administratively possible, of course, to seize all the inadequately managed land in Kenya, but a threat, or even a hint, of action should be enough to spur a great flurry of agricultural development. Then, too, any action along these lines would have to be carried out judiciously, to avoid appearances reminiscent of colonial coercion. However, after all the qualifications have been made, it remains clear that government action is possible and that it could win at least the necessary degree of popular support. The only serious block to action is within Kenya's leadership ranks, among the many influential people who themselves are holders of inadequately managed land. The big question is whether this block can be overcome.

Overcoming it would be an important achievement. A campaign to ensure that as much as possible of Kenya's farmland is being worked by capable and committed farmers combines strong elements of social justice with economic good sense. Other paths to Kenya's development are far less certain. We do not know whether Kenya's industrial bourgeoisie will be able to build toward a prosperous future, as Leys hopes, or become a factor contributing to stagnation and dependency, as Kaplinsky and Langdon fear. What is beyond dispute is that Kenya's great wealth and variety of agricultural resources, both human and material, are capable of making a contribution to prosperity that is second to none. The question of whether and how that contribution will be made is the most important one facing Kenyans in the 1980s.

Appendix

Plot No. _____, _____ Scheme

Social and Economic Information
 1 Name; age.
 2 Are you the owner of this plot?
 3 a. Are you the manager?
   b. How many acres does this plot have?
 4 What do you produce on this farm?
 5 How many acres of each? / How many head of each?
 6 Which of these are sold?
 7 Which are consumed on the shamba?
 8 Which produce do you find the most profitable?
 9 Do you find any of the produce suggested by the agricultural assistant unsuitable or unprofitable?
10 Which produce?
11 Why?
12 Do you find the instalment periods for your loan repayments convenient?
13 Do you find the loan repayments rather high, about right, or rather low
   in comparison to what your farm produces? Explain your answer.
14 How many adults live on your plot?
15 How many children live on your plot?
16 How many families are on the plot?
17 How many of these are labourers?
18 Friends?
19 Relatives?

20 Explain 17, 18, and 19.
21 How are the relatives related and what are their rights on the land?
22 How do they come to have these rights?
23 Are you doing any other business together?
24 Do you make more use of casual or regular labour?
25 Why? (Probe on relative usefulness of casual and regular labour.)
26 What do regular labourers usually get here for their work? (In cash and in kind.)
27 What is the usual daily wage for casual labour?
28 Explain wages further.
29 Do you own or have interest in land outside the scheme? Specify.
30 Do you do any work for pay outside of your plot? Specify.
31 Do you own or participate in any enterprise outside of this plot? Specify.
32 Do you meet regularly with family or kin that live anywhere outside of this scheme?
33 How are you related to them?
34 How often do you visit each other?
35 Do you help each other? How?
36 Do you find these exchanges beneficial to you? How?
37 How far have you gone in school?
38 What work did you do before coming to settlement?
39 How many children of school age do you have?
40 How many of these are in school?
41 Where are they going to school?
42 Have any of your children completed school? At what level?
43 To what level do you plan to educate your children that are in school?
44 What would you like your children to become?

Discussion Questions
1 Leadership in the co-operative society.
2 Participation or leadership in *harambee* or other community projects.
3 Local, area, or county councils.
4 Schools.
5 Church.
6 KANU activities.
7 How and when the settler came.
8 His economic and family situation before coming.
9 His experiences in the Emergency.
10 His experiences with land consolidation.
11 How have kinship ties changed since the Emergency?

12 How has the management of a farm changed since the Emergency?

13 Have new opportunities for advancement arisen since the Emergency? How are they different from the old ones?

14 Are there better jobs and investments than agriculture? What are they?

15 What are the best opportunities these days for young people?

16 Where would it be best to own a farm and what kind of farm would be best?

Notes

CHAPTER 1

1 The phrase was popularized by Elspeth Huxley in *White Man's Country: Lord Delamere and the Making of Kenya*, 2 vols (London: Chatto and Windus 1935).

2 R.S. Odingo, *The Kenya Highlands: Land Use and Agricultural Development* (Nairobi: East African Publishing House 1971), 40

3 T.J. Byres, 'Agrarian Transition and the Agrarian Question,' *Journal of Peasant Studies* 4, no. 3 (1977): 258

4 Ibid.

5 Arghiri Emmanuel, *Unequal Exchange: A Study of the Imperialism of Trade* (London: NLB 1972), appendix 4

6 Two representative examples of this literature are Andre Gunder Frank, *Capitalism and Underdevelopment in Latin America: Historical Studies of Chile and Brazil* (New York: Monthly Review Press 1969); and Samir Amin, *Accumulation on a World Scale: A Critique of the Theory of Underdevelopment* (New York: Monthly Review Press 1974).

7 Colin Leys, *Underdevelopment in Kenya: The Political Economy of Neo-Colonialism* (London: Heinemann 1975), 255 and passim

8 Ibid., 255

9 Nicola Swainson, *The Development of Corporate Capitalism in Kenya 1918–77* (Berkeley: University of California 1980)

10 Leys, 'Underdevelopment and Dependency: Critical Notes,' *Journal of Contemporary Asia* 7, no. 1 (1977): 92

11 Ibid.

12 Leys, 'Capital Accumulation, Class Formation and Dependency: The Significance of the Kenyan Case,' in *Socialist Register* (London: Merlin Press 1978), 245. Italics in original

13 Ibid., 262

14 See, for example, Rafael Kaplinsky, J.S. Henley, and Colin Leys, 'Debate on "Dependency" in Kenya,' *Review of African Political Economy* 17 (1980): 83–113.

15 Steven W. Langdon, *Multinational Corporations in the Political Economy of Kenya* (London: Macmillan 1981), 194; see also 195 and passim.

16 Leys, 'Politics in Kenya: The Development of Peasant Society,' *British Journal of Political Science* 1, no. 3 (1971): 307–37

17 Ibid., 320

18 Ibid., 322

19 Ibid., 314

20 Michael Cowen, 'Commodity Production in Kenya's Central Province,' in Judith Heyer et al., *Rural Development in Tropical Africa* (London: Macmillan 1981), 141. See also Cowen and Kabiru Kinyanjui, 'Some Problems of Income Distribution in Kenya' (Nairobi: Institute for Development Studies 1977), mimeo.

21 Cowen in Heyer et al., *Rural Development ...*, 140 and passim

22 Ibid., 140

23 The term is Cowen's.

24 Much of the basis for our understanding of peasant society was laid by A.V. Chayanov, most of whose work was published in the 1920s. See *The Theory of Peasant Economy*, ed. Daniel Thorner et al. (Homewood, Ill.: Irwin 1966). A much-read, or at least much-quoted, recent work is Teodor Shanin, *The Awkward Class: Political Sociology of Peasantry in a Developing Society: Russia 1910–25* (Oxford: Clarendon 1972).

25 Chayanov, 'Peasant Farm Organization,' *The Theory of Peasant Economy*, 39–41

26 Karl Marx, *Surveys from Exile*, ed. David Fernbach (New York: Random House 1973), 116, 239–41

27 Hyden, *Beyond Ujamaa in Tanzania: Underdevelopment and an Uncaptured Peasantry* (Berkeley: University of California 1980)

CHAPTER 2

1 Jomo Kenyatta, *Facing Mount Kenya: The Tribal Life of the Gikuyu* (London: Secker and Warburg 1961), 26. The book was first published in 1938. Kenyatta's spelling of the name of his people, 'Gikuyu,' is more correct than mine, 'Kikuyu,' in that it better reflects the correct pronunciation. But both the correct spelling and the correct pronunciation have been all but abandoned in English, even by Kikuyus themselves.

2 Michael Cowen, 'The Agrarian Problem: Notes on the Nairobi Discussion,' *Review of African Political Economy* 20 (1981): 59. See also A.L. Njonjo, 'The Africanization of the "White Highlands": A Study in Agrarian Class Struggle in Kenya 1950–75,' PHD thesis, Princeton, 1977.

3 Not 'tribe.' If that usage was ever justified, it would have had to be on the grounds that the groups bearing that designation partook of pre-modern technologies and forms of organization. Today, with most people integrated into capitalist and/or bureaucratic society, even that justification is gone and, in practice, 'tribe' simply means 'non-white ethnic group.' Clearly, then, the term has become an odious one. In political scholarship and journalism, it is a particularly unfortunate usage, because it tends to give uninitiated readers a badly distorted picture of reality, projecting atavistic images that no longer correspond to reality – if they ever did.

4 A good article on this subject is Rada and Neville Dyson-Hudson, 'Subsistence Herding in Uganda,' *Scientific American*, February 1969: 76–89.

5 Generalizations about so-called tribal law are difficult to make. Max Gluckman, in trying to do so nevertheless, gets around the difficulty by building his discussion upon the Lozi, whom he characterizes as 'strikingly representative' in the matter of land law among cultivators. He says that 'one right of Lozi citizenship, to which all men who are accepted as subjects are entitled, is a right to building and to arable land ...,' *Politics, Law and Ritual in Tribal Society* (Chicago: Aldine 1965), 37.

6 The presentation that follows is documented in John Middleton and Greet Kershaw, *The Central Tribes of the Northeastern Bantu* (London: International African Institute 1965), 23–9, 46–53.

7 Ibid., 25–6

8 Ibid., 51

9 Peter Marris and Anthony Somerset, *African Businessmen: A Study of Entrepreneurship and Development in Kenya* (London: Routledge and Keagan Paul 1971), ch. 2. See also Michael Cowen, 'Differentiation in a Kenya Location,' East African Universities Social Science Council, no. 16 (Nairobi 1972), 2–3

10 Marris and Somerset, *African Businessmen*, 33–4

11 A sizeable livestock holding added to a man's position in his community, both by the prestige it conferred and by the purchasing power it gave him. See, inter alia, Jomo Kenyatta, *Facing Mount Kenya*, 64–5.

12 Elspeth Huxley, *White Man's Country: Lord Delamere and the Making of Kenya*, 2 vols (London: Chatto and Windus 1935), 80–1

13 Among the best sources on the process of European settlement are the following: Kenya Land Commission (hereinafter KLC), *Report*, Cmd. 4556

(London: His Majesty's Stationery Office 1934); M.P.K. Sorrenson, *Origins of European Settlement in Kenya* (Nairobi: Oxford University Press 1968), chs 11–13. See also W.T.W. Morgan, 'The "White Highlands" of Kenya,' *The Geographical Journal* 129, part 2 (June 1963): 140–55; and Carl G. Rosberg and John Nottingham, *The Myth of 'Mau Mau': Nationalism in Kenya* (New York: Praeger 1966), chapter 1.

14 Huxley, *White Man's Country*, 81
15 Sorrenson, *Origins of European Settlement in Kenya*, 233
16 Ibid., 181–2
17 Ibid., 217. Italics in original
18 According to Kikuyu custom, rights of redemption for all land acquired from another *mbari*, except by sale, are never lost. (Middleton and Kershaw, *The Central Tribes of the Northeastern Bantu*, 50.) In other words, if the Kikuyus in question believed they were granting a tenancy to the foreigners, they would also believe that they could revoke the transaction later by paying compensation.
19 Sorrenson, *Origins of European Settlement in Kenya*, 180
20 The commission recommended the distribution of £2000 and the addition of some acreage to the Kikuyu reserve in compensation for the losses. KLC, *Report*, part 1, chapters 8–9. See also Sorrenson, *Origins of European Settlement in Kenya*, 180–1. It is important to note that the commission's calculations of Kikuyu land losses did not reflect lost *githaka* rights. The *Report* accepted the colonial position that Africans could lay claim only to land actually under cultivation, not to the entire *githaka*.
21 Ibid., 184
22 Ibid., 191
23 KLC, *Report*, 187, para. 642
24 Quoted in Sorrenson, *Origins of European Settlement in Kenya*, 195
25 KLC, *Report*, 188, para. 649
26 Sorrenson, *Origins of European Settlement in Kenya*, 211
27 Ibid., 211, and KLC, *Report*, 214, para. 768
28 Sorrenson, *Origins of European Settlement in Kenya*, 212–13
29 Ibid., 213–14
30 Ibid., 215; KLC, *Report*, 273, para. 1047
31 Ibid., 272–81, para. 1030–75
32 The Kenya Land Commission *Report* calls them the Lumbwa.
33 Ibid., 302, 305, para. 1149, 1165
34 Ibid., 302, para. 1150
35 The pressure on Chepalungu came from several quarters. In addition to the European demand just cited (the commission's reference to them is

ibid., 306–7, para. 1171, 1173), there had been a proposal that the area be used to accommodate some members of the Dorobo tribe (ibid., 258, 306, para. 978, 1170). In addition, Chepalungu had been a Kipsigis apiary, generating 'a very large trade in honey' (ibid., 306, para. 1172). The commission sought to resolve these conflicting claims by recommending that not more than 4000 hectares of Chepalungu's 264 square kilometres be made available to Europeans. (Significantly, this area was to be chosen by colonial authorities 'in consultation with the local European community.') The remainder of Chepalungu, the commission recommended, should be set aside as a reserve for Kipsigis and Dorobo people (ibid., 306–7, para. 1167, 1176).

36 Ibid., 1, para. 2
37 The clearest information (for non-technical purposes) on Kenya's large-scale agriculture is in World Bank, 'Project for the Development and Settlement of Land in the Scheduled Areas' (Nairobi 1961), para. 6–7, mimeo. Other sources: R.S. Odingo, *The Kenya Highlands: Land Use and Agricultural Development* (Nairobi: East African Publishing House 1971); and Colony and Protectorate of Kenya, *The Agrarian Problem in Kenya: Note by Sir Philip Mitchell, Governor of Kenya* (Nairobi: Government Printer 1948).
38 Ibid., 37
39 The legally correct term was 'native lands' or 'native land units.' 'Native reserves,' strictly speaking, meant areas reserved for future use (Y.P. Ghai and J.P.W.B. McAuslan, *Public Law and Political Change in Kenya: A Study of the Legal Framework of Government from Colonial Times to the Present* [Nairobi: Oxford University Press 1970], p 92).
40 World Bank, 'Project for the Development and Settlement of Land ...,' para. 5
41 East African Royal Commission, *Report*, Cmd. 9475 (London: Her Majesty's Stationery Office 1955), 54, para. 3
42 Act No. 33 of 1918. See Ghai and McAuslan, *Public Law and Political Change in Kenya*, 83–4 and 94–7. See also East African Royal Commission, *Report*, chapter 6.
43 Ghai and McAuslan, *Public Law and Political Change in Kenya*, 83–4

CHAPTER 3

1 This story is pieced together from a variety of works. A rich source throughout is Y.P. Ghai and J.P.W.B. McAuslan, *Public Law and Political Change in Kenya: A Study of the Legal Framework of Government from Colonial*

Times to the Present (Nairobi: Oxford University Press 1970), which has been undeservedly ignored. In many cases, other writers either owe Ghai and McAuslan an unacknowledged debt or are reinventing the wheel. An equally ambitious, but less successful, work is Gavin Kitching, *Class and Economic Change in Kenya: The Making of an African Petite Bourgeoisie 1905–70* (New Haven: Yale University Press 1980), which presents masses of data and argument focusing generally on the agrarian system, but is curiously unable to reach clear conclusions. Another useful source is East African Royal Commission, (hereinafter EARC) *Report*, Cmd. 9475 (London: Her Majesty's Stationery Office 1955). The best source on Kenya's agrarian labour system up to 1930 is Richard D. Wolff, *The Economics of Colonialism: Britain and Kenya 1870–1930* (New Haven: Yale University Press 1974). A more detailed, but less incisive, study is R.M.A. van Zwanenberg, *Colonial Capitalism and Labour in Kenya 1919–39* (Nairobi: East African Literature Bureau 1975). The classic source on the post-war development of the agrarian system in Central Province (which set the pattern for the rest of the country) is M.P.K. Sorrenson, *Land Reform in the Kikuyu Country* (Nairobi: Oxford University Press 1967). Although this is a storehouse of data, it suffers from unclarity – so much so that, as recently as 1977, Michael Cowen took other writers to task for their failure to understand what Sorrenson *really* said about class formation (Cowen and Kabiru Kinyanjui, 'Some Problems of Income Distribution in Kenya,' Institute for Development Studies [Nairobi 1977], section 3, p. 2). Most of Sorrenson's readers have, at various points, been left in doubt as to what he *really* meant. Non-agrarian aspects of class formation have been touched upon in many works, and are generally quite well known to students of Kenya's history and politics, but are not covered systematically anywhere. The task of this chapter, therefore, is to draw together material from a wide variety of sources, summarize it, and, of course, relate it to this study's argument.

2 Plural of *muhoi* (see chapter 2)
3 Swahili for 'European,' i.e. 'white man'
4 Rebmann M. Wambaa and Kenneth King, 'The Political Economy of the Rift Valley: A Squatter Perspective,' Historical Association of Kenya, Annual Conference, 1972, 1
5 R.S. Odingo, *The Kenya Highlands: Land Use and Agricultural Development* (Nairobi: East African Publishing House 1971), 31, 40
6 EARC, *Report*, 163, para. 46; see also 164–5, para. 51.
7 Odingo, *The Kenya Highlands*, 32
8 Kenya Land Commission (hereinafter KLC), *Report*, Cmd. 4556 (London: His Majesty's Stationery Office 1934), 144, para. 498

9 Ghai and McAuslan, *Public Law and Political Change in Kenya*, 95–6

10 M.P.K. Sorrenson, *Land Reform*, 39

11 Ghai and McAuslan, *Public Law and Political Change in Kenya*, 96

12 Ibid., 121–22; EARC, *Report*, 164–7, para. 51–60. See also Sorrenson, *Land Reform*, 80–1.

13 EARC, *Report*, 166–7, para. 59–60

14 Interview in Ol'Kalou West Settlement Scheme, Nyandarua District, 21 July 1971. Administrative officers shared the ex-squatter's sentiment. In a series of interviews in 1971, administrators responsible for areas where ex-squatters had been settled after independence complained repeatedly that the squatters' work background had left them peculiarly unprepared for taking over the management of their own small farms.

15 Peter Marris and Anthony Somerset, *African Businessmen: A Study of Entrepreneurship and Development in Kenya* (London: Routledge and Kegan Paul 1971), 46

16 Ibid., 49

17 Ibid., 48. See also John Anderson, *The Struggle for the School*, (Nairobi: Longman 1970), 107, for another reference to the trade with European settlers.

18 Marris and Somerset refer to this type of trade in a context that suggests it was taking place no later than the 1930s (*African Businessmen* 49). One of the respondents interviewed for the present study told of having engaged in a motorized version of the same trade during a later period. He said he bought eggs and potatoes from squatters in the Dundori area of what is today called Nyandarua District and then hired a truck for Shs 60/- a trip to take them into Nakuru, where he sold them to Asians and Africans who had stalls in the market there. Interview in Ol'Kalou West Settlement Scheme, Nyandarua District, 9 August 1971

19 A number of respondents in the present study told of having engaged in such enterprises as these during the colonial era. See also Waruhiu Itote, *'Mau Mau' General* (Nairobi: East African Publishing House 1967), 32–4; and Marris and Somerset, *African Businessmen*, 51.

20 Colony and Protectorate of Kenya, *Sessional Paper No. 77 of 1956–57*; *The Development Programme, 1957–60* (Nairobi: Government Printer 1957), 14, para. 53

21 John Anderson, *The Struggle for the School*, 76, 107. Harry Thuku, *An Autobiography* (Nairobi: Oxford University Press 1970), 11–18

22 Anderson, *The Struggle for the School*, 107

23 Ibid., 108–9, 136–8

24 B.A. Ogot and J.A. Kieran, *Zamani: A Survey of East African History* (Nai-

robi: East African Publishing House and Longman 1968), 266; Anderson, *The Struggle for the School*, 113–28. See also Carl G. Rosberg and John Nottingham, *The Myth of 'Mau Mau': Nationalism in Kenya* (New York: Praeger 1966), 125–31, 179–81.

25 Anderson, *The Struggle for the School*, 138
26 Ibid., 22
27 Ibid., 141
28 Ibid., 46
29 Ibid., 46. The sluggishness of the colonial government's response to African needs – even in this final period of comparatively earnest effort – can be gauged by comparing it with what an inexperienced new regime was able to achieve after independence. In addition to the 82 African secondary schools of 1963, 36 Asian and European schools had to abandon their racial exclusiveness – a total, therefore, of 118 government-aided secondary schools in 1963. By 1968, after only five years of independence, that number had grown to 232. In its last 18 years, therefore, the colonial government had helped to establish 78 African secondary schools; in the first five years of independence 114 had been added to that total (ibid., 150).
30 Tom Mboya, *Freedom and After* (London: Andre Deutsch 1963), 142
31 Anderson, *The Struggle for the School*, 76–9
32 Ibid., 123
33 Mboya, *Freedom and After*, 137–41
34 Anderson, *The Struggle for the School*, 139–40
35 Another Marxist argument is that the development of capitalist agriculture in African areas was slowed by the loss of manpower to European areas as the latter recruited labour. See Colin Leys, *Underdevelopment in Kenya: The Political Economy of Neo-Colonialism* (London: Heinemann 1975), 31. This could be true, and would not be incompatible with the argument advanced in these pages, since two factors might simultaneously contribute to the same phenomenon. However, Leys' point is speculative. He offers no direct evidence.
36 EARC, *Report*, 54, para. 3; 286, para. 19–20. KLC, *Report*, 147, para. 510; *The Agrarian Problem in Kenya: Note by Sir Philip Mitchell, Governor of Kenya* (Nairobi: Government Printer 1948), 12–13, para. 32. Sir Philip blames overpopulation, in the case of the Kikuyus, on the fact that 'they have bred so freely' (ibid., 11, para. 29), a subtle appeal to the racial and sexual prejudices of many conservative English people of his generation. But it seems impossible to escape the conclusion that the congestion would not have occurred had European settlement not closed the Kikuyu frontier.

37 Anglicization of *mashamba*, the Swahili word for 'cultivated fields' or, more broadly, 'farms'

38 EARC, *Report*, 287, para. 22. See also M.P.K. Sorrenson, *Land Reform*, 38–9, 42–3, 75–7; and KLC, *Report*, 146–8, para. 507–12.

39 EARC, *Report*, 287, para. 22–3; Sorrenson, *Land Reform*, 39

40 Sorrenson, *Land Reform*, 74–5

41 EARC, *Report*, 287–8, para. 23

42 Sorrenson, *Land Reform*, 40; see also KLC, *Report*, 142, para. 492(6); 149, para. 516, 518.

43 Sorrenson, *Land Reform*, 78. Cf. EARC, *Report*, 287–8, para. 23.

44 Ghai and McAuslan, *Public Law and Political Change in Kenya*, 93–4; Sorrenson, *Land Reform*, 41–3. Desire to limit competition from African producers may also have been a factor. See Leys, *Underdevelopment in Kenya*, 34.

45 Ghai and McAuslan, *Public Law and Political Change in Kenya*, 110; see also 111–13.

46 EARC, *Report*, 103, para. 25

47 The commitment to improved African agriculture was made explicit in the so-called Swynnerton Plan, a blueprint of proposed reforms for the latter part of the 1950s (Colony and Protectorate of Kenya, *A Plan to Intensify the Development of Agriculture in Kenya* [Nairobi: Government Printer 1954]).

48 Ghai and McAuslan, *Public Law and Political Change in Kenya*, 114

49 Ibid., 115

50 Ibid., 114

51 On this subject, see Sorrenson, *Land Reform*.

52 But not so very much, perhaps. Sorrenson (ibid., 229–31) appears to leave considerable room for doubt.

53 World Bank, 'Project for the Development and Settlement of Land in Scheduled Areas' (Nairobi 1961), para. 5, 9, mimeo. The European figure is not strictly comparable because it includes produce retained on the farm while the African figure refers only to produce sold.

54 Some of the available population figures are obviously inexact and have been subject to conflicting interpretations, but the population increase and the Kikuyu majority hold true by any interpretation. The Kenya Land Commission (*Report*, 144, para. 490–9) does not distinguish clearly between squatters and other Africans resident outside of their own reserves, such as town dwellers and residents of other reserves. As a result, the KLC figure of about 150 000 Africans employed outside their reserve – 110 000 of them Kikuyus – is interpreted by Sorrenson (*Land Reform*, 80) to mean

total number living outside their reserve, while the East African Royal Commission (*Report*, 164, para. 47) implies it means resident labourers (squatters) only. In either case, the 1945 figures of 203 000 squatters on European farms and in the forests (ibid.) – about 120 000 of them Kikuyus (Sorrenson, *Land Reform*, 81) – represent an increase. In 1945, the Kikuyus remained a majority of the squatter population, but a smaller majority than earlier, an indication that the economic pressures that had affected large numbers of Kikuyus from the early days of settlement were, by the mid-1940s, having a growing effect on other ethnic groups.

55 Ibid., 80
56 Ibid., 82; Rosberg and Nottingham, *The Myth of 'Mau Mau,'* 331
57 Two accessible and succinct accounts may be found in Sorrenson, *Land Reform*, chapters 5–6, and Rosberg and Nottingham, *The Myth of 'Mau Mau,'* chapters 8–9.
58 The official view of Mau Mau was that it was irrational and the oaths were pointed to as evidences of atavism and savagery. That view is defended by F.C. Corfield in *Historical Survey of the Origins and Growth of Mau Mau*, Cmd. 1030 (London: Her Majesty's Stationery Office 1960). Rosberg and Nottingham (*The Myth of 'Mau Mau'*) argue that the Land Freedom Army was a nationalist organization pursuing rational objectives and that the appeal to tradition in the oaths does not constitute savagery. A first-hand account of oathing may be found in Waruhiu Itote, *'Mau Mau' General* (Nairobi: East African Publishing House 1967), appendix A.
59 Calculated from J.S. Goldthorpe and F.B. Wilson, *Tribal Maps of East Africa and Zanzibar* (Kampala: East African Institute of Social Research 1960), 10.
60 Ghai and McAuslan, *Public Law and Political Change in Kenya*, 122
61 A certain amount of ambiguity surrounds the term 'Rift Valley.' In the first instance, it is a geographical term. But in common parlance as well as in various historical writings it is not unusual to find it used more or less synonymously with 'White Highlands.' This use is especially frequent vis-à-vis squatters and in contrast to the reserves. Thus in the term 'Rift Valley squatter' or in such a phrase as 'leaving the reserves to go to the Rift,' it is not the geographical boundaries but rather those of the White Highlands that are being referred to.
62 Rosberg and Nottingham, *The Myth of 'Mau Mau,'* 285–6
63 Sorrenson, *Land Reform*, 98–9
64 Fred Majdalany, *State of Emergency: The Full Story of Mau Mau* (Boston: Houghton Mifflin 1963), 221
65 Rosberg and Nottingham, *The Myth of 'Mau Mau,'* 295–6. See also Sorren-

son, *Land Reform*, 105–9, for evidence on the economic position of loyalists.

66 Sorrenson, *Land Reform*, 114–15, 118, 231, 240–1
67 Ibid., 101–3. For one of several personal accounts of detention, see J.M. Kariuki, *'Mau Mau' Detainee* (London: Oxford University Press 1963), chapters 4–8.
68 Colonial government figures, cited in Rosberg and Nottingham, *The Myth of 'Mau Mau,'* 303
69 Sorrenson, *Land Reform*, 234
70 Kenya Legislative Council, *Debates*, 16 November 1960, cols 553, 567
71 Colony and Protectorate of Kenya, *Land Tenure and Control Outside the Native Lands*, Sessional Paper No. 10, 1958–59 (Nairobi: Government Printer 1959), 1, para. 1
72 Itote, *'Mau Mau' General*, 30–1
73 Rosberg and Nottingham, *The Myth of 'Mau Mau,'* 208
74 Montagu Slater, *The Trial of Jomo Kenyatta*, 2nd edition (London: Secker and Warburg 1955), 192. This book contains a useful summary and analysis of the trial's voluminous proceedings.
75 Ibid., 242
76 Majdalany, *State of Emergency*, 195
77 Odingo, *The Kenya Highlands*, 58
78 World Bank, 'Project for the Development and Settlement of Land in the Scheduled Areas' (Nairobi 1961), para. 11, mimeo.

INTRODUCTION TO PART II

1 I have advanced that thesis myself in 'The Political Economy of Land in Kenya: The Case of the Million-Acre Settlement Scheme,' PH D thesis, University of Toronto, 1977. In this study, I present what now seems to me a more nuanced and more plausible interpretation.

CHAPTER 4

1 The national politics of this period are described in George Bennet and Carl G. Rosberg, *The Kenyatta Election: Kenya 1960–61* (London: Oxford University Press 1961); and George Bennet, *Kenya: A Political History. The Colonial Period* (London: Oxford University Press 1963). Useful personal accounts may be found in Tom Mboya, *Freedom and After* (London: Andre Deutsch 1963); Jomo Kenyatta, *Suffering without Bitterness: The Founding of the Kenya Nation* (Nairobi: East African Publishing House 1968); Oginga

Odinga, *Not Yet Uhuru: An Autobiography* (London: Heinemann 1967), and Sir Michael Blundell, *So Rough a Wind* (London: Weidenfeld and Nicolson 1964).

2 Land Development and Settlement Board (hereinafter LDSB), *A Review of the Activities of the Land Development and Settlement Board* (1962), para. 2, mimeo, from the Kenya National Archives (hereinafter KNA), 3/121, Office of the President

3 Ibid., appendix 1; Kenya Agriculture Ordinance No. 8 of 1955; Agriculture (Amendment) Bill, No. 47 of 1960

4 Kenya Legislative Council, *Debates*, 16 October 1960, col. 537

5 World Bank, 'Project for the Development and Settlement of Land in the Scheduled Areas' (Nairobi 1961), para. 11, mimeo

6 Ibid.

7 From the Kenya government's application to the World Bank, as quoted in LDSB, *A Review ...*, para. 14

8 Ibid., para. 8, 22, 44; World Bank, 'Project for the Development and Settlement of Land ...,' para. ii

9 Ibid., para. 26

10 Ibid.

11 LDSB, *A Review ...*, para. 1

12 Ibid., para. 6

13 Ibid., para. 27; World Bank, 'Project for the Development and Settlement of Land ...,' para. 31. IBRD stands for International Bank for Reconstruction and Development, i.e. World Bank.

14 Calculated from East African Royal Commission, *Report*, Cmd. 9475 (London: Her Majesty's Stationery Office 1955), 167, para. 60.

15 LDSB, *A Review ...*, para. 2–3

16 'Loan Agreement (Land Settlement and Development Project) between Colony and Protectorate of Kenya and International Bank for Reconstruction and Development' (Loan No. 303 KE), 29 November 1961, Recital D, supplied by World Bank, Nairobi. Cf. LDSB, *A Review ...*, para. 7

17 'Loan Agreement,' sections 2.02(b) and 3.01

18 Ibid., sections 5.01(d), 5.01(e), 5.02(a), 5.09; cf. World Bank, 'Project for the Development and Settlement of Land ...,' para. 47

19 LDSB, *A Review ...*, para. 44

20 Ibid.

21 World Bank, 'Project for the Development and Settlement of Land ...,' para. vi

22 Ibid., para. 29; LDSB, *A Review ...*, para. 19

23 LDSB, 'Valuation Policy and Procedure,' 12 October 1962, para. 6, KNA 3/113, Office of the President

24 At the same time, it placed a ceiling on the profits that might be made by such speculation in cases where the speculator bought the land at a price lower than the 1959 market value – a point emphasized by former colonial civil servants C.P.R. Nottidge and J.R. Goldsack in *The Million-Acre Settlement Scheme 1962–66* (Nairobi: Department of Settlement n.d.), 11–12. On the other hand, Nottidge and Goldsack reveal that the effective date of the policy, originally set at the beginning of 1960, was later changed to January 1961. If they are right in maintaining that the policy had the effect of preventing (unlimited) speculation, then the change in its effective date opened a loophole for any speculators who may have bought land at bargain prices during 1960.

25 Hans Ruthenberg, *African Agricultural Development Policy in Kenya, 1962–65* (Berlin: Springer-Verlag 1966), 80–1

26 LDSB, 'Valuation Policy and Procedure,' para. 2(c)

27 A.W. Thompson, 'Valuation: Tea and Sugar Land,' n.d., KNA, 3/113. The LDSB had expected to pay an average of less than £13 per acre for land World Bank, 'Project for the Development and Settlement of Land ...,' para. 29.

28 LDSB, *A Review* ..., para. 14; 'Valuation Policy and Procedure,' para. 2. Italics added

29 Ibid., para. 2(c)

30 Ruthenberg, *African Agricultural Development* ..., 68. Ruthenberg forgets, evidently, that it was independent Kenya, not Britain, that shouldered the bulk of the costs.

31 LDSB, *A Review* ..., para. 44

32 World Bank, 'Project for the Development and Settlement of Land ...,' para. 44

33 At Ol'Kalou Location, Nyandarua District, on 4 November 1971

34 Carl G. Rosberg and John Nottingham, *The Myth of 'Mau Mau': Nationalism in Kenya* (New York: Praeger 1966), 295–6

35 Rebmann M. Wambaa and Kenneth King, 'The Political Economy of the Rift Valley: A Squatter Perspective,' Historical Association of Kenya, Annual Conference, 1972, 17–18

36 P.D. Abrams for the director of settlement to the chief commissioner, 25 April 1963; reply from R.E. Wainwright, chief commissioner, 29 April 1963; LDSB minutes of 24 October 1962, 12 December 1962, 23 January 1963, 27 February 1963, 30 April 1963, 24 May 1963, KNA 3/121; IBRD-CDC Settlement Schemes Loans and Planning Committee (LDSB), minutes of

22 August 1962, 11 January 1963, 8 February 1963, 10 May 1963, KNA 3/119

37 LDSB, *A Review ...*, para. 47

CHAPTER 5

1 Quoted by Margery Perham in 'What Place Now for Kenya's Settlers?' *Kenya Weekly News*, 8 March 1963 (reprinted from *The Times*, London, 20 February 1963), 24

2 Ibid.

3 Oginga Odinga, *Not Yet Uhuru: An Autobiography* (London: Heinemann 1967), 226; cf. Gary Wasserman, *Politics of Decolonization: Kenya Europeans and the Land Issue 1960–65* (London: Cambridge University Press 1976, 98–100

4 Sir Michael Blundell, *So Rough a Wind* (London: Weidenfeld and Nicholson 1964), 298–9

5 Quoted in Jomo Kenyatta, *Suffering without Bitterness: The Founding of the Kenya Nation* (Nairobi: East African Publishing House 1968), 163–4

6 Ibid., 164

7 Colin Leys, *Underdevelopment in Kenya: The Political Economy of Neo-Colonialism* (London: Heinemann 1975), 36–7

8 Land Development and Settlement Board (hereinafter LDSB), *A Review of the Activities of the Land Development and Settlement Board* (1962), para. 5, mimeo

9 World Bank, 'Project for the Development and Settlement of Land in the Scheduled Areas' (Nairobi 1961), para. 78, mimeo

10 Ibid., para. 49

11 LDSB, *A Review ...*, appendix I.

12 LDSB minutes, 25 September 1962, Kenya National Archives (hereinafter KNA), 3/121, Office of the President

13 A.C. Loggin, acting chief executive officer, LDSB, to the Colonial Office, 13 January 1963, KNA 3/121. A fuller statement of the policy may be found in LDSB, 'Valuation Policy and Procedure,' 12 October 1962, KNA 3/113, Office of the President. Cf. the statement of LDSB as it stood before the Million-Acre Scheme in LDSB, *A Review ...*, para. 14.

14 Hans Ruthenberg, *African Agricultural Development Policy in Kenya 1962–65* (Berlin: Springer-Verlag 1966), 68

15 LDSB minutes, 30 April 1963, KNA 3/121

16 Ibid., 22 August 1962

17 Ibid. Later, the number of compassionate case farms was increased to 160

(Statistics Division, Ministry of Finance and Economic Planning, *An Economic Appraisal of the Settlement Schemes, 1964–65 to 1967–68*, Farm Economic Survey Report No. 27 [Nairobi: Government Printer 1971], para. 2.14).

18 Land and Agricultural Bank of Kenya, *Annual Report, 1963*, 4; *Annual Report, 1964* (Nairobi) 4; LDSB, 'Finance for the Land and Agricultural Bank of Kenya: Memorandum to the Secretary of State,' KNA 3/119, Office of the President; LDSB, 'Chairman's Report,' 31 March 1963, para. 6, KNA 3/121

19 Director of settlement's Planning Committee, minutes of 18 and 19 September 1962, KNA 3/116, Office of the President

20 Calculated from Republic of Kenya, *Department of Settlement Annual Report 1968–69*, appendix I. Only one yeoman scheme – Chepsir, near Kericho, which supports thirty-five families at Shs 5000/- target incomes – survived in the Million-Acre program.

21 A puzzling aspect of the World Bank's reduced financial support is that it was not written into the supplemental loan agreement that was drawn up to reflect changes in the program and which reads as if IBRD funding were unchanged, although in other respects the revised agreement reflects the changes that took place after the introduction of the Million-Acre Scheme. For example, the figure for CDC funding is changed to reflect the new circumstances, while the provisions for one-third support by the CDC and two-thirds by the IBRD remain as before, and as they were in reality. But, in apparent defiance of simple arithmetic, the World Bank figure is copied unchanged from the original loan agreement. See 'Supplemental Agreement (Land Development and Settlement Project) between Kenya and International Bank for Reconstruction and Development and United Kingdom of Great Britain and Northern Ireland' (Loan No. 303 KE), 2 April 1964; cf. 'Loan Agreement (Land Development and Settlement Project) between Colony and Protectorate of Kenya and International Bank for Reconstruction and Development' (Loan No. 303 KE), 29 November 1961.

22 LDSB, *A Review* ..., para. 15. The board calculated that if the land had been bought at the valuer's price and subdivided, plots that could be sold for £200 each would have been bought at an average of £425 each. Each plot, therefore, would require a subsidy of £225, or more than 50 per cent, at a time when the government subsidy on high-density land purchase amounted to about 30 per cent (calculated from ibid., para. 7, 15).

The board's judgment that the land had been overvalued later won an oblique confirmation from the prospective sellers themselves. They 'informed the Board that they were prepared to negotiate sale at a lower figure' and the Kinangop scheme went ahead after all (ibid., para. 15).

23 Ibid.

24 Ibid. No reason was given for the chairman's resignation.

25 LDSB minutes 25 July 1962, KNA 3/121. See also LDSB circular to members of the Provincial Administration, 31 August 1962, KNA 4/99, Ministry of Agriculture; and LDSB, *A Review ...*, para. 12.

26 LDSB minutes, 22 August 1962, KNA 3/121

27 Interpretation of settlement legislation in World Bank, 'Project for the Development and Settlement of Land ...,' para. 48

28 LDSB meeting, 23 January 1963, KNA 3/121

29 Several examples of the chief executive officer's liaison role are recorded in the minutes of the director of settlement's Planning Committee, KNA 3/116, Office of the President. See especially minutes of December 1962 and January 1963 meetings. See also LDSB minutes, passim.

30 For an explanation of the term 'settlement charge,' see LDSB, *A Review ...*, para. 30.

31 In some cases there appears to have been an additional charge for the soil conservation services that were part of the process of preparing the land for smallholder occupation. See director of settlement's Planning Committee, minutes of 22 April 1963 (KNA 3/116), but note also the entry about settlement charges in the minutes of 6 May 1963.

32 The consolidation of development credit into a single, ten-year loan did not take place until 1964–65, as it took some time to hammer out a decision about the appropriate way of handling loans for a plethora of different types of purchases. Information meeting for SSOs, minutes, 5 February 1963, and director of settlement's Planning Committee, minutes of 22 April 1963 and 6 May 1963, KNA 3/116; Department of Settlement, *Annual Report, 1964–65* (Nairobi: Government Printer 38)

33 Director of settlement's Planning Committee, 21 January 1963, KNA 3/116; SSOs' meeting, 5 February 1963; Department of Settlement, *Annual Report, 1963–64* (Nairobi: Government Printer), 54

34 Information meeting for SSOs, minutes, 5 February 1963, KNA 3/116

35 Calculated from Department of Settlement, *Annual Report, 1970* (Nairobi: Government Printer), 67

36 Statistics Division, Ministry of Finance and Economic Planning, *An Economic Appraisal ...*, para. 2.14; C.P.R. Nottidge and J.R. Goldsack, *The Million-Acre Settlement Scheme 1962–66* (Nairobi: Department of Settlement n.d.), 7–8

37 A.M. Mercer, 'Ol'Kalou Salient: Background to Policies, with Some Notes on Organization and Practical Farming Problems' (Nyahururu, Kenya:

Nyandarua District Commissioner 1966), mimeo. For information on the Salient's later development, see Department of Settlement, *Annual Report: 1966–67*, 45; ibid., *1967–68*, 28–9.

38 Note, for example, the following from a meeting of settlement and agricultural officials: '... three areas on the wet land on the Kinangop [are to] be planned on a co-op basis ... This is essential because these areas are completely unsuitable for High Density Settlement because of the extent of vlei [i.e. waterlogged] land.' Notes on a meeting held 19 August 1963, KNA 4/98, Agriculture

39 In many cases, two sos during the first year of settlement, when one was often needed to supervise the large-scale farming, which was being phased out, while a second oversaw settlement.

40 Department of Settlement, *Annual Report 1962–63*, 27–32, mimeo

41 P.H. Brown for chief commissioner to permanent secretary, Ministry of Land Settlement and Water Development, 3 August 1962, KNA 3/113, Office of the President

42 Department of Settlement, *Annual Report 1962–63*, 24; ssos' meeting, 5 February 1963

43 Kenya, *Report of the Regional Boundaries Commission*, Cmd. 1899 (London: Her Majesty's Stationery Office 1962), 9–13

44 Ibid., para. 39

45 LDSB, minutes of 23 January 1963, KNA 3/121

46 LDSB, 'Memorandum: Kikuyu Settlement Schemes; Priority Terms for Allocation of Plots,' 27 February 1963, KNA 3/121

47 Central Land Board, *Annual Report 1963–64* (Nairobi: Government Printer); Kenya, Independence Constitution, section 198 (1) (d). A good description of these arrangements may be found in Y.P. Ghai and J.P.W.B. McAuslan, *Public Law and Political Change in Kenya: A Study of the Legal Framework of Government from Colonial Times to the Present* (Nairobi: Oxford University Press 1970), 292–5.

48 Such criticisms were voiced by Hans Ruthenberg, *African Agricultural Development Policy in Kenya* 1962–65; R.S. Odingo in 'Land Settlement in the Kenya Highlands' (in *Education, Employment and Rural Development*, ed. James A. Sheffield [Nairobi: East African Publishing House 1967], 149); and even the director of settlement, who lobbied against his own program in his 1962–63 *Annual Report* (Nairobi: Department of Settlement 1963). These criticisms are discussed in Christopher Leo, 'The Failure of the "Progressive Farmer" in Kenya's Million-Acre Settlement Scheme,' *Journal of Modern African Studies* 16, no. 4 (1978): 622–3 and passim.

49 Blundell, *So Rough a Wind*, chapter 14

50 As late as 1967, four years after independence, ranching and plantation

areas had 'hardly been touched' by African purchases, according to R.S. Odingo, *The Kenya Highlands: Land Use and Agricultural Development* (Nairobi: East African Publishing House 1971), 191–2.

51 For a more detailed account of the internal divisions within the settler community – and of the political conflicts that grew out of those divisions – see Wasserman, *Politics of Decolonization*.

52 Nottidge and Goldsack, *The Million-Acre Settlement Scheme* 1962–66, 1

53 Republic of Kenya, *Statistical Abstract 1968* (Nairobi: Government Printer), 79. The 1968 issue of the *Abstract* has been selected at random. The same information appears in earlier issues as well.

54 The defilement metaphor, if that is how it was intended, is that of the Land Development and Settlement Board in 'Finance for the Land and Agricultural Bank of Kenya: Memorandum to the Secretary of State,' 8 February 1963, KNA 3/119. Significantly, perhaps, the word 'untouched,' or 'undisturbed,' appears repeatedly in colonial documents describing the rationale for block purchase.

55 Ibid.

56 Ibid.

57 LDSB, minutes of 25 July 1962, KNA 3/121

58 'Land for sale outside the Million Acre Scheme would only be purchased by the Board under the terms of the IBRD-CDC Schemes ...' That ruled out everything except the yeoman scheme, because peasant settlement was, by definition, excluded from integration into the highlands (LDSB, minutes of 25 September 1962, KNA 3/121).

59 LDSB, minutes of 12 December 1962, KNA 3/121

60 Ibid., 25 September 1962

61 LDSB, 'Finance for the Land and Agricultural Bank of Kenya: Memorandum to the Secretary of State,' KNA 3/119

62 Calculated from Ruthenberg, *African Agricultural Development in Kenya* 1962–65, 87

63 Department of Settlement, *Annual Report 1962–63*, 6

64 Ibid., 7. Since they had been bought at inflated prices in order to assist the sellers, they had to be resold at a loss.

65 Calculated from ibid., 8–14

66 Department of Settlement, *Annual Report 1967–68*, 3

CHAPTER 6

1 Land Development and Settlement Board (hereinafter LDSB), *A Review of the Activities of the Land Development and Settlement Board* (1962), para. 5, mimeo, from Kenya National Archives (hereinafter KNA) 3/121, Office of the President

2 C.P.R. Nottidge and J.R. Goldsack, *The Million-Acre Scheme 1962–66*, mimeo (Nairobi: Department of Settlement n.d.), 1

3 Gary Wasserman, *Politics of Decolonization: Kenya Europeans and the Land Issue 1960–65* (London: Cambridge University Press 1976), 128

4 Kenya Legislative Council, *Debates*, 16 November 1960, col. 553

5 Department of Settlement, *Annual Report 1962–63*, 8–14, mimeo

6 LDSB, minutes of 12 December 1962, KNA, 3/121

7 Labour officer, Thomson's Falls to R.F. Jennings, Box 22, Rumuruti, 8 March 1963, from LAB. 1/Vol II, Nyandarua district commissioner, Nyahururu.

8 Labour officer to J.J. Smith, Box 290, Thomson's Falls, 13 March 1963, ibid.

9 LDSB, 'Memorandum: Kikuyu Settlement Schemes; Priority Terms for Allocation of Plots,' 27 February 1963, KNA 3/121, Office of the President.

10 A variety of evidence (including reports of individual instances as well as officials' observations of trends) points to these events. For example, in March 1963, the permanent secretary, Ministry of Land Settlement and Water Development, noted that the Wanjohi Stock Farms in Nyandarua were 'becoming a security problem on account of squatters' (director of settlement's Planning Committee, meeting of 18 March 1963, KNA 3/116). In May, the deputy minister of settlement reported that there had been 'a mass influx of landless and unemployed Kikuyu onto the schemes in the Central Province, particularly at Kipipiri [in Nyandarua]' (HMG Settlement Schemes Loans and Planning Committee [LDSB], meeting of 10 May 1963, KNA 3/120). In July, the regional government agent in Nyandarua commented, in a letter to his superior in Nyeri, about 'the numerous problems which are now beginning to appear in this District as more and more landless Kikuyu are showing their fierce determination to obtain a slice of the settlement cake' (regional government agent, Nyandarua, to civil secretary, Central Region, Nyeri, 16 July 1963, from LAB. 1/Vol. II, Nyandarua district commissioner, Nyahururu). Toward the end of 1963, Nyandarua agricultural authorities were concerned about a farm on Turasha Ridge which had been taken over by squatters (district agricultural officer, Nyandarua, to regional agricultural officer, Nyeri, 12 November 1963, KNA 4/98, Agriculture). In the sample of formerly landless and unemployed people who were interviewed for the present study, a number related the odysseys that led them through squatter villages, temporary residences, and a variety of jobs to settlement. The 1963–64 *Annual Report* of the Department of Settlement related that Nyandarua had suffered 'an invasion of people hoping to be granted land' (p. 30).

11 LDSB, minutes of 12 December 1962, KNA 3/121

12 Ibid. and minutes of 23 January 1963
13 Director of settlement's Planning Committee, minutes of 21 January 1963, KNA 3/116; LDSB, 'Memorandum: Kikuyu Settlement Schemes; Priority Terms for Allocation of Plots,' KNA 3/121
14 Ministry of Lands and Settlement, 'Proposed Nyandarua Settlement Plan,' 4 September 1963, KNA 4/98
15 Rebmann M. Wambaa and Kenneth King, 'The Political Economy of the Rift Valley: A Squatter Perspective,' Historical Association of Kenya, Annual Conference, 1972, 18
16 Ibid.
17 LDSB, A Review ..., para. 9
18 D.M. Frost, Box 55, South Kinangop, to the Nyandarua district commissioner, 12 June 1963, from LAB.l/Vol. II, Nyandarua district commissioner, Nyahururu
19 Kenya Legislative Council, Debates, 19 October 1962, col. 228
20 Ibid., 23 October 1962, col. 244
21 HMG Settlement Scheme Loans and Planning Committee (LDSB), minutes of 8 February 1962, KNA, 3/120
22 R.J.F. Wheeler, regional government agent, Nyandarua District, 16 September 1963, from LAB. 1/Vol. II, Nyandarua district commissioner, Nyahururu
23 LDSB, minutes of 15 November 1962, KNA 3/121
24 Director of settlement's Planning Committee, minutes of 5 October 1962, KNA 3/116
25 Ibid., meeting of 17 December 1962
26 LDSB, minutes of 23 January 1963 and 24 May 1963, KNA 3/121
27 Ibid., 30 April 1963
28 Department of Settlement, Annual Report 1963–64 (Nairobi: Government Printer), 4
29 Director of settlement's Planning Committee, minutes of 7 December 1962, KNA 3/116
30 LDSB, 'Memorandum: Kikuyu Settlement Schemes; Priority Terms for Allocation of Plots,' KNA 3/121
31 Ibid. That estimate included provision for legal Kikuyu labourers in settlement areas for other ethnic groups. In addition to providing for these people, it was also necessary to take into account the fact that, wherever there was low-density settlement, landless and unemployed people would be displaced who would have to be absorbed into high-density schemes elsewhere.
32 Ibid.

33 LDSB, minutes of 25 September 1962 and 27 February 1963, KNA 3/121

34 Kenya Legislative Council, *Debates*, 23 October 1962, col. 250; confirmed in interviews for the present study

35 LDSB, minutes of 25 July 1962, KNA 3/121

36 Interview on 20 March 1972

37 SSOS' meeting, 5 February 1962, KNA 3/116

38 Director of settlement's Planning Committee, 2 April 1963, KNA 3/116

39 Meeting of officials concerned with settlement in Nyandarua District, 19 July 1963, KNA 4/98. Any plans that went beyond the five per cent limit, it was noted, would require approval of the director of settlement's Planning Committee.

40 Director of settlement's Planning Committee, minutes of 18 and 19 September 1962, KNA 3/116

41 LDSB, minutes of 24 May 1963, KNA 3/121

42 Leslie Brown, 'Contrasts in High Density Schemes,' *Kenya Weekly News*, 23 July 1965, 8

43 A.M. Mercer, 'Ol' Kalou Salient: Background to Policies, with some Notes on Organization and Practical Farming Problems,' mimeo (Nyahururu: Nyandarua District Commissioner 1966), 6

44 Nyandarua District, *Annual Report 1964* (Nyahururu: Nyandarua District Commissioner), mimeo

45 In the case of tea, the board resisted a demand that all potential tea land be purchased at 'enhanced' prices. The board limited its concession to land that could in fact be developed for tea in the near future and that was readily accessible to processing and marketing facilities. In the *cause célèbre* of the Kinangop, discussed in chapter 5, the board disavowed an obviously inflated land assessment. As late as February 1963 the board refused an appeal from landowners in the Turbo-Kipkarren area for higher valuations (LDSB meeting of 27 February 1963, KNA 3/121

46 C.P.R. Nottidge for director of settlement to acting PAO, Nyeri, 23 May 1963, KNA 4/97, Agriculture

47 Minutes of 17 December 1962, KNA 3/116

48 Director of settlement's Planning Committee, minutes of 24 April 1963, KNA 3/116

49 W. Keir, DAO, South Kinangop, 26 April 1963, KNA 4/97, Agriculture

50 Nottidge and Goldsack, *The Million-Acre Scheme 1962–66*, 15

51 The value of two acres of subsistence cultivation varies with the fertility of the soil and the value of the crops that can be grown in it. Here is a sample calculation for maize, which seems as good an example as any. In the sample budgets reprinted in Nottidge and Goldsack (ibid.), the antici-

pated net annual income from two acres of maize ranges from Shs 168/- (assuming a yield of eight bags per acre) to 410/- (assuming twelve bags). In these two cases, the high-density settler's subsistence is worth Shs 632/- and 390/- less, respectively, than the low-density settler's allotment of Shs 800/-. If we subtract that difference from the Shs 500/- annual target income, we find that a family of settlers are earning a negligible income or none at all. In terms of their obligation to meet loan repayments, they have become participants in the cash economy. But their standard of living remains at the subsistence level: Instead of winning them a peasant's freedom to move back and forth between the subsistence and cash economies (see chapter 1), their acquisition of land has trapped them into the worst of both worlds.

52 Meeting of officials concerned with settlement in Nyandarua District, 19 July 1963, KNA 4/98

53 Ministry of Lands and Settlement, 'Proposed Nyandarua Settlement Plan,' 4 September 1963, KNA 4/98

54 L.H. Brown, 'Safari Report,' 23 May 1963, KNA 4/97

55 Nottidge and Goldsack, The Million-Acre Scheme 1962–66, 28–30

56 Republic of Kenya, African Socialism and its Application to Planning in Kenya (Nairobi: Government Printer 1965), para. 103

57 Department of Settlement, Annual Report 1965–66 (Nairobi: Government Printer), 48

58 Department of Settlement, Annual Report 1963–64, 4

59 Ibid., 1965–66, 53

60 LDSB, 'Memorandum: Kikuyu Settlement Schemes; Priority Terms for Allocation of Plots,' 27 February 1963, KNA 3/121

61 This was confirmed in an interview (on 4 November 1971) with Edward Muceru Ayub, who was a field-level settlement official in the period following internal self-government, and in numerous interviews and casual conversations with people who participated in the lotteries.

62 Letter from chairman, Nyandarua District Agricultural Committee, 2 April 1964, and reply from regional government agent, Nyandarua, KNA 4/97; see also Nyandarua District, Annual Report 1964, 5. Settlers themselves and some settlement administrators seem to lack the regional government agent's reticence. In Nyandarua in the early 1970s it was taken for granted that patronage had played a role in settler selection, both before and after independence. The areas settled before internal self-government were sometimes called 'Ngala's land,' a reference to Ronald Ngala, the late KADU leader. Some settlement schemes were regarded as

loyalist strongholds and others were universally assumed to be freedom fighter schemes. See chapter 7.

63 Ibid., 2, 5, 9. The DC appears to have meant 18 000 landless *families* rather than *people*. The 6800 families receiving famine relief alone would have totalled more than 18 000 people.

64 DC Nyandarua to SSO Thomson's Falls, 17 May 1965, LAB. 4/1/II, Nyandarua district commissioner, Nyahururu.

65 Nyandarua District, *Annual Report 1964*, 1

66 Ibid., 7

67 Stephen Mathia Muratha, Pesi Settlement Scheme, to SSO Thomson's Falls, 28 August 1963, LAB. 1/Vol. II, Nyandarua district commissioner, Nyahururu; Kimani, son of Kariuki, Silanga Settlement Scheme, to SO Silanga, 13 February 1965; Njoroge Kamau, Sabugo Settlement Scheme, to SO Sabugo, 15 February 1965; Chege Gakuya, South Kinangop Scheme, to DC Nyandarua, April 1965, LAB. 4/1/II, Nyandarua District Commissioner, Nyahururu

68 J.S. Reid, Thomson's Falls, to regional government agent, Nyandarua, 8 March 1965; A.R. Swift, Thomson's Falls, to district commissioner, May 1965; H. Retief, Thomson's Falls, to regional government agent, Nyandarua, 12 June 1965; S.N. Mariga, Nakuru, to DC Nyandarua, 13 September 1965, LAB. 1/Vol. II, Nyandarua district commissioner, Nyahururu; Nelson K. Ngethe, Nakuru, to DC Nyandarua, 13 February 1965, LAB. 4/1/II, Nyandarua district commissioner, Nyahururu

69 Nyandarua district commissioner to Mathia Muratha, 10 September 1965, LAB.4/1/II

70 Nyandarua District, *Annual Report 1964*, 2

71 Regional government agent, Nyandarua, 15 December 1964, LAB. 1/Vol. II, Nyandarua district commissioner, Nyahururu

72 Special Commissioner (Squatters), 'Procedure on the Registration of Squatters and the Subsequent Investigations' (circular SCS 28/20), 25 September 1965, LAB. 1/Vol. II, Nyandarua district commissioner, Nyahururu; Republic of Kenya, *Development Plan 1970–74* (Nairobi: Government Printer), para. 8.50

INTRODUCTION TO PART III

1 Michael Cowen, 'Commodity Production in Kenya's Central Province,' in Judith Heyer et al., *Rural Development in Tropical Africa* (London: Macmillan 1981), 141

CHAPTER 7

1 See chapter 5

2 Calculated from Department of Settlement, *Annual Report 1970* (Nairobi: Government Printer), appendix G. These totals include the so-called co-operative units of the Ol'Kalou Salient as well as regular high- and low-density schemes.

3 A reminder that this is Swahili for 'freedom'; it is the word used for 'independence.'

4 Cf. Jomo Kenyatta, *Suffering without Bitterness: The Founding of the Kenya Nation* (Nairobi: East African Publishing House 1968), 241

5 The accuracy of that report was confirmed by officials. Cf. 'Land: A Way of Life,' *Daily Nation*, Nairobi, 14 February 1973, 19.

6 Cf. Colin Leys, *Underdevelopment in Kenya: The Political Economy of Neo-Colonialism* (London: Heinemann 1975), 234ff

7 L.N. Mucemi, district agricultural officer, Nyandarua District, to SSO Kinangop, 19 February 1964, Kenya National Archives (hereinafter KNA) 4/97, Agriculture

8 Ibid., 2 March 1964. See also Mucemi's letter of 12 March 1964, ibid.

9 Interview with Mayikuva Shirandula, SO, Nyansiongo Complex, Sotik, 10 May 1971

10 Interview with G. Nalyanya, senior assistant agricultural officer, Turbo, 18 May 1971

11 Interview with Japheth Nyakwara, senior assistant agricultural officer, Nyahururu, 22 April 1971

12 Statistics Division, Ministry of Finance and Economic Planning, *An Economic Appraisal of the Settlement Schemes 1964–65 to 1967–68*, Farm Economic Survey Report No. 27 (Nairobi: 1971), para. 2.8

13 The average plot size was 10.4 hectares (Department of Settlement, *Five-Year Review and Annual Report 1967–68* [Nairobi: Government Printer], appendix L).

14 Department of Settlement, *Annual Report 1963–64* (Nairobi: Government Printer), 5

15 The figure arrived at was 34.2 per cent. It was derived as follows: The acreage of the three special plots, as given by their owners $(90 + 99 + 100 = 289)$ was added to the average plot size (25.8 acres) times seven (180.6), on the assumption that the remaining plots held by former white-collar workers were of average size. Ol'Kalou West's seven z-plots (estimated at 700 acres) were reduced to the scale of the 40 per cent random

sample (result: 280 acres). The total acreage of the scheme (5483) was similarly reduced (result: 2193.2). Thus 40 per cent of the middle-class acreage (749.6) comes to 34.2 per cent of 40 per cent of the total acreage.

16 Z.B. Shimechero, special commissioner (squatters) to district commissioner, Nyandarua, 10 September 1965, LAB. 4/1/II, Nyandarua district commissioner, Nyahururu

17 Interview with G. Kithenji, district officer, Ol'Kalou Division, 1 November 1971

18 Interview with Appolo Ngumba wa Ndurubu, chief, Ol'Kalou Location, 22 September 1971

19 The observations were made 1) in the course of the Ol'Kalou West and Passenga surveys, which included extensive discussions of settlers' relations with kin, with squatters, and with farm labourers; 2) in interviews with settlement administrators, a number of whom proved to be well informed and articulate on the subject of social relations within settlement; and 3) in numerous casual conversations with Africans from all walks of life.

20 It seems likely that this initial absence of squatters from low-density settlement – and their presence in high-density schemes – was a further effect of the IBRD restrictions discussed in chapter 6. As noted, the World Bank's insistence on high development standards – and the eagerness of government officials to meet those standards – helped to set a pattern of favouritism for low-density settlement. The clearing of squatters from low-density schemes, and not from high-density ones, was undoubtedly part of that pattern. In later years, as data indicate, the policy of differentiation was continued – whether out of inertia, fear of World Bank inspections, or simply because low-density settlers were in a better position to defend their interests than were poor settlers.

21 Interview with G. Nalyanya, senior assistant agricultural officer, Turbo area, 18 May 1971

22 Interview with John Paul Odero, senior assistant agricultural officer, Sotik, 10 May 1971

23 Interview with Japheth Nyakwara, senior assistant agricultural officer, Nyahururu, 22 April 1971

CHAPTER 8

1 Hans Ruthenberg, *African Agricultural Development Policy in Kenya, 1962–65* (Berlin: Springer-Verlag 1966), 72–3

2 See World Bank, *Assault on World Poverty: Problems of Rural Development,*

Education, and Health (Baltimore: Johns Hopkins 1975); and Uma Lele, *The Design of Rural Development: Lessons from Africa* (Baltimore: Johns Hopkins 1975)

3 Department of Settlement, *Annual Report 1962–63* (Nairobi:), 3–4, mimeo

4 Statistics Division, Ministry of Finance and Economic Planning, *An Economic Appraisal of the Settlement Schemes 1964–65 to 1967–68*, Farm Economic Survey Report No. 27 (Nairobi: 1971), para. 4.32

5 Hans-Wilhelm von Hauguwitz, *Some Experiences with Smallholder Settlement in Kenya 1963–64 to 1966–67* (Munich: Weltforum Verlag 1971), part E, section V

6 See, *inter alia*, S.N. Hinga and Judith Heyer, 'The Development of Large Farms,' in *Agricultural Development in Kenya: An Economic Assessment* (Nairobi: Oxford University Press 1976), 222–54.

7 Two useful sources are Heyer and J.K. Waweru, 'The Development of the Small Farm Areas,' ibid., 187–221; and Heyer, 'Agricultural Development Policy in Kenya' in Heyer et al., *Rural Development in Tropical Africa* (London: Macmillan 1981), 90–120.

8 Hinga and Heyer, 'The Development of Large Farms'

9 Republic of Kenya, *Development Plan 1974–78* (Nairobi: Government Printer), 199–200

10 Apollo L. Njonjo 'The Africanization of the "White Highlands": A Study in Agrarian Class Struggle in Kenya 1950–75,' PH D, Princeton, 1977, 471

11 Ibid., 494–6

12 Ibid., 505–6

13 Ibid., 497–509

14 Ibid., 498–9

15 Ibid., 509

16 Ward Ashcroft and Parkman Ltd (East Africa), *Large Farm Sector Study*, vol. 1 (Nairobi: Ministry of Agriculture 1977), 1

17 Much of the same figures may be found in what, in March 1983, was the department's most recent annual report – the one for 1976! See appendix A of the report.

18 Ministry of Co-operatives and Social Services, *Survey of Large-Scale Co-operative Farms* (Nakuru 1973), 3

19 Ibid., 5

20 Ward Ashcroft and Parkman Ltd, *Large Farm Sector Study*, 1–2

21 Ibid., 4

22 Ibid., 8

23 Ibid., 7

24 Ibid., 10–11

25 Ibid., 10

26 Ibid., 12

27 'Land Companies: What Future?' *Daily Nation*, 17 February 1983, 6

28 Nicola Swainson, *The Development of Corporate Capitalism in Kenya, 1918–77* (Berkeley: University of California 1980), 206; italics in original. For news reports on Kihika see, *inter alia*, *Weekly Review*, Nairobi, 18 February 1983, 4–6; and *Daily Nation*, Nairobi, 17 February 1983, 6

29 Njonjo, 'The Africanization of the "White Highlands,"' 536

30 Robert Buijtenhuijs, *Mau Mau: Twenty Years After: The Myth and the Survivors* (The Hague: Mouton 1973), 134–9

31 Department of Settlement, *Annual Report, 1974* (Nairobi), 3

32 Ibid., *1975*, 2

33 According to the World Bank, Kenya's average annual population growth in the 1970s was 3.4 per cent and the projected rate for the 1980s and 1990s is 4.1 per cent (*World Development Report 1982* [New York: Oxford University Press]).

34 Interviews with settlement administrations, 22 May 1971 and 18 June 1971

35 Interview on 23 February 1983

36 Ashcroft and Parkman Ltd, *Large Farm Sector Study*

37 Ibid., 11. In the context of the study, it appears as if 'farms with few owners' is intended to include individually owned farms.

38 Republic of Kenya, *Development Plan 1979-83*, Part II (Nairobi: Government Printer), 283

39 Republic of Kenya, *Development Prospects and Policies* (Sessional Paper No. 4), 1982, 19

40 *Weekly Review*, 29 April 1983, 8

41 Chapter 318, section 187

Bibliography

BOOKS, ARTICLES, AND THESES

Amin, Samir. *Accumulation on a World Scale: A Critique of the Theory of Underdevelopment*. 2 vols. New York: Monthly Review Press 1974

Anderson, John. *The Struggle for the School*. Nairobi: Longman 1970

Apter, David. *Ghana in Transition*. New York: Atheneum 1963

Baran, Paul A. *The Political Economy of Growth*. New York: Monthly Review Press 1957

Bennett, George. *Kenya: A Political History. The Colonial Period.* London: Oxford University Press 1963

Bennett, George and Carl G. Rosberg. *The Kenyatta Election: Kenya 1960–61.* London: Oxford University Press 1961

Blundell, Sir Michael. *So Rough a Wind*. London: Weidenfeld and Nicolson 1964

Buijtenhuijs, Robert. *Mau Mau: Twenty Years After: The Myth and the Survivors.* The Hague: Mouton 1973

Byres, T.J. 'Agrarian Transition and the Agrarian Question.' *Journal of Peasant Studies* 4, no. 3 (1977)

Chayanov, A.V. *The Theory of Peasant Economy*. Edited by Daniel Thorner et. al. Homewood, Illinois: Irwin 1966

Cowen, Michael. 'The Agrarian Problem: Notes on the Nairobi Discussion.' *Review of African Political Economy* 20 (1981)

– 'Commodity Production in Kenya's Central Province.' In *Rural Development in Tropical Africa*, edited by Judith Heyer et al. London: Macmillan 1981

– 'Differentiation in a Kenya Location.' East African Universities Social Science Council, no. 16. Nairobi 1972

Cowen, Michael and Kabiru Kinyanjui. 'Some Problems of Income Distribution in Kenya.' Institute for Development Studies. Nairobi 1977. Mimeo

Emanuel, Arghiri, *Unequal Exchange: A Study of the Imperialism of Trade*. London: NLB 1972

Fordham, Paul. *The Geography of African Affairs*. Harmondsworth: Penguin 1963

Frank, Andre Gunder. *Capitalism and Underdevelopment in Latin America: Historical Studies of Chile and Brazil*. New York: Monthly Review Press 1969

Ghai, Y.P., and J.P.W.B. McAuslan. *Public Law and Political Change in Kenya: A Study of the Legal Framework of Government from Colonial Times to the Present*. Nairobi: Oxford University Press 1970

Gluckman, Max. *Politics, Law and Ritual in Tribal Society*. Chicago: Aldine 1965

Goldthorpe, J.S. and F.B. Wilson. *Tribal Maps of East Africa and Zanzibar*. Kampala: East African Institute of Social Research 1960

Harbeson, John W. 'Land Reform and Politics in Kenya, 1954–70.' *Journal of Modern African Studies* (August 1971)

– *Nation-building in Kenya: The Role of Land Reform*. Northwestern University, Evanston, 1973

Heyer, Judith, Pepe Roberts, and Gavin Williams. *Rural Development in Tropical Africa*. London: Macmillan 1981

Heyer, Judith, J.K. Maitha, and W.M. Senga. *Agricultural Development in Kenya: An Economic Assessment* Nairobi: Oxford University Press 1976

Hoskyns, Catherine. *The Congo since Independence: January 1960–December 1961*. London: Oxford University Press 1965

Huxley, Elspeth. *White Man's Country: Lord Delamere and the Making of Kenya*. 2 vols. London: Chatto and Windus 1935

Hyden, Goran. *Beyond Ujamaa in Tanzania: Underdevelopment and an Uncaptured Peasantry*. Berkeley: University of California, 1980

Itote, Waruhiu. *'Mau Mau' General*. Nairobi: East African Publishing House 1967

Kaplinsky, Rafael, J.S. Henley, and Colin Leys. 'Debate on "Dependency" in Kenya.' *Review of African Political Economy* 17 (1980)

Kariuki, J.M. *'Mau Mau' Detainee*. London: Oxford University Press 1963

Kenyatta, Jomo. *Facing Mount Kenya*. London: Secker and Warburg 1938

– *Suffering without Bitterness: The Founding of the Kenya Nation*. Nairobi: East African Publishing House 1968

Kitching, Gavin. *Class and Economic Change in Kenya: The Making of an African Petite Bourgeoisie 1905–70*. New Haven: Yale University Press 1980

Langdon, Steven W. *Multinational Corporations in the Political Economy of Kenya*. London: Macmillan 1981

Lele, Uma. *The Design of Rural Development: Lessons from Africa*. Baltimore: Johns Hopkins 1975

Leo, Christopher. 'The Failure of the "Progressive Farmer" in Kenya's Million-Acre Settlement Scheme.' *Journal of Modern African Studies* 16, no. 4 (1978)

— 'The Political Economy of Land in Kenya: The Case of the Million-Acre Settlement Scheme.' PHD dissertation, University of Toronto, 1977

— 'Who Benefited from the Million-Acre Scheme? Toward a Class Analysis of Kenya's Transition to Independence.' *Canadian Journal of African Studies* 15, no. 2 (1981)

Leys, Colin. 'Capital Accumulation, Class Formation and Dependency: The Significance of the Kenyan Case.' *Socialist Register*. London: Merlin Press 1978

— 'Politics in Kenya: The Development of Peasant Society.' *British Journal of Political Science* 1, no. 3 (1971)

— 'Underdevelopment and Dependence: Critical Notes.' *Journal of Contemporary Asia* 7, no. 1 (1977)

— *Underdevelopment in Kenya: The Political Economy of Neo-Colonialism 1964–71*. London: Heinemann 1975

Majdalany, Fred. *State of Emergency: The Full Story of Mau Mau*. Boston: Houghton Mifflin 1963

Marris, Peter, and Anthony Somerset. *African Businessmen: A Study of Entrepreneurship and Development in Kenya*. London: Routledge and Kegan Paul 1971

Mboya, Tom. *Freedom and After*. London: Andre Deutsch 1963

Middleton, John, and Greet Kershaw. *The Central Tribes of the Northeastern Bantu*. London: International African Institute 1965

Morgan, W.T.W. 'The "White Highlands" of Kenya.' *The Geographical Journal*, (June 1963)

Njonjo, A.L. 'The Africanization of the "White Highlands": A Study in Agrarian Class Struggle in Kenya 1950–1975.' PHD dissertation, Princeton, 1977

Odinga, Oginga. *Not Yet Uhuru: An Autobiography*. London: Heinemann 1967

Odingo, Richard S. 'Land Settlement in the Kenya Highlands.' In *Education, Employment and Rural Development*, edited by James A. Sheffield. Nairobi: East African Publishing House 1967

— *The Kenya Highlands: Land Use and Agricultural Development*. Nairobi: East African Publishing House 1971

Ogot, B.A., and J.A. Kieran. *Zamani: A Survey of East African History*. Nairobi: East African Publishing House and Longman 1968

Rosberg, Carl G., and John Nottingham. *The Myth of 'Mau Mau': Nationalism in Kenya*. New York: Praeger 1966

Ruthenberg, Hans. *African Agricultural Development Policy in Kenya, 1962–65*. Berlin: Springer-Verlag 1966

Shanin, Teodor. *The Awkward Class; Political Sociology of Peasantry in a Developing Society: Russia 1910–25*. Oxford: Clarendon 1972

Sheffield, James A., ed. *Education, Employment, and Rural Development*. Nairobi: East African Publishing House 1967

Slater, Montagu. *The Trial of Jomo Kenyatta*. 2nd edition. London: Secker and Warburg 1955

Sorrenson, M.P.K. *Land Reform in the Kikuyu Country*. Nairobi: Oxford University Press 1967

– *Origins of European Settlement in Kenya*. Nairobi: Oxford University Press 1968

Swainson, Nicola. *The Development of Corporate Capitalism in Kenya 1918–77*. Berkeley: University of California 1980

Thuku, Harry. *An Autobiography*. Nairobi: Oxford University Press 1970

van Arkadie, Brian. 'Dependency in Kenya.' In Centre of African Studies, University of Edinburgh, *Developmental Trends in Kenya* (proceedings of an April 1972 seminar)

van Zwanenberg, R.M.A. *Colonial Capitalism and Labour in Kenya 1919–39*. Nairobi: East African Literature Bureau 1975

von Haugwitz, Hans-Wilhelm. *Some Experiences With Smallholder Settlement in Kenya, 1963–64 to 1966–67*. Munich: Weltforum Verlag 1971

Wambaa, Rebmann M., and Kenneth King. 'The Political Economy of the Rift Valley: A Squatter Perspective.' Historical Association of Kenya. Annual Conference (1972)

Wasserman, Gary. 'The Adaptation of a Colonial Elite to Decolonization: Kenya Europeans and the Land Issue 1960–65.' PHD dissertation, Columbia University, 1973

– 'Continuity and Counter Insurgency: The Role of Land Reform in Decolonizing Kenya 1962–70.' *Canadian Journal of African Studies* 7 no. 1 (1973)

– 'The Independence Bargain: Kenya Europeans and the Land Issue 1960–62.' *Journal of Commonwealth Political Studies* (July 1973)

– *Politics of Decolonization: Kenya Europeans and the Land Issue 1960–65*. London: Cambridge University Press 1976

Wolff, Richard D. *The Economics of Colonialism: Britain and Kenya 1870–1930*. New Haven: Yale University Press 1974

World Bank. *Assault on World Poverty: Problems of Rural Development, Education and Health*. Baltimore: Johns Hopkins 1975

– *World Development Report, 1982*. New York: Oxford University Press

KENYA GOVERNMENT PUBLICATIONS

African Socialism and Its Application to Planning in Kenya. 1965
A Plan to Intensify the Development of Agriculture in Kenya. 1954
Central Land Board. *Annual Report 1963–64.*
Department of Settlement. *Annual Reports.* 1962–70 and 1974–76
Development Plan 1970–74, 1974–78, 1979–83.
Development Prospects and Policies. Sessional Paper No. 4. 1982
Land and Agricultural Bank of Kenya. *Annual Reports.* 1963–64
Land Tenure and Control outside Native Lands. Sessional Paper No. 10. 1958–59
Legislative Council. *Debates.* 1960, 1962
Ministry of Co-operatives and Social Services. *Survey of Large Scale Co-operative Farms.* Nakuru 1973
Ministry of Finance and Economic Planning, Statistics Division. *An Economic Appraisal of the Settlement Schemes 1964–65 to 1967–68.* Farm Economic Survey Report No. 27. 1971
Nottidge, C.P.R., and J.R. Goldsack. *The Million-Acre Settlement Scheme 1962–1966.* Nairobi: Department of Settlement
Statistical Abstract 1968
The Agrarian Problem in Kenya: Note by Sir Philip Mitchell, Governor of Kenya. 1948
The Development Programme 1957–60. Sessional Paper No. 77. 1956–57
Ward Ashcroft and Parkman Ltd (East Africa). *Large Farm Sector Study.* Vol. 1. Ministry of Agriculture 1977

BRITISH GOVERNMENT PUBLICATIONS

Corfield, F.C. *Historical Survey of the Origins and Growth of Mau Mau.* Cmd. 1030. 1960
East African Royal Commission (EARC). *Report.* Cmd. 9475. 1955
Kenya. *Report of the Regional Boundaries Commission.* Cmd. 1899, 1962
Kenya Land Commission (KLC). *Report.* Cmd. 4556. 1934

KENYA GOVERNMENT FILES

Kenya National Archives (KNA). Minutes of the Land Development and Settlement Board and its committees; records of the administration of settlement at headquarters and in Nyandarua District. 3/113, 3/116, 3/119, 3/120, 3/121, Office of the President; 4/97, 4/98, 4/99, Agriculture

Nyandarua district commissioner, Thomson's Falls. Correspondence files of the Labour Officer (LAB. 1/Vol. II; LAB. 4/1/II); Nyandarua District, *Annual Report 1964*; A.M. Mercer, 'Ol'Kalou Salient: Background to Policies with Some Notes on Organization and Practical Farming Problems' (1966)

FILES OF THE WORLD BANK (IBRD), NAIROBI

Loan Agreements for the supply of development funds to the IBRD-CDC settlement scheme (Loan No. 303KE).
'Project for the Development and Settlement of Land in the Scheduled areas' (1961)

PERIODICALS

Daily Nation. Nairobi. Various issues, 1970–83
Kenya Weekly News. Various issues, 1965
Weekly Review. Nairobi. Various issues, 1983

Index

absentee landowners. *See* landownership
acreage (hectarage) conversion scale
138–9, 181
African-American Students Foundation 53; *see also* Mboya, Tom
African Land Development Board
(ALDEV) 56
African Land Utilization and Settlement Board (ALUS). *See* African
Land Development Board
agrarian system: class analysis 187–
94; and economic development 8–
12; future of 194–8; transformation 72, 149
Agreement of 1904 49
Agreement of 1911 49
agriculture: contributions to capitalist
development 10; development
of 11; post-independence 53–7;
technological advancement 169–
70; *see also* cash-crop agriculture,
large-scale agriculture, market
agriculture, plantation agriculture,
small-scale agriculture, *and* subsistence agriculture
Agriculture Act 198

ahoi 45, 55
anti-guerilla warfare 60
area settlement controllers (ASCs) 108
assisted-owner scheme 116, 118
auxiliary bourgeoisie. *See* class system
Ayub, Edward Muceru, LDSB administration 83–4, 86

Baring, Sir Evelyn 58
block purchase 115
Blundell, Michael, New Kenya Party
90, 112
Board of Agriculture 73, 102
boundaries 152
bourgeoisie. *See* class system
Boy, Juma 197
British government: and land-transfer
strategies 92, 93, 144; compensation 89; land subsidies 81; support
for high density 94
Brown, Leslie, H., agricultural official 136, 140
Buijtenhuijs, Robert 186
'bush politicians' 158
Byres, T.J. 10–11, 21

capital accumulation, African: post-